METHODS OF RANDOMIZATION
IN EXPERIMENTAL DESIGN

Quantitative Applications in the Social Sciences

A SAGE PUBLICATIONS SERIES

Series/Number 07-171

METHODS OF RANDOMIZATION IN EXPERIMENTAL DESIGN

Valentim R. Alferes
University of Coimbra

Los Angeles | London | New Delhi
Singapore | Washington DC

Los Angeles | London | New Delhi
Singapore | Washington DC

FOR INFORMATION:

SAGE Publications, Inc.
2455 Teller Road
Thousand Oaks, California 91320
E-mail: order@sagepub.com

SAGE Publications Ltd.
1 Oliver's Yard
55 City Road
London EC1Y 1SP
United Kingdom

SAGE Publications India Pvt. Ltd.
B 1/I 1 Mohan Cooperative Industrial Area
Mathura Road, New Delhi 110 044
India

SAGE Publications Asia-Pacific Pte. Ltd.
3 Church Street
#10-04 Samsung Hub
Singapore 049483

Printed in the United States of America

A catalog record of this book is available from the Library of Congress.

9781452202921

This book is printed on acid-free paper.

Acquisitions Editor: Helen Salmon
Editorial Assistant: Kaitlin Perry
Production Editor: Brittany Bauhaus
Copy Editor: Diane DiMura
Assistant Editor: Kalie Koscielak
Typesetter: C&M Digitals (P) Ltd.
Proofreader: Jeff Bryant
Indexer: Sylvia Coates
Cover Designer: Candice Harman
Marketing Manager: Nicole Elliott
Permissions Editor: Adele Hutchinson

12 13 14 15 16 10 9 8 7 6 5 4 3 2 1

BRIEF CONTENTS

DETAILED CONTENTS

LIST OF FIGURES AND TABLES

Chapter 3

Chapter 4

Appendices

ABOUT THE AUTHOR

Valentim R. Alferes is Professor of Psychology at the University of Coimbra, Portugal, where he has been teaching courses in social psychology and research methods in psychology at the undergraduate and graduate levels for over 20 years. His main scientific interests and publications are in the domains of sexuality, close relationships, dyadic data analysis, and experimental design. He has delivered lectures and conducted workshops on methodological and statistical topics at several Portuguese universities and has also maintained an SPSS Syntax Files website since 2002. He earned a PhD in social psychology from the University of Coimbra in 1995.

SERIES EDITOR'S INTRODUCTION

Like many other aspects of the development of statistics in the 20th century, the fundamental idea of randomization in experimental design originated with R. A. Fisher. Today, the randomized comparative experiment is generally considered the "gold standard" for inferring causation from statistical data.

As is commonly taught in basic classes on statistics and research methods, randomized assignment of subjects to conditions ensures that the manipulated factors in an experiment are independent of the unobserved causes of the outcome variable, at least within the bounds of chance. If, therefore, an association is observed between manipulated factors and the outcome, it can unambiguously be attributed to the experimental manipulations, again within the bounds of chance—as quantified, for example, in a p value. Unlike in observational data, in a randomized comparative experiment, association does imply causation.

As a practical matter, however, experiments in the behavioral and, especially, social sciences can fall prey to a number of difficulties:

- Although an effect may unambiguously be attributed to an experimental manipulation, specifically what it is about the manipulation that produces the effect may remain ambiguous. The effect may be due to what are sometimes termed "hidden biases," as would be the case, for example, when a new teaching method appears better than an old one not because of its intrinsic superiority but rather because of the relative enthusiasm of the teachers who implement it. For this reason, careful experimenters try to match experimental conditions as closely as possible so as to control extraneous influences, and they employ techniques such as "double-blind" manipulations (in which the experimenter and the subject are both unaware of the treatment to which the subject is assigned) where these are possible.
- Subjects employed in behavioral experiments are typically convenience samples, drawn prototypically as volunteers from introductory psychology courses. Even a carefully conducted experiment, therefore, doesn't provide a statistical basis for generalizing beyond re-randomization of the subjects at hand (what Campbell and his colleagues famously termed the "internal validity" of the study) to some larger population of individuals ("external validity").

- It is diffcult to mobilize in a laboratory the kinds of social and psychological forces that typically are of interest to social and behavioral researchers, and when it is possible to do so—Milgram's now classic experiments on obedience to authority provide a striking example—experimental studies may raise serious ethical issues.
- A distinction must often be drawn between "intention to treat," which can be randomized, and the actual application of experimental treatments. In medical research, for example, some experimental subjects may refuse treatment, take treatment irregularly or imperfectly, or drop out of a study, while some control subjects may independently seek alternative treatment.
- Experimental studies tend to be expensive and time-consuming in comparison with non-experimental research conducted on similar numbers of individuals, and therefore experiments often employ a relatively small number of subjects.

Valentim Alferes's monograph on *Methods of Randomization in Experimental Design* discusses some of these issues in the opening and concluding chapters, but it speaks most directly to the last point. Writing in the Campbell tradition, which addresses methodological along with purely statistical issues, Professor Alferes explains, carefully and in detail, how to design experiments so as to use resources efficiently and in a manner that does not compromise the internal validity of the research. He considers both between-subjects designs, in which subjects are assigned independently to different experimental conditions, and within-subject designs, in which more than one treatment is administered to each subject.

The monograph focuses on the *design* of experimental research rather than, as is more common, on the statistical *analysis* of experimental data. The monograph is therefore a valuable and logically prior complement to traditional texts that describe, for example, the analysis of variance of experimental data. After all, one must design an experiment before collecting and analyzing data, and the experimental design will in large part determine how informative the data are.

Alferes's monograph will naturally be of most interest to behavioral and social scientists—such as many psychologists and experimental economists—who conduct experimental research. But I believe, in addition, that a clear understanding of experimental design is also useful to researchers who analyze quasi-experimental and purely observational data, if only as a point of comparison to achieve a deeper understanding of how statistics can inform causal inferences.

—*John Fox*
Series Editor

PREFACE

This book is about *randomization* and *local control* procedures in experimental design. Using Fisher's (1925/1970, 1935/1966) terminology, this is a book about the devices required for an *unbiased* and *efficient* estimation of treatment causal effects. In Campbell's (1986) words, this is a book about the conditions that maximize the validity of *local molar causal inferences*, ruling out potential threats to internal and statistical conclusion validity.

Aiming to be a conceptual systematization and a practical tool for advanced undergraduates, graduate students, and researchers in the social, behavioral, educational, and health sciences who need to understand random assignment procedures and design randomized experiments, the book can be read as a supplementary text in *experimental design* and *research methods* courses, as well as a companion volume for the *experimental design and analysis of variance* monographs included in the QASS series (e.g., Volumes 1, 12, 23, 54, 74, 84, 98, and 125). While those volumes are centered on statistical analysis issues, this one focuses on design issues. To adopt the Campbellian framework, which provides the rationale for the book, it relates primarily to internal validity and some specific aspects of statistical conclusion validity and only tangentially to data analysis or statistical testing. It could also be directly related to Volume 35 (*Introduction to Survey Sampling*), in the sense that both books focus on random processes. However, random sampling is an external validity issue, while random assignment is a matter of internal validity.

Chapter 1 introduces the basic structure of randomized experiments and the theoretical foundations of randomization and local control in the context of the Campbellian approach to the validity of scientific inferences (Campbell, 1957; Campbell & Stanley, 1966; Cook & Campbell, 1979; Shadish, Cook, & Campbell, 2002). Randomized experiments can be conceived of as controlled experiments in the three meanings of *control* described by Boring (1954): (1) a *restraint* (constancy of environmental or situational nuisance variables and equivalence of personal or dispositional nuisance variables via random assignment of experimental units); (2) a *guide* or *directing* (systematic variation of experimental factors); and (3) a *check* or *verification* (manipulation check and reliable recording of outcome measures). Valid local inferences, a preliminary condition of generalized inferences (representation and extrapolation), presuppose the establishment of covariation (*statistical conclusion validity*) and causality (*internal validity*). Randomization procedures are conceptualized as a central feature of internal validity, while local control procedures are presented as a complementary tool for the maximization of statistical conclusion validity. More specifically, randomization is the fundamental condition to obtain unbiased estimates of treatment effects, excluding plausible rival explanations based on systematic differences between experimental units (*selection bias*, a threat to internal validity); local control increases the efficiency (or precision) of these estimates by reducing the *heterogeneity of experimental units* (a threat to statistical conclusion validity).

In addition to the basic principles of experimentation (*replication, randomization*, and *local control*) introduced by Fisher (1925/1970, 1935/1966) and their embodiment in the Campbellian framework, Chapter 1 gives the key definition of causal effects in the context of Rubin's (1974, 2006, 2007) *potential outcomes approach* to experimentation and quasi-experimentation and presents two advanced organizers for the core contents of Chapters 2 and 3: (1) a classification of experimental designs in connection with the corresponding methods of randomization and (2) a synthesis of the common designations given to the manipulated, controlled, and measured variables in randomized experiments.

Chapter 2 deals with randomization of between-subjects designs and is organized around the types of limitations imposed on random assignment: (a) *procedural constraints* (number of available units per experiment, number of intended units in each experimental condition, or equal-size homogeneous blocks) and (b) *substantive restrictions* (restrictions to randomization based on the intrinsic characteristics of experimental units). The main procedures for random assignment of units to experimental conditions in *completely randomized designs* (only procedural constraints) and *restrictedly randomized designs* (blocks or strata defined by substantive restrictions) are described and illustrated from Section 2.2 to Section 2.4. *Sequential assignment* adaptations and variations of these procedures are then presented in Section 2.5.

After an overview of the basic assumptions and the specific threats (*carryover effects* of the previous periods) to the validity of scientific inferences (Section 3.1), Chapter 3 summarizes the structural properties of within-subjects designs and gives a synopsis of the main randomization procedures (Section 3.2). From Section 3.3 to Section 3.6, *random counterbalancing, positional counterbalancing, nonrestricted sequential counterbalancing,* and *restricted sequential counterbalancing* are described and illustrated with reference to one-treatment designs. The final section deals with the adjustment of counterbalancing schemes to factorial within-subjects designs.

Chapters 2 and 3 are self-contained in the sense that all randomizations, including the ones implying unequal probabilities of assignment or adaptive randomization procedures, were executed based on the tables given in Appendices 1 (*Random Numbers*), 2 (*Permutations, Arrangements, and Combinations*), and 3 (*Latin squares*), using the MS-Word "Tables" menu and the "Sort" command to associate systematically and randomly ordered lists of experimental units and treatment replications. The application to "real-world randomizations" of the methods described and illustrated in Chapters 2 and 3 could be entirely done with the same resources. Needless to say, the use of basic random number generators (RNG), like those incorporated in spreadsheets and statistical software or available interactively on the Internet, can allow the reader to skip the tedious and error-prone task of picking digits from tables of random numbers. A better solution consists in the adoption of specialized software, provided that the available randomization methods are compatible with the procedural constraints and substantive restrictions underlying the experimental design. In the companion website of this monograph (www.sagepub.com/alferes), along with other supplementary materials, the reader can freely download IBM SPSS and R versions of SCRAED, a package that performs *simple and complex random assignment in experimental design*, including the 18 randomization methods presented in Chapters 2 and 3.

Virtually all books about *experimental design* or *research methods* discuss random assignment or random allocation procedures. However, illustrations are frequently limited to simple random assignment, and authors often presume that students and researchers can properly deal with complex designs without further explanations and technical details. This state of affairs can result in nonoptimal designs and deficient reporting of randomization procedures in scientific journals. In Chapters 2 and 3, instead of presenting randomization methods as stand-alone tools, emphasis is placed on the interdependence between local control and random assignment strategies (i.e., *error control design*) and the structural features of design layouts (i.e., *treatment design*). In Chapter 4, the interfaces with the third component of experimental design (i.e., *sampling and observational design*) are discussed in the context of the main activities involved in planning and monitoring randomized experiments (Section 4.1), and some theoretical and technical details of randomization methods omitted in the two previous chapters, along with general guidelines for data analysis, are also given (Section 4.2). The concluding section is a brief guide to the standards for reporting randomized experiments in the social, behavioral, educational, and health sciences.

Having in mind Donald Campbell's remark in his brilliant "Foreword" to the now classic *Case Study Research* by Robert Yin (1984)—"More and more I have come to the conclusion that the core of the scientific method is not experimentation per se but the strategy connoted by the phrase *plausible rival hypotheses*" (Campbell, 1984, p. ix)—we hope that this monograph will help readers improve the current practice of designing and reporting randomized experiments.

Acknowledgments

I would like to thank two anonymous reviewers for their helpful comments on a draft of this monograph; Professor John Fox, the editor of the QASS Series, for his valuable feedback and continuous encouragement; and Mariza Estêvão for her help and support.

CHAPTER 1. RANDOMIZED EXPERIMENTS

1.1 Nature and Structure of Randomized Experiments

In broad terms, methods are the linking procedures between theory and data. They embody the theoretical hypothesis in the research design, specifying the conditions and technical devices to collect, analyze, and interpret relevant basic information (raw data). In the nomothetic or quantitative approach, as opposed to the idiographic or qualitative one, methods of empirical investigation are usually classified on the basis of the structural properties of the underlying design and the degree to which they allow valid causal inferences.

Leaving out *theoretical innovation, research synthesis and evaluation* (including meta-analysis and bibliometric surveys), and *documental studies* focused on previously archived materials, all investigations based either on *self-reports* (via self-administered questionnaires or interviews) or on *direct observation of research participants* fall into one of the three main categories: (1) *experimental,* (2) *quasi-experimental,* and (3) *nonexperimental* research (see Figure 1.1; see also Alferes, 2012, for a methodological classification of theoretical and empirical studies in psychology and related disciplines). As the reader can verify from the decision chart shown in Figure 1.1, this classification scheme—inspired by the Campbellian approach to the validity of causal inferences (Campbell, 1957; Shadish et al., 2002)—is organized around two key attributes of empirical studies: (1) *systematic variation of the presumed causes* (independent variables manipulation) and (2) *use of randomization procedures.* The presence of the first attribute separates *experimental* and *quasi-experimental* research from *nonexperimental* research; the presence of the second one separates *randomized experiments* (experimental designs) from *nonrandomized experiments* (quasi-experimental designs). The specific use of randomization procedures in experimental design depends on the manipulation strategy adopted by the researcher: (a) each unit is only exposed to *one* experimental condition and the randomization procedure is used to determine what exactly is that condition (*between-subjects designs*), or (b) each unit is exposed to *two or more* experimental conditions and the randomization procedure is used to determine the order in which the conditions will be presented (*within-subjects designs*).

As stated in the opening paragraph of the Preface, this book is about experimental designs and the devices required for an *unbiased* and *efficient* estimation of treatment causal effects. Formally speaking, a causal effect is

1

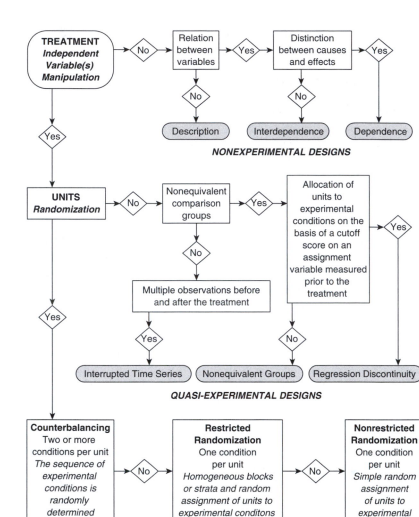

Figure 1.1 Decision chart for the classification of experimental, quasi-experimental, and nonexperimental designs according to the Campbellian approach

the difference between what happens when an experimental unit is subjected to a treatment and what would happen if it was not subjected to the same treatment or, which is equivalent, the difference between the responses of an experimental unit when simultaneously subjected to two alternative treatments (differential causal effect). Stated in another way, the inference of a causal effect requires counterfactual evidence. Yet, regarding a concrete experimental unit, it is impossible to obtain such evidence: We are unable to apply and not apply a treatment (or apply two alternative treatments) to an experimental unit at the same time.

A tentative solution for this problem could be either the comparison of the responses of two units (one receiving and one not receiving the treatment or one receiving the treatment and the other the alternative treatment) or the comparison of the responses of the same unit observed in two successive periods. However, this time, the counterfactual evidence is equivocal: In the first case, the treatment effect is completely confounded with the intrinsic characteristics of the experimental unit; in the second case, the treatment effect is completely confounded with any systematic or random variation potentially associated with the different periods of observation. A better solution, and the only one really feasible, is to replicate the experiment with other experimental units. Provided that certain assumptions are verified, having observations from several units can allow us to separate the treatment effect from "subjects" and "temporal sequence" effects.

What we have been saying is the core content of Rubin's causal model (Rubin, 1974, 2006, 2007; see also Rubin, 2004, for a pedagogical introduction), which defines a causal effect in terms of the mean difference in the potential outcomes between those who were submitted and those who were not submitted to a treatment, as long as the experimenter can guarantee what Rubin calls *stable-unit-treatment-value assumption* (SUTVA). Among other things, this assumption states that the potential outcome of one unit must not be affected by the actual assignment (to experimental conditions) of the remaining units. More precisely, SUTVA is a twofold assumption. First, it implies that there are *no hidden or different versions of the treatments*; that is, the selected treatment levels (or treatment level combinations) are administrated without any modification from the beginning to the end of the experiment. Second, it implies *no interference or interaction between subjects* who are receiving different treatment levels (or treatment level combinations). If we are dealing with a randomized experiment, this means that the independence condition introduced by the initial randomization must be preserved during the experiment to avoid potential contamination effects resulting from interactions between subjects assigned to distinct experimental conditions. Some authors subsume randomization procedures under the

SUTVA rubric, despite the clear statement of Rubin (2007, 2010) that substantive assumptions must be distinguished from the underlying assignment mechanism.

Rubin's causal model can be seen as an elaboration of the three fundamental principles of experimentation introduced by Fisher (1935/1966): (1) *replication*, (2) *randomization*, and (3) *local control*. The first principle implies the recording of observations from several units to estimate causal effects (mean differences). Randomization guarantees that the estimate is a nonbiased one. Local control ensures more precision in the estimation (i.e., a more efficient nonbiased estimator; for a synthesis of the properties of statistical estimators, see Fox, 2009). Stated in another way, randomization rules out alternative explanations based on the intrinsic characteristics of experimental units, whereas local control reduces the magnitude of random noise (residual variability) in the experiment.

In addition to the elaboration of Fisher's principles, a distinctive feature of Rubin's causal model is the replacement of the *observed outcomes notation* with the *potential outcomes notation* underlying his contrafactual approach to experimentation (*randomized experiments*) and quasi-experimentation (*observational studies*, according to the terminology introduced by Cochran [1965, 1983] and popularized by Rosenbaum [2002, 2010] and Rubin himself [Cochran & Rubin, 1973; Rubin, 1973]). In the context of this introductory chapter, it is sufficient to remark that the potential outcomes notation, initially proposed by Neyman (1923/1990), constitutes a coherent framework for the analysis of randomized and nonrandomized experiments and is particularly relevant in cases where the conditions established by the initial randomization are broken throughout the experiment and the SUTVA is violated. We will revisit this issue in the final chapter, which is centered on practical matters and the guiding principles of data analysis.

For now, we will be returning to the basics of experimental design, reproducing an extended definition given by Kirk (1995), in which the nature and the structure of randomized experiments are clearly detailed:

> The term experimental design refers to a plan for assigning subjects to experimental conditions and the statistical analysis associate with the plan. The design of an experiment to investigate a scientific or research hypothesis involves a number of interrelated activities:
>
> (1) Formulation of statistical hypotheses that are germane to the scientific hypothesis. A *statistical hypothesis* is a statement about (a) one or more parameters of a population or (b) the functional form of a population. Statistical hypotheses are rarely identical to scientific hypotheses; they are testable formulations of scientific hypotheses.

(2) Determination of the experimental conditions (independent variable) to be used, the measurement (dependent variable) to be recorded, and the extraneous conditions (nuisance variables) that must be controlled.

(3) Specification of the number of subjects (experimental units) required and the population from which they will be sampled.

(4) Specification of the procedure for assigning the subjects to the experimental conditions.

(5) Determination of the statistical analysis that will be performed. (pp. 1–2)

In the next section, these "interrelated activities" involved in experimental design are discussed in the broader context of the validity of causal inferences, and the main structural features of randomized experiments (*experimental factors*, *pseudofactors*, *classificatory factors*, and *outcome measures*) are conveniently described. Section 1.3 gives an overview of experimental designs in connection with methods of randomization and must be read as an advanced organizer for the core contents of Chapters 2 and 3. This introductory chapter ends with a brief section devoted to important terminological and notational issues.

1.2 Experimental Design and Validity of Scientific Inferences

Scientific hypotheses are conjectural statements about the relationships between theoretical constructs, empirically represented by particular events or realizations (called operationalizations or measurements). In the nomothetic tradition, relational or causal connections specified in the hypothesis are (ideally) theory driven. Inferences from data (particular observables) to the hypothesis (corroboration, falsification) are the realm of the scientific enterprise and must be distinguished from statistical inferences, which are about estimating population parameters from sampling particulars (Meehl, 1990). Study designs are the embodiment of the theoretical hypothesis, and their structural features define the conditions and constraints of scientific inference.

We can easily define the structural features of experimental designs by relying on the well-known Lewinian truism, which states that "in general terms, behavior (B) is a function (F) of the person (P) and of his environment (E), $B = F(P, E)$" (Lewin, 1946/1997, p. 337). First, *behavioral measures* (B) are *dependent variables* (outcome measures). Second, *environmental* or *situational variables* (E) susceptible of being manipulated are *experimental factors* (independent variables, treatments, or interventions). Third, *personal* or *dispositional variables* (P) are *classificatory factors*, which are ideally controlled by random assignment of units to experimental conditions. Finally, *pseudofactors*—that is, environmental or situational variables other than the focal or primary experimental factors—can be incorporated in the design (as secondary experimental factors), locally controlled (by holding them constant), or statistically handled (by measurement and subsequent modeling as covariables). When *classificatory factors*—conceptualized either as randomization restrictions (blocks or strata) or as measured covariables (substantive dispositional moderators)—are included in the design, they are occasionally labeled *passive independent variables* and contrasted with *true* (i.e., manipulated) or *active independent variables*.

A substantive classification of classificatory factors, experimental factors, outcome measures, and pseudofactors is given in Table 1.1, where some disciplinary traditions in experimental research are also identified. Using the terminology proposed by Cronbach (1982) to describe the basic

Table 1.1 Classification of Experimental Factors, Classificatory Factors, Pseudofactors, and Outcome Measures in Randomized Experiments

---

I. Experimental Factors (Independent Variables)   *Treatments*

  A. Physical Manipulations

   • Variations in physical settings (*ecological tradition*)
   • Variations of specific stimuli (*experimental psychology tradition*)

  B. Biological Manipulations

   • Biophysiological treatments and interventions (e.g., drugs, chemical therapies, chirurgical interventions; *pharmacological* and *evidence-based medicine traditions*)
   • Physical exercise and diet regimen (*sports* and *nutritional sciences traditions*)

  C. Psychosocial Manipulations

   • Variations in social stimuli and situations (*Festinger's tradition in social psychology*)
   • Variations in the *cognitive definition* (instructional manipulations) of social situations, physical settings and stimuli, or internal states (*experimental psychology tradition*; *social cognition experiments tradition*; *Schachter's tradition in social psychology*)
   • Variations of response contingencies (e.g., schedules of reinforcement; *Skinner's behaviorist tradition*)
   • Systematic psychological (e.g., psychotherapies) or social interventions (e.g., educational programs; *social experimentation tradition*; *evaluation studies tradition*)

  D. Combinations of Physical, Biological, and Psychosocial Manipulations

---

II. Classificatory Factors (Personal or Dispositional Variables)   *Units*

A. Biosocial Markers (gender, age, nationality, ethnicity, socioeconomic status, educational level, political and religious affiliations, sexual orientation, family and relationships status, structural characteristics of social and professional networks, etc.)

B. Physical Attributes and Organismic Variables

C. Personality Traits and (Enduring) Motivational-Emotional Dispositions

D. Cognitive Abilities and Styles

E. Frames of Reference (e.g., ideologies, shared social representations, etc.), Values, and Social Attitudes

III. Pseudofactors (Environmental or Situational Variables)   *Settings*

A. All the variables classified under *I—Experimental Factors*—but not being the focal target (i.e., active independent variables) in the current experiment

B. Socio-Institutional and Ecological Contexts and Temporal Structure of Experiments

IV. Outcome Measures (Dependent Variables)[a]   *Observations*

A. Self-Report Measures (rating scales; questionnaires and interviews; etc.)

B. Observational Measures

- Overt behaviors (including verbal behavior and expression of behavioral intentions, as well as performances in standardized tasks or psychological and educational tests)
- Biophysiological measures

C. Accretion and Erosion Measures ("behavioral fossils")

Note. This classification is restricted to randomized experiments with human beings or animals as experimental units, omitting typical manipulations and measures in agricultural, physical, or technological research.

[a]Classification of self-report and observational measures is based on Aronson, Ellsworth, Carlsmith, and Gonzalez (1990). Accretion and erosion measures are extensively presented and discussed in Webb, Campbell, Schwartz, Sechrest, and Grove (1981).

elements of experimental designs (UTOS: *units, treatments, observations, and settings*), the relationships between these elements are depicted in the lower left panel of Figure 1.2.

Figure 1.2 is a graphical representation of the widely known Campbellian approach to the validity of scientific inferences (Campbell, 1957;

8

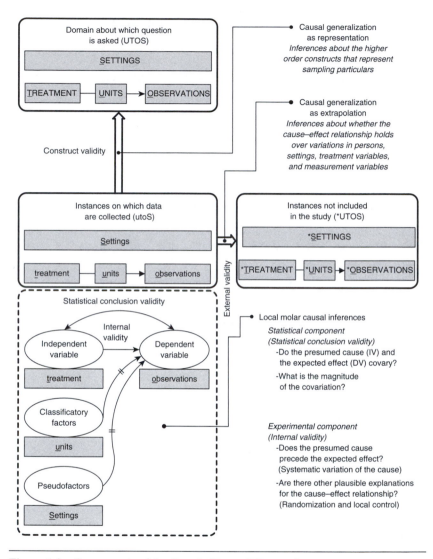

Figure 1.2   Components of the Campbellian validity typology

Campbell & Stanley, 1966; Cook & Campbell, 1979; Shadish & Cook, 2009; Shadish et al., 2002). To state it briefly, scientific claims are evaluated by the degree to which the underlying design allows the researcher to *make* and to *generalize* local causal inferences. Making valid local causal inferences is synonymous with giving unequivocal evidence of covariance between the presumed causes and the expected effects and, simultaneously, ruling out alternative explanations for the observed relationship. That is, the validity of local causal inferences depends on the statistical and experimental components of the research design (see *statistical conclusion validity* and *internal validity* in the lower right panel of Figure 1.2). Generalization of causal relationships requires a twofold approach: (1) generalizing from sampling particulars to higher order constructs (causal generalization as representation, or *construct validity*) and (2) generalizing the local causal relationship to other persons and instances not included in the study (causal generalization as extrapolation, or *external validity*) (see the two upper panels of Figure 1.2).

The four dimensions of the validity of scientific inferences (external, construct, internal, and statistical conclusion validity) can be thought of as the organizing principles for the main areas of the methodological field (*sampling, measurement, design,* and *analysis*), matching, term by term, the critical challenges that all researchers must deal with: (1) to extrapolate from observed samples to target populations, (2) to guarantee that their empirical realizations adequately represent the theoretical constructs involved in the scientific hypothesis, (3) to establish causality, and (4) to model the data ensuring that the underlying statistical relationships are not spurious. The first section of Chapter 4—focusing on practical matters related to planning and monitoring randomized experiments—is organized around the most common strategies to overcome potential drawbacks in local (Subsection 4.1.2) and generalized (Subsection 4.1.1) causal inferences.

1.3 Randomized Experiments and Methods of Randomization

In Section 1.1, experimental designs are contrasted with nonexperimental and quasi-experimental designs and classified into two broad categories according to the researcher's manipulation strategy: (1) *between-subjects* versus (2) *within-subjects designs*. Additionally, between-subjects designs are split into *completely randomized designs* and *restrictedly randomized designs*, on the basis of the restrictions (blocking or stratifying) imposed on random assignment procedures (see Figure 1.1). This classification scheme can be elaborated to account for other features of experimental design, such as the number of treatments, the pattern of treatment level combinations, and the introduction of control devices other than randomization and blocking (e.g., single and multiple pretest–posttest observations, covariates, or concomitant variables).

Relying on the *elementary building blocks* of randomized experiments (*CR—completely randomized, RB—randomized block*, and *LS—Latin square* basic designs) and their possible combinations, Kirk (1995, 2003a) proposes a very useful classification of factorial extensions of one-treatment designs. Excluding the examples of four "systematic designs" and two miscellaneous designs, Kirk (2003a, p. 11) lists 34 randomized designs, classified on the basis of six criteria: (1) the *number of treatments* (one vs. two or more treatments), (2) the *absence/presence of covariates* (analysis of variance [ANOVA] vs. analysis of covariance [ANCOVA] designs), (3) the *randomization procedures* used (simple random assignment vs. blocking prior to random assignment), (4) the *structure of factorial designs* (crossed vs. hierarchical designs), (5) the *absence/presence of confounding in crossed designs*, and (6) the *type of hierarchical designs* (complete vs. partial nesting). Ignoring ANCOVA designs, whose structure is similar to the equivalent ANOVA designs, and grouping together the variants and extensions of *incomplete block* (Designs 4) and *Latin square* (Designs 5) designs, we get the 22 designs listed in Figure 1.3.

Adopting an analysis-centered perspective, Kirk (1995, 2003a) subsumes within-subjects or repeated measures designs under the rubric *cross-over design*, a special type of the randomized block design where each block is formed by a single experimental unit that is observed in all experimental conditions (see Chapter 3, Table 3.3, Design 6N). This classification of within-subjects designs is consistent with the underlying statistical model of Design 6N, which for computational purposes is precisely the same. However, as Kirk (1995) observes, compared with designs containing homogeneous but different units per block, the cross-over design has distinct interpretations and generalizes to different target populations. More important in the context of this book, the counterbalancing procedures applying to Design 6N and to other types of cross-over designs are quite different from the random assignment procedures used in the between-subjects designs, and therefore, we have chosen to handle within-subjects designs randomization in a separate chapter (Chapter 3). For the rest, Figure 1.3 can be taken as an outline for the description of random assignment and blocking procedures in between-subjects designs (Chapter 2). The distinct types of the one-factor cross-over design (Designs 6 in Figure 1.3) and their factorial extensions are listed and labeled in Table 3.3 (Chapter 3). The main randomization methods described and illustrated in Chapters 2 and 3 are named and sequentially numerated in Tables 1.2 and 1.3.

This arrangement of the core contents of this monograph fits a widely used organization scheme in statistical analysis and research

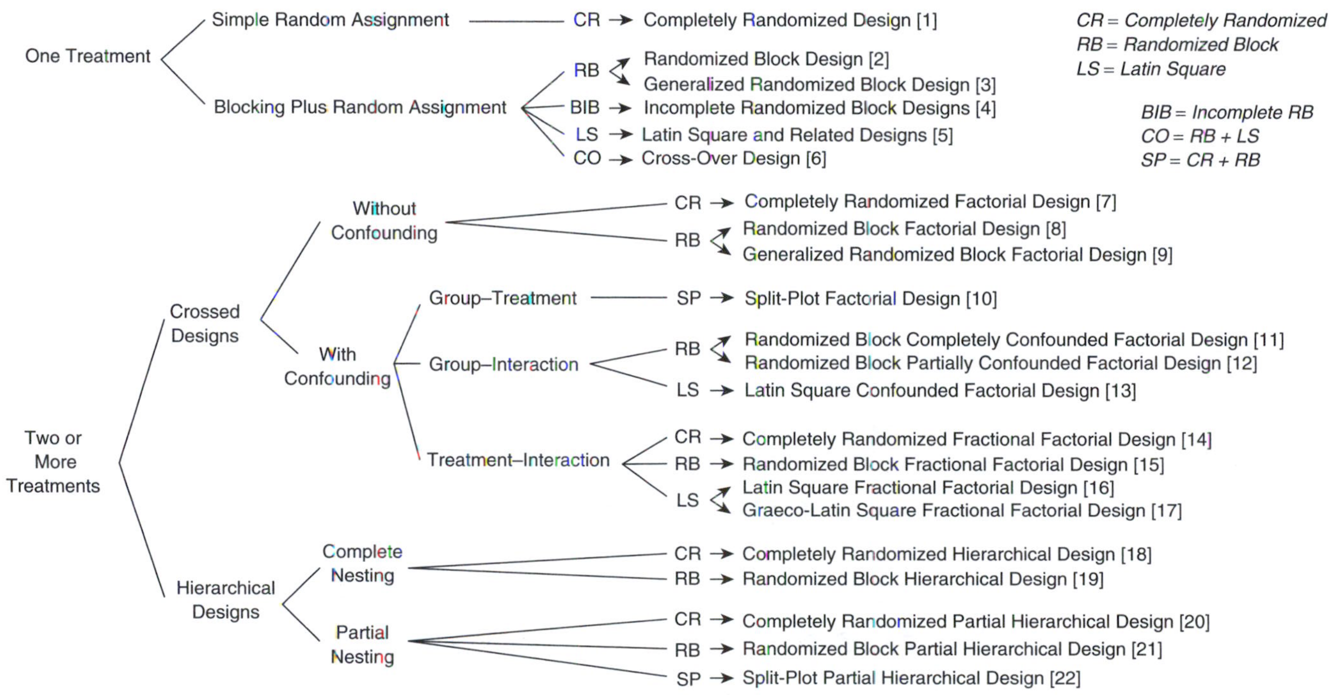

Figure 1.3 Classification of randomized experiments (based on Kirk, 1995, 2003a)

One Treatment

Simple Random Assignment ———— CR → Completely Randomized Design [1]

Blocking Plus Random Assignment

RB → Randomized Block Design [2]
RB → Generalized Randomized Block Design [3]
BIB → Incomplete Randomized Block Designs [4]
LS → Latin Square and Related Designs [5]
CO → Cross-Over Design [6]

Two or More Treatments

Crossed Designs

Without Confounding

CR → Completely Randomized Factorial Design [7]
RB → Randomized Block Factorial Design [8]
RB → Generalized Randomized Block Factorial Design [9]

With Confounding

Group–Treatment — SP → Split-Plot Factorial Design [10]

Group–Interaction

RB → Randomized Block Completely Confounded Factorial Design [11]
RB → Randomized Block Partially Confounded Factorial Design [12]
LS → Latin Square Confounded Factorial Design [13]

Treatment–Interaction

CR → Completely Randomized Fractional Factorial Design [14]
RB → Randomized Block Fractional Factorial Design [15]
LS → Latin Square Fractional Factorial Design [16]
LS → Graeco-Latin Square Fractional Factorial Design [17]

Hierarchical Designs

Complete Nesting

CR → Completely Randomized Hierarchical Design [18]
RB → Randomized Block Hierarchical Design [19]

Partial Nesting

CR → Completely Randomized Partial Hierarchical Design [20]
RB → Randomized Block Partial Hierarchical Design [21]
SP → Split-Plot Partial Hierarchical Design [22]

CR = Completely Randomized
RB = Randomized Block
LS = Latin Square

BIB = Incomplete RB
CO = RB + LS
SP = CR + RB

Table 1.2 Methods of Randomization of Between-Subjects Experimental
Designs

Method of Randomization		Comments	Design[a]
Nonrestricted Randomization			
SRA-ep	Simple Random Assignment with equal probabilities (Method 1)	—	1, 7, 14, 18, 20
SRA-up	Simple Random Assignment with unequal probabilities (Method 2)	—	1, 7, 14, 18, 20
SRA-es	Simple Random Assignment with forced equal sizes (Method 3)	—	1, 7, 14, 18, 20
SRA-us	Simple Random Assignment with forced unequal sizes (Method 4)	—	1, 7, 14, 18, 20
SRA-es-s	Simple Random Assignment with forced equal sizes—Sequential Assignment (Method 5)	Variation of Method 3 (Time Blocking)	1, 7, 14, 18, 20
SRA-us-s	Simple Random Assignment with forced unequal sizes—Sequential Assignment (Method 6)	Variation of Method 4 (Time Blocking)	1, 7, 14, 18, 20
Restricted Randomization: Blocking			
BRA-rb	Blocked Random Assignment with one blocking variable (Method 7)	Extension of Method 3	2, 3, 8, 9, 15, 19, 21
BRA-2s	Two-Step Blocked Random Assignment (Method 8)	Method 3 combined with Method 7	4, 10, 11, 12, 22
BRA-Ls	Two-Way Blocked Random Assignment: Latin Squares (Method 9)	Extension and restriction of Method 7	5A, 13, 16

Method of Randomization		Comments	Design[a]
BRA-GLs	Blocked Random Assignment Via Graeco-Latin Squares (Method 10)	Extension of Method 9	5B, 17
Restricted Randomization: Stratifying			
StrRA-c	Stratified Random Assignment: Nonsequential procedure (Method 11)	Extension of Method 3 plus Last Replication Correction	*Section 2.4*
StrRA-s	Stratified Random Assignment: Sequential procedure (Method 12)	Extension of Methods 3 (Time Blocking)	*Subsection* 2.5.3
Restricted Randomization: Minimizing Treatment Imbalance			
MIN	Minimization (Method 13)	Combination of Methods 1 and 2	*Subsection* 2.5.4

[a]For design designation, see Figure 1.3.

Table 1.3   Methods of Randomization of Within-Subjects (Cross-Over) Experimental Designs

Method of Randomization		Comments
Nonsequential Counterbalancing		
RC-ro	Random Counterbalancing (Method 14)	Variation of Method 7
PC-Ls	Positional Counterbalancing (Method 15)	Variation of Method 9
Sequential Counterbalancing		
SC-nr	Nonrestricted Sequential Counterbalancing (Method 16)	Application of Method 3 to Specific Sequences of Treatments
SC-rs	Restricted Sequential Counterbalancing: The Same Sequences per Group (Method 17)	Extension of Method 16
SC-rd	Restricted Sequential Counterbalancing: Different Sequences per Group (Method 18)	Extension of Method 17

Note. These methods apply to variations and factorial extensions (Designs 6A–6V—see Table 3.3) of Design 6 (Cross-Over Design—see Figure 1.3).

design reference books (e.g., Anderson, 2001; Keppel & Wickens, 2007; Maxwell & Delaney, 2004; Tabachnick & Fidell, 2007; Winer, Brown, & Michels, 1991). Shadish et al. (2002, p. 258), adopting a more methodological approach and omitting blocking and stratifying procedures, present diagrams for nine randomized experiments classified according to three criteria: (1) the *inclusion of pretests* (posttest-only designs vs. pretest–posttest designs), (2) the *number of experimental factors* (one-factor vs. two-factor designs), and (3) the *manipulation strategies* used (between-subjects vs. within-subjects designs). From the randomization perspective adopted here, eight designs are completely randomized designs (three variations of the *pretest–posttest design*, three variations of the *posttest-only design*, the *longitudinal design*, and the *factorial design*), and the remaining one (*cross-over design*) is a within-subjects or repeated measures design.

1.4 Terminological and Notational Issues

The designation under which *randomized experiments* are known varies according to the dominant traditions in each scientific discipline (e.g., *randomized controlled trials* or *randomized clinical trials* in medicine and the health sciences) and, even within the same discipline, researchers use different labels, as is the case in some areas of psychology, where *true experiments*, defined as the "gold standard" of experimentation, are contrasted with quasi-experiments, which are done without prior random assignment of subjects to experimental conditions (see Figure 1.1). The same goes for the labels currently applied to the major categories of experimental designs: (a) *between-subjects designs* are also called *independent group designs* and (b) *within-subjects designs* are known under the interchangeable names of *repeated measures designs* and *cross-over designs* (see Figure 1.1). The terminology is even more diverse when we consider the designations given to the manipulated, controlled, and measured variables in a randomized experiment, as the reader can notice on a careful inspection of Table 1.4.

Finally, a word of caution concerning the precise meaning of the key terms *treatment*, *treatment level* (also called *treatment arm* in some areas of medicine and the health sciences), *treatment level combination*, and *experimental condition*. *Experimental conditions* correspond to the differential features of the independent variable(s) manipulation or treatment(s) implementation. In one-factor experiments, the number of experimental conditions is identical to the *levels of the treatment*,

Table 1.4   Common Designations Given to Manipulated, Controlled, and Measured
Variables in Randomized Experiments

Causes (*Explanatory Factors*)				Effects
Experimental Factors and Pseudofactors[a] *Environmental/situational variables*		Classificatory Factors[a] *Personal/dispositional variables*		
Manipulated	Controlled	Included in the design	Controlled by randomization	Observations
• Experimental factor • Treatment • Independent variable (active) • Experimental variable • Stimulus (variable) • Intervention • Program • Primary factor	• Pseudofactor[b] • Settings[b] • Contextual variable[b]	• Blocking variable • Matching variable • Stratifying variable • Independent variable (passive) • Prognostic factor	• Subject variable • Intrinsic variable • Individual characteristics or attributes • Individual difference variable • Personality variable • Organismic variable	• Dependent variable • Measure • Outcome (measure) • Response (variable) • Behavioral variable

[a]Classificatory factors (i.e., personal or dispositional variables) and pseudofactors (i.e., all environmental or situational variables with the exception of the focal or primary experimental factors) are generically named *nuisance*, *extraneous*, or *confounding* variables. When explicitly measured and incorporated in data analysis, they are also referred to as *covariates* or *concomitant variables*.

[b]Pseudofactors, settings, or contextual variables (sometimes called *nonspecific factors*) are ideally controlled by holding them constant throughout the experiment. Alternatively, they can also be incorporated in the design as covariates or secondary experimental factors. In some circumstances, pseudofactors can be handled as blocking variables (e.g., *time blocking*).

while in (multi)factorial experiments, this number equals the number of *treatment level combinations* included in the design. To make a fair trade-off between clarity of exposition and economy of words, avoiding misunderstandings and giving the reader a consistent frame of reference, we have adopted in this monograph the notational system depicted in Table 1.5.

Table 1.5 Notational System for Treatments and Treatment Levels in Between-Subjects and Within-Subjects Experimental Designs

Design	Treatments	Treatment Levels
Between-Subjects Designs (Chapter 2)		
One treatment[a]	T	$T_1, T_2, T_3, \ldots$
Two or more treatments[b]	A	$A_1, A_2, A_3, \ldots$
	B	$B_1, B_2, B_3, \ldots$
	C	$C_1, C_2, C_3, \ldots$
	[...]	[...]
Within-Subjects Designs (Chapter 3)		
One treatment[c]	*No labeling*	A, B, C, ...
Two or more treatments		
Only within-subjects treatments[d]	W	$W_1, W_2, W_3, \ldots$
	X	$X_1, X_2, X_3, \ldots$
	[...]	[...]
At least one between-subjects treatment[e]		
Within-subjects treatments		*The same as previous*
Between-subjects treatments	T_A	$T_{A1}, T_{A2}, T_{A3}, \ldots$
	T_B	$T_{B1}, T_{B2}, T_{B3}, \ldots$
	[...]	[...]

[a] Subsections 2.2.1 and 2.3.1 to 2.3.4, and Sections 2.4 and 2.5
[b] Subsections 2.2.2 and 2.3.5
[c] Sections 3.1 to 3.6
[d] Subsection 3.7.1
[e] Subsection 3.7.2

CHAPTER 2. BETWEEN-SUBJECTS DESIGNS RANDOMIZATION

2.1 Randomization and Local Control

In spite of recent advances in the design and analysis of nonrandomized experiments (e.g., Rosenbaum, 2002, 2010; Rubin, 2006) and innovative approaches to the inference of causality in nonexperimental studies (e.g., Pearl, 2009), the randomized experiment has remained the best strategy when the researcher's main objective is to establish causal relationships. Needless to say, a large number of interesting and crucial problems cannot (yet?) be approached with experimental methods, namely, complex cognitive and affective *meditational process* in the behavioral sciences (Kenny, 2008) or *social phenomena* whose nature and structure inhibit the deliberate and systematic variation of their causal conditions and the effective control of contextual features. In any case, it is not by virtue of hidden or transcendental properties but for supplying a coherent and unified framework to infer causality that the randomized experiment plays a central role in the "scientific enterprise." This framework, with roots in David Hume's conceptualization of causal process and John Stuart Mill's methods of inductive logical reasoning, includes the demonstration of *temporal precedence*, the assessment of *covariation*, and the exclusion of *alternative explanations* for the observed phenomena.

This chapter is focused on the third distinctive feature of randomized experiments: exclusion of alternative explanations by random assignment and local control of the "heterogeneity" of experimental units. These principles of experimentation—introduced by Ronald Fisher (1925/1970, 1935/1966) in the beginning of the 20th century—can be thought of as central devices for making *local molar causal inferences*, as they have been conceptualized by Donald Campbell and colleagues (Campbell, 1957, 1986; Campbell & Stanley, 1966; Cook & Campbell, 1979; Shadish & Cook, 2009; Shadish et al., 2002) for more than 50 years.

Drawing causal inferences by excluding plausible rival explanations for experimental effects is an unfinished task that we are obliged to pursue, and the aid of some guidelines may make this task less painful. It is exactly with this purpose, and not as a kind of an "experimental design recipe book," that the so-called threats approach to scientific inferences developed by Campbell and colleagues is introduced in Figure 2.1, as a frame of reference for understanding the role of randomization and local control in experimental design. Figure 2.1 reproduces the lower panel of Figure 1.2, where the experimental and statistical components of valid local inferences

18

are schematized, and adds an organized list of internal and statistical conclusion validity threats to the picture (for the evolution and revisions of the
initial version of validity threats presented by Campbell in 1957, we recommend the firsthand reports given in Campbell, 1986; Campbell & Stanley,
1966; Cook & Campbell, 1979; Shadish et al. 2002).

The "group" of validity threats shown at the top of Figure 2.1 is a generic
one and concerns the central aim of experimentation: *estimation and evaluation of the magnitude of causal effects*. We shall return to this topic in
Chapter 4. The remaining four groups of threats are classified in terms of
their proximity to the structural features of randomized designs, as they were
presented in Chapter 1. The first group (*ambiguous temporal precedence*

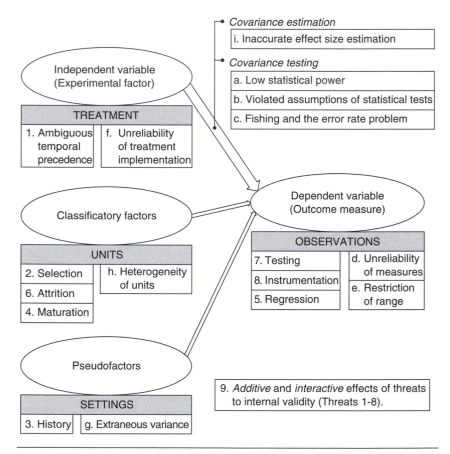

Figure 2.1 Local molar causal inferences: Threats to *internal validity* (Threats 1–9)
and to *statistical conclusion validity* (Threats *a–i*)

and *unreliability of treatment implementation*) is directly related to independent variable manipulation and is not a focal issue in the context of this chapter. The same is true for the second group of threats subsumed under the dependent variables measurement (*testing, instrumentation*, and *regression* for internal validity; *unreliability of measures* and *restriction of range* for statistical conclusion validity). Note that rigorously speaking *regression artifacts* are relational threats underlying all structural features (for an outstanding review and conceptualization, see Campbell & Kenny, 1999).

The last two groups of threats are more directly related to our purposes. Unwanted but systematic variations of environmental or situational factors other than experimental factors—threats to internal validity generically labeled as *history*—as well as contextual random noise (*extraneous variance*) can confound the effect of the independent variable. The environmental or situational factors can be controlled by holding them constant or by their inclusion in the design as blocking variables (e.g., time blocking), covariables, or secondary experimental factors. Random noise is inevitably a source of the residual (error) variance and must be considered in the data analysis stage.

Finally, the threats grouped under the *Units* box are the main concern of randomization and local control procedures. Technically speaking, the aim of *randomization* is to prevent the systematic bias associated with the intrinsic characteristics of experimental units in case they have been assigned to experimental conditions on the basis of some nonrandom criteria, hence the designation *selection* or *selection bias* for this threat to internal validity. In addition to the systematic bias potentially introduced by selection, the overall "heterogeneity" of experimental units, as is the case for situational random noise, increases the residual (error) variance, and therefore the net effect of the experimental treatment vanishes. *Local control* is the main strategy to deal with the overall "heterogeneity" of experimental units. Note that randomization also plays a role in the control of *additive and interactive effects* of selection with other threats to internal validity, namely, *attrition* (also called *experimental mortality*) and *maturation* (psychobiological changes in experimental units that may be confounded with the effects of the independent variables manipulation). Also observe that randomization per se doesn't rule out the main effects of attrition and maturation, and therefore other control devices (pre- and posttest measures for attrition and multiple-pretest observations for maturation) must be added to the experimental design (see Shadish et al., 2002). In the final chapter, these threats to internal and statistical conclusion validity, as well as some threats classified under the rubrics construct and external validity in the Campbellian framework, will be discussed in connection with the *potential outcomes approach* to experimentation proposed by Rubin (1974, 2006, 2007).

From a more statistical point of view, random assignment is the funda-mental device to obtain an unbiased estimate of the experimental effects by ensuring the independence of observations and making the error terms in the statistical model uncorrelated with the terms standing for the experimental effects (for a more comprehensive discussion of statistical issues, see Chapter 4). On the other hand, local control or blocking can be seen as a complementary technique for eliminating or reducing the het-erogeneity of units in the experiment and, this way, allowing a more *precise* (*efficient*) and unbiased estimate of causal effects. To speak about *reducing* or *eliminating* the heterogeneity of experimental units is a some-what misleading shortcut to refer to the role of local control in experi-mental design. Rigorously speaking, local control, or blocking, doesn't reduce any "heterogeneity" of experimental units. What blocking actually does is to distribute the units homogeneously across the experimental conditions on the basis of their scores (values) on the blocking variable (theoretically related with the outcome measure), which is—in the data analysis stage—incorporated in the statistical model in such a way that the variability in the outcome measure associated with it is subtracted from the residual variability (variability on the outcome measures within conditions). Saying it in other words, in the *zero-order elimination of heterogeneity of experimental units* strategy (completely randomized designs) the total variance in the outcome measure is divided into *system-atic variance* (theoretically explained by the systematic variation of the experimental factors) and random or *residual variance* (theoretically explained by all "insufficiently" controlled sources of error). In blocking (*one or more ways of elimination of heterogeneity*), the variability attrib-utable to the blocking variables is considered as systematic variability and subtracted from the residual or error variability, which becomes smaller, thereby allowing a more efficient estimation of the causal effect of the experimental treatment.

In conclusion, the main reason for randomization is to prevent threats to internal validity, namely, *selection* and related threats. The reason for choosing restrictedly randomized designs, instead of completely random-ized designs, is primarily a statistical conclusion validity issue: to circum-vent the potential heterogeneity of research units. In this sense, restrictedly randomized designs can be thought of as error-purifying designs (Weiss, 2006). For the same reason, a within-subjects (repeated measures or cross-over) design constitutes an ideal error-purifying design, in which the het-erogeneity of units is theoretically zero. Unfortunately, there are other problems underlying within-subjects designs (see Sections 3.1 and 3.2).

Before proceeding with the practical features of randomization and local control, it is convenient to distinguish between a *randomization plan* and a *design layout* (i.e., the specification of design structure, namely, the nature and number of treatments and treatment levels and the desired pattern of treatment level combinations). Federer and Balaam (1973), in a systematic bibliography of theoretical, methodological, and statistical literature on experimental investigations, adopt the expressions *experiment design* and *treatment design* for these two complementary features of experimentation. The former label applies to the way treatments are arranged in an experiment, which is the basis for the classification of experimental designs according to the strategies of randomization and elimination of the heterogeneity of experimental units: *zero-way elimination* (e.g., completely randomized designs), *one-way elimination* (e.g., randomized block designs), *two-way elimination* (e.g., Latin square designs), *three-way elimination* (e.g., Graeco-Latin square designs), and *four- and higher-way elimination* (e.g., Hyper-Graeco-Latin square and other complex designs). In contrast, *treatment design* refers to the actual selection of treatments, including the selection of treatment levels (e.g., selection on the basis of previous regression analysis, dose–response studies, fixed vs. random factors, etc.), handling more than one treatment (e.g., factorial designs), confounding, nesting, and fractional replication.

Hinkelmann and Kempthorne (2008) make a similar distinction between *treatment design* (the same label given by Federer & Balaam, 1973) and *error control design* (their label for *experiment design*) and present *sampling and observation design* as a third component of experimental design. In light of these distinctions, this chapter focuses primarily on *experiment* or *error control* design. However, instead of presenting randomization methods as stand-alone tools, emphasis is placed on the interdependence between random assignment strategies and the structural features of experimental designs (*treatment design*). *Sampling and observational design* issues will be briefly discussed in the final chapter.

Taking a practical approach, random assignment or random allocation is the process of associating, term by term, a *systematically ordered list* of treatment levels or treatment level combinations with a *randomly ordered list* of available experimental units (simple random assignment, SRA) or with *multiple randomly ordered lists* of available experimental units within homogeneous blocks (blocked random assignment, BRA) or strata (stratified random assignment, StrRA). It is formally equivalent to matching a randomly ordered list of treatment level replications to a systematically ordered list of available units (e.g., names in alphabetical order, order of enrollment in the experiment, etc.). For example, in "captive" or *nonsequential assignment* (i.e., in situations where all experimental units are available at the onset of the experiment; Sections 2.2–2.4), we associate a systematically ordered list of treatment replications to a randomly permuted list of units (i.e., identification numbers [IDs] in the allocation frame are randomly ordered), so that the reader can easily grasp the structure of the experiment in conjunction with the final allocation of units. In *sequential assignment* (Section 2.5), considering the allocation procedural constraints, we associate a randomly permuted list of treatment replications to a systematically ordered list of IDs ($1-n$) corresponding to the order of the units enrollment in the experiment.

When properly done—that is, when the systematically ordered list is exhaustive and unambiguous, the correspondence between ID numbers and units is kept unchangeable through the experiment, and the random mechanism underlying the randomly ordered list is a nonfaulty one—this association process ensures that each experimental unit has a nonzero probability of being allocated to a particular treatment level (or treatment level combination) or, which is the same, that each treatment level (or treatment level combination) has a nonzero probability of being assigned to a particular experimental unit. Ideally, this probability should be equal for all units or treatment levels. Local and procedural constraints, substantive restrictions, and the practical or theoretical relevance of specific intended comparisons can result in or justify unequal probabilities of assignment. In any case, theoretical probabilities of assignment must be specified in advance (see Subsection 4.2.1 for a discussion of assignment mechanisms and underlying probabilities).

The remaining sections of this chapter are organized around the type of limitations imposed on random assignment: (a) *procedural constraints* (number of available units per experiment and number of intended units in each experimental condition; equal-size homogeneous blocks of experimental units) and (b) *substantive restrictions* (restrictions based on the intrinsic characteristics of experimental units—classificatory factors). Section 2.2 deals with simple random assignment in *completely randomized designs*, that is, designs that contain only procedural constraints. Sections 2.3 and 2.4 deal with *restrictedly randomized designs*, that is, designs involving substantive restrictions, in which experimental units are grouped in homogeneous blocks (*randomized block* and *Latin square designs*) or strata prior to random assignment. Randomization and local control procedures are first described and illustrated with one-treatment designs and then extended to factorial designs. From Section 2.2 to Section 2.4, all procedures are presented on the assumption that the *allocation frame* (i.e., a systematically ordered list of all units numerated from 1 to n) is available at the onset of the experiment ("captive" or nonsequential assignment). Adjustments of these procedures to sequential assignment and adaptive randomization strategies (e.g., minimization) are described in Section 2.5.

2.2 Completely Randomized Designs

2.2.1 Basic Design

When the researcher "follows the old standard *rule of one variable*, [holding] all the conditions constant except for one factor which is his *experimental factor* or his *independent variable*" (Woodworth, 1938, p. 2) and he or she has no compelling reasons to engage in local control of classificatory factors, the randomization plan consists in assigning at chance the *t* treatment levels to the *N* available experimental units (or, which is the same, assigning at chance the *N* experimental units to the *t* treatment levels). The resulting design is called *Completely Randomized Design* (Design 1; see Figure 1.3), and the randomization procedure is known as SRA. This is the most basic experimental design and one of the three elementary "building blocks" of complex experimental designs (Kirk, 1995; the remaining two elementary building blocks are the one-factor randomized block design and the Latin square design—see Section 1.3 and Subsections 2.3.1 and 2.3.4).

Rigorously speaking, SRA implies equal probabilities of assignment, which means that each experimental unit has an equal probability of being assigned to each of the treatment levels included in the design (Method 1: *Equal Probabilities of Assignment*). With a finite and small number of available experimental units, Method 1 seldom conduces to a balanced design, that is, a design in which all treatment levels are equally replicated. The search for balanced designs, whose properties express an ideal trade-off between costs and power of experiments and allow simplicity in the data analysis stage, often justifies the introduction of procedural constraints to ensure that all experimental conditions have the same number of experimental units (Method 3: *Forced Equal Sizes*). On the other hand, Method 4—*Forced Unequal Sizes*—can be used on the basis of the theoretical or practical relevance of specific comparisons, which are made with greater power than less relevant comparisons. Finally, Method 2—*Unequal Probabilities of Assignment*, also known as *Biased Coin Method* (Efron, 1971)—is of special interest in the context of the adaptive randomization procedures discussed in Subsection 2.5.5 (for a more detailed discussion of the probabilistic nature of the basic SRA methods, see Subsection 4.2.1).

To carry out SRA, we begin by associating, term by term, a series of random numbers to the entries of an allocation frame. Units in the allocation frame must be unambiguously identified and sequentially numerated (1–*n*). Table 2.1 shows such an allocation frame with 20 experimental units, ordered alphabetically by name and numerated from 1 to 20 (note that any other systematic criterion could be used to order the units, as long as the correspondence between ID numbers and units is kept unchangeable from the beginning to the end of the study). The associated series of random numbers could be produced by any random numbers generating mechanism (see Appendix 1) or simply taken from an existing table of random numbers. Throughout this monograph, we have used Table A1.1 to get series of random numbers drawn from a uniform distribution in the interval [.000, .999]. For example, having randomly picked number 6 in the intersection of Row 27 and Column 13 of Table A1.1 as the starting point and having decided in advance to read the table vertically (down columns instead of across rows or diagonals, from top to bottom and from left to right), to select numbers with three digits (digits occurring in the random selected column and in the two immediately adjacent columns), and to divide these numbers by 1,000 (in order to obtain a random uniform series between .000 and .999), we got the series of 20 random numbers shown in Table 2.1, beginning in .621 and ending in .143 (for a detailed description of this procedure and alternative procedures for using tables of random numbers, see Appendix 1).

Table 2.1   Completely Randomized Design: Allocation Frame and Random Numbers (RN) (Design 1; Methods 1, 2, 3, and 4)

Allocation Frame and Random Numbers			Allocation Frame Sorted by Random Numbers		
ID	Unit	RN	ID	Unit	RN
1	Andy	.621	18	Ted	.037
2	Bill	.388	8	Gene	.048
3	Bob	.546	20	Walt	.143
4	Chris	.205	17	Ron	.199
5	Dave	.641	4	Chris	.205
6	Don	.616	13	Mike	.245
7	Frank	.721	12	Larry	.334
8	Gene	.048	2	Bill	.388
9	Hal	.973	11	Ken	.469
10	Jack	.833	15	Pete	.494
11	Ken	.469	3	Bob	.546
12	Larry	.334	6	Don	.616
13	Mike	.245	1	Andy	.621
14	Nick	.852	5	Dave	.641

Allocation Frame and Random Numbers			Allocation Frame Sorted by Random Numbers		
ID	Unit	RN	ID	Unit	RN
15	Pete	.494	7	Frank	.721
16	Phil	.764	16	Phil	.764
17	Ron	.199	10	Jack	.833
18	Ted	.037	14	Nick	.852
19	Tom	.911	19	Tom	.911
20	Walt	.143	9	Hal	.973

RN: Table A1.1 (Rows: 27–46; Columns: 13–15).

In the next step, we sort the ID numbers (units) by the random series (see the last three columns of Table 2.1; also repeated in Table 2.2) and assign the treatments levels according to the intended SRA method (see Table 2.2). For *forced sizes* methods (Methods 3 and 4), we simply associate the randomly ordered list of units with the systematically ordered list of treatment level replications. For instance, in Method 3—*Forced Equal Sizes*—the randomization plan contains five replications for each treatment level (T1, T2, T3, and T4), which are systematically ordered in the sixth column of Table 2.2. According to the random permutation of their ID numbers, Ted, Gene, Walt, Ron, and Chris are assigned to Treatment Level T1; Mike, . . ., and Pete to T2, and so forth. With the understanding that a different number of replications is systematically listed for each treatment level (in our example, 7, 3, 3, and 7 replications, respectively), random assignment in Method 4—*Forced Unequal Sizes*—is analogous to that in Method 3 (see last column of Table 2.2).

For *a priori probabilities* methods (Methods 1 and 2), the randomization strategy capitalizes on the procedure we have used to draw random numbers. More specifically, in Method 1—*Equal Probabilities*—the probability that a three-digit random number drawn from a uniform distribution within the interval [.000, .999] falls in one of the four equal-length intervals ([.000, .250[, [.250, .500[, [.500, .750[, and [.750, .999]) is exactly $p = 1/4 = .25$. As a result, all the units (Ted, Gene, Walt, Ron, Chris, and Mike) whose associated random numbers fall in the interval [.000, .250[are assigned to Treatment Level T1; those in the interval [.250, .500[are assigned to Treatment Level T2, and so on (see fourth column of Table 2.2). Likewise, in Method 2—*Unequal Probabilities*—the probabilities for the intervals [.000, .400[, [.400, .600[, [.600, .800[, and [.800, .999] are $p_1 = .40$, $p_2 = .20$, $p_3 = .20$,

Table 2.2 Completely Randomized Design: Procedures for Allocation of 20 Units (See Table 2.1) to Four Treatment Levels (T1, T2, T3, and T4) (Design 1; Methods 1, 2, 3, and 4)

			Treatment allocation			
Allocation Frame Sorted by Random Numbers (RN)			A priori probabilities		Forced sizes	
			Equal	Unequal	Equal	Unequal
ID	Unit	RN	$p = .25$	$p_{1-4} = .40, .20, .20, .20$	$n = 5$	$n_{1-4} = 7, 3, 3, 7$
18	Ted	.037	T1	T1	T1	T1
8	Gene	.048	T1	T1	T1	T1
20	Walt	.143	T1	T1	T1	T1
17	Ron	.199	T1	T1	T1	T1
4	Chris	.205	T1	T1	T1	T1
13	Mike	.245	T1	T1	T2	T1
12	Larry	.334	T2	T1	T2	T1
2	Bill	.388	T2	T1	T2	T2
11	Ken	.469	T2	T2	T2	T2
15	Pete	.494	T2	T2	T2	T2
3	Bob	.546	T3	T2	T3	T3
6	Don	.616	T3	T3	T3	T3
1	Andy	.621	T3	T3	T3	T3
5	Dave	.641	T3	T3	T3	T4
7	Frank	.721	T3	T3	T3	T4
16	Phil	.764	T4	T3	T4	T4
10	Jack	.833	T4	T4	T4	T4
14	Nick	.852	T4	T4	T4	T4
19	Tom	.911	T4	T4	T4	T4
9	Hal	.973	T4	T4	T4	T4

and $p_4 = .20$, respectively. The random assignment procedure is similar to the one for Method 1 (see fifth column of Table 2.2). Note that in *a priori probabilities* methods there is no need to sort the allocation frame by random numbers: Once the random series is drawn, the assignment is automatically done. In the example, we have sorted the allocation frame to permit a quick contrast between the four basic methods of SRA.

Although Method 1—*Equal Probabilities of Assignment*—corresponds to the formal definition of SRA, Method 3—*Forced Equal Sizes*—in view of the aforementioned reasons (optimal trade-off between the costs and power of experiments and data analysis facilities) is the standard choice in completely randomized designs. However, when the number of units per experiment is not a multiple of the number of treatments, Method 3 cannot conduce to an equal number of subjects (n_s) per experimental condition. In this situation, the reader may adopt one of the following procedures for treatment exclusion of the last replication: (a) elimination of treatments based on theoretical/practical relevance, (b) elimination of the last treatment(s), and (c) random elimination of treatments. This may appear to be a nonissue, because when applying the forced equal sizes strategy in a completely randomized design the difference between the number of experimental units assigned to different treatment levels cannot be greater than 1. Nevertheless, when Method 3 is applied within strata in the stratified random assignment (see Section 2.4) and there is no compelling reason to adopt procedure (a), the choice of procedure (b) instead of procedure (c) can result in severe imbalance.

To carry out procedure (c) we draw a random permutation of treatments order (see Appendix 2), and we apply this permutation to the last treatment replication. For instance, if only 19 units are available in the allocation frame for Design 1 (see Table 2.2), all treatment levels will be replicated four times but only three of them will be replicated five times. Supposing we have picked from Table A1.1 the random permutation of four digits: 2, 4, 1, 3 (Rows: 35–50; Column: 19); then treatment T3's fifth replication will be excluded from the systematically ordered list of treatments included in Table 2.2: T1, T1, T1, T1, T1, T2, T2, T2, T2, T2, T3, T3, T3, T3, T4, T4, T4, T4, T4. A generalization of procedure (c)—which we have called *last replication correction* (LRC)—to stratified random assignment is presented in Section 2.4.

2.2.2 Factorial Designs

The "old standard *rule of one variable*" is no longer the dominant strategy in experimental design. For theoretical or "economical" reasons, researchers in the social, behavioral, educational, or health sciences run experiments with two or more independent variables hoping to analyze the patterns of interaction (moderation effects) in the determination of the outcome response.

According to the pattern of treatment level combinations, completely randomized factorial designs can be classified into *crossed* or *hierarchical* (nested) designs. The former category applies to designs where all possible combinations of treatment levels are included (see Design 7: *Completely Randomized Factorial Design*; Table 2.3). The latter one refers to designs where at least the levels of one treatment are not completely crossed with the levels of a second treatment (see Design 18: *Completely Randomized Hierarchical Design*; Table 2.3). With more than two treatments, it is possible to have simultaneously crossed and nested factors (partial nesting). For instance, in Design 20—*Completely Randomized Partial Hierarchical Design* (see Table 2.3)—Treatment C is crossed with Treatments A and B, but Treatment B is nested in Treatment A. Finally, when some possible treatment level combinations are omitted from crossed designs, at the expense of confounding treatment and interaction effects, the designs are called *completely randomized fractional factorial designs* (e.g., Design 14 in Table 2.3 is a *one-half fraction* of the corresponding completely randomized factorial design with four treatments—A, B, C, and D—and two levels per treatment).

Nesting structures and fractional replication are complex topics in *treatment design* (design layout) and are out of the scope of the present monograph (for trustworthy presentations and discussions, see Hinkelmann & Kempthorne, 2005, 2008; Kirk, 1995). However, from the *error control design* perspective, the randomization of completely randomized factorial designs is a mere extension of the single-factor completely randomized design. More precisely, instead of treatment levels, treatment level combinations included in the layout are assigned to experimental units. For instance, in the four designs depicted in Table 2.3, the available experimental units would be randomly assigned to *eight* (Design 7), *four* (Design 18), *eight* (Design 20), and *eight* (Design 14) experimental conditions or treatment level combinations. Any of the four basic SRA methods could be used, but Method 3—*Forced Equal Sizes*—remains the standard choice.

2.3 Restrictedly Randomized Designs: Blocking

Restricted randomization is the combination of SRA with local control procedures. On the basis of their intrinsic characteristics, experimental units are arranged in homogeneous groups (blocks or strata) prior to random assignment. Random assignment within homogeneous groups rules

Table 2.3 Layouts of Completely Randomized Factorial Designs (Designs 7, 14, 18, and 20)

Design 7—Completely Randomized Factorial Design					Design 18—Completely Randomized Hierarchical Design			
	B_1	B_2	B_3	B_4		B_1	B_2	B_3	B_4
A_1	A_1B_1	A_1B_2	A_1B_3	A_1B_4	A_1	A_1B_1	A_1B_2		
A_2	A_2B_1	A_2B_2	A_2B_3	A_2B_4	A_2			A_2B_3	A_2B_4

Note. Treatments A and B are crossed.   *Note.* Treatment B is nested in treatment A.

Design 20—Completely Randomized Partial Hierarchical Design

	B_1		B_2		B_3		B_4	
	C_1	C_2	C_1	C_2	C_1	C_2	C_1	C_2
A_1	$A_1B_1C_1$	$A_1B_1C_2$	$A_1B_2C_1$	$A_1B_2C_2$				
A_2					$A_2B_3C_1$	$A_2B_3C_2$	$A_2B_4C_1$	$A_2B_4C_2$

Note. Treatments A and C, as well as treatments B and C, are crossed, but treatment B is nested in treatment A.

Design 14—Completely Randomized Fractional Factorial Design

		C_1		C_2	
		D_1	D_2	D_1	D_2
A_1	B_1	$A_1B_1C_1D_1$			$A_1B_1C_2D_2$
	B_2		$A_1B_2C_1D_2$	$A_1B_2C_2D_1$	
A_2	B_1		$A_2B_1C_1D_2$	$A_2B_1C_2D_1$	
	B_2	$A_1B_1C_1D_1$			$A_2B_2C_2D_2$

Note. One-half fraction of a completely randomized factorial design with four treatments (A, B, C, and D) and with two levels per treatment.

out alternative explanations to treatment effects based on the individual attributes of experimental units (classificatory factors). Blocking and stratifying reduce the overall "heterogeneity" of units or, which is the same, minimize the residual variability or error term in ANOVA models, allowing a more precise estimation of treatment effects.

Procedural constraints make the distinction between blocking and strati-fying. In blocking, the number of units per block must be equal to or a multiple of the number of experimental conditions, with the exception of incomplete blocks, in which this number is smaller than the number of experimental conditions, but it is the same for all blocks. In stratifying, the number of experimental units varies across strata, and treatments are unequally replicated within each stratum. In this section, we describe ran-domization methods applying to homogeneous blocks of experimental units. The next section deals with stratified random assignment.

2.3.1 Randomized Block Design

Using Federer and Balaam's (1973) terminology, randomized block designs illustrate the *one-way elimination* of the heterogeneity of the exper-imental units. In randomized block designs, the researcher begins by arrang-ing the available experimental units in equal-size homogeneous groups (blocks), on the basis of individual scores (values) on the *blocking variable*. The blocking variable can be any classificatory factor (see Section 1.2), as long as the information it conveys is theoretically relevant for dependent variable prediction. Saying it in another way, the choice of the blocking vari-able must be carefully made, with the understanding that its role in the minimization of residual variability is a function of the expected correlation with the outcome measure. Vis-à-vis the measurement scale, the blocking variable can be a *nonmetric* (nonordered categories and ordered categories; nominal and ordinal scales) or a *metric* (continuous variable; interval and ratio scales) variable.

Suppose you are studying the impact of extrinsic motivation (a treatment with three levels: *high*, *medium*, and *low* incentives) on academic achieve-ment (outcome measure) and you have good reasons to suspect that stu-dents' cognitive abilities (classificatory factor) could diminish the expected relationship "Higher incentives → Better achievement." Instead of assign-ing at random the available experimental units to the three treatment levels (SRA; completely randomized design), you could assess students' IQ (intelligence quotient) prior to randomization, place them in homogeneous blocks on the basis of their IQ level, and finally proceed to random assign-ment of treatment levels within each block. If the number of units per block is the same as the number of treatment levels, so that in each block only one experimental unit is assigned to each treatment level, your randomization strategy is called BRA (Method 7) and the resulting design is a *Randomized Block Design* (Design 2). With this strategy, you have controlled the vari-ability of cognitive abilities within experimental conditions (local control) and therefore created the optimal circumstances for a more precise estima-tion of the effect of motivation on academic achievement.

The adopted blocking and randomization procedures are illustrated in Tables 2.4 and 2.5, assuming that 18 experimental units (students) have been enrolled and are available at the onset of the experiment. For example, Gabby, Deb, and Nancy, according to their IQ scores, have been placed in Block 6 (see Table 2.4); in line with the associated random numbers, they have been allocated to Treatment Levels T1, T3, and T2, respectively (see Table 2.5). Note that in the allocation frame for BRA, the IDs are sequentially

Table 2.4   Randomized Block Design: Allocation Frame and Random Numbers (RN) (Design 2; Method 7)

Units and Blocking Variable Scores (IQ)		Allocation Frame Sorted by Blocking Variable and Random Numbers				
Unit	IQ	Block	ID	Unit	IQ	RN
Aggie	109	1	1	Nan	134	.261
Bea	130	1	2	Sue	132	.742
Betty	121	1	3	Bea	130	.119
Cathy	120	2	1	May	126	.615
Deb	100	2	2	Glad	124	.827
Flo	115	2	3	Lucy	123	.178
Gabby	103	3	1	Betty	121	.568
Glad	124	3	2	Cathy	120	.773
Hill	108	3	3	Terry	117	.797
Lucy	123	4	1	Pam	116	.180
May	126	4	2	Rosie	116	.507
Nan	134	4	3	Flo	115	.042
Nancy	98	5	1	Aggie	109	.544
Pam	116	5	2	Hill	108	.668
Rosie	116	5	3	Viv	105	.282
Sue	132	6	1	Gabby	103	.130
Terry	117	6	2	Deb	100	.729
Viv	105	6	3	Nancy	98	.166

RN: Table A1.1 (Rows: 9–26; Columns: 31–33).

Table 2.5   Randomized Block Design: Allocation of 18 Units (Grouped in Six Blocks of 3 Units—See Table 2.4) to Three Treatment Levels (T1, T2, and T3) (Design 2; Method 7)

	Block 1					Block 2			
ID	Unit	IQ	RN	Treatment	ID	Unit	IQ	RN	Treatment
3	Bea	130	.119	T1	3	Lucy	123	.178	T1
1	Nan	134	.261	T2	1	May	126	.615	T2
2	Sue	132	.742	T3	2	Glad	124	.827	T3
	Block 3					Block 4			
ID	Unit	IQ	RN	Treatment	ID	Unit	IQ	RN	Treatment
1	Betty	121	.568	T1	3	Flo	115	.042	T1
2	Cathy	120	.773	T2	1	Pam	116	.180	T2
3	Terry	117	.797	T3	2	Rosie	116	.507	T3
	Block 5					Block 6			
ID	Unit	IQ	RN	Treatment	ID	Unit	IQ	RN	Treatment
3	Viv	105	.282	T1	1	Gabby	103	.130	T1
1	Aggie	109	.544	T2	3	Nancy	98	.166	T2
2	Hill	108	.668	T3	2	Deb	100	.729	T3

assigned within blocks, which themselves are also sequentially numerated (1–*n*). Note also that Method 7—*Blocked Random Assignment*—is simply the application of SRA (Method 3: *Forced Equal Sizes*) within the blocks included in the allocation frame.

2.3.2 Generalized Randomized Block Design

When the number of experimental units per block is greater than the number of treatment levels (*t*) but is fixed at any multiple of this number (*kt*, where *k* is any integer ≥2), using Method 7—*Blocked Random Assignment*—produces a *Generalized Randomized Block Design* (Design 3). The randomization procedure is identical to the procedure for the *Randomized Block Design* (Design 2), with the exception that in each block two or more experimental units are assigned to each treatment level. Tables 2.6 and 2.7

Table 2.6   Generalized Randomized Block Design: Allocation Frame and
Random Numbers (RN) (Design 3; Method 7)

Units and Blocking Variabe (Gender)		Allocation Frame Sorted by Blocking Variable and Random Numbers				
Unit	Gender	Block	ID	Unit	Gender	RN
Abbie	Female	1	1	Art	Male	.580
Art	Male	1	2	Bernie	Male	.671
Bernie	Male	1	3	Chuck	Male	.570
Bonny	Female	1	4	Ernie	Male	.281
Chuck	Male	1	5	Jim	Male	.250
Cindy	Female	1	6	Leo	Male	.145
Denny	Female	1	7	Rick	Male	.249
Ernie	Male	1	8	Steve	Male	.065
Jim	Male	1	9	Tony	Male	.082
Jody	Female	2	1	Abbie	Female	.385
Leo	Male	2	2	Bonny	Female	.184
Lora	Female	2	3	Cindy	Female	.931
Mel	Female	2	4	Denny	Female	.162
Reggie	Female	2	5	Jody	Female	.346
Rick	Male	2	6	Lora	Female	.949
Steve	Male	2	7	Mel	Female	.715
Tony	Male	2	8	Reggie	Female	.913
Vonna	Female	2	9	Vonna	Female	.713

RN: Table A1.1 (Rows: 21–38; Columns: 9–11).

show the allocation frame, the randomization procedure, and the final allocation for a generalized randomized block design with three treatment
levels (T1, T2, and T3) and a nominal blocking variable: *gender* of the
experimental units.

Table 2.7 Generalized Randomized Block Design: Allocation of 18 Units (Grouped in Two Blocks of 9 Units—See Table 2.6) to Three Treatment Levels (T1, T2, and T3) (Design 3; Method 7)

		Block 1					Block 2		
ID	Unit	Gender	RN	Treatment	ID	Unit	Gender	RN	Treatment
8	Steve	Male	.065	T1	4	Denny	Female	.162	T1
9	Tony	Male	.082	T1	2	Bonny	Female	.184	T1
6	Leo	Male	.145	T1	5	Jody	Female	.346	T1
7	Rick	Male	.249	T2	1	Abbie	Female	.385	T2
5	Jim	Male	.250	T2	9	Vonna	Female	.713	T2
4	Ernie	Male	.281	T2	7	Mel	Female	.715	T2
3	Chuck	Male	.570	T3	8	Reggie	Female	.913	T3
1	Art	Male	.580	T3	3	Cindy	Female	.931	T3
2	Bernie	Male	.671	T3	6	Lora	Female	.949	T3

The option between Design 2 (*Randomized Block Design*, also called *Complete Randomized Block Design*; see Hinkelmann & Kempthorne, 2008) and Design 3 (*Generalized Randomized Block Design*) is simultaneously a procedural and a substantive (theoretical) issue, as it depends on having enough homogeneous experimental units to form larger size blocks and the expected relationship between the experimental factor and the blocking variable. More precisely, in randomized block designs, the interaction between the blocking variable and the experimental factor is completely confounded with the residual variance (crossing both variables in the design layout gives rise to *one* experimental unit per cell), and therefore only the main effects for both variables can be estimated. In contrast, generalized randomized block designs, in which each cell has at least two experimental units, allow the estimation of the interaction effect besides the main effects of the experimental factor and the blocking variable (see Subsection 4.2.2). Briefly stated, when larger size blocks are possible and some kind of interaction between the independent and the blocking variable can be anticipated, the best option is the generalized randomized block design.

As Kirk (1995) remarks, this design is often misspelled in empirical research reports and confounded with the two-factor *Completely Randomized Factorial Design* (Design 7; see Table 2.3). The confusion comes from the fact that both designs share the same underlying statistical model; however the Completely Randomized Factorial Design has two true experimental factors (active independent variables), whereas the Generalized Randomized Block Design is limited to one active independent variable (the experimental factor) and one passive independent variable (the blocking variable; see Table 1.4 for terminological details).

2.3.3 Incomplete Randomized Block Designs

When the number of treatment levels is large and the distribution of observed scores (values) on the blocking variable doesn't recommend the arrangement of available experimental units in blocks of size equal to or a multiple of the number of experimental conditions, a strategy to circumvent the problem consists in the formation of a homogeneous block whose size is smaller than the number of treatment levels. In this situation, the design layout must include a fixed number of treatment level arrangements, selected in such a way that all pairwise associations between treatment levels within blocks are equally replicated.

Design 4A in Table 2.8 corresponds to this requirement in the sense that every pairwise association of the six treatment levels (1, 2, 3, 4, 5, and 6) occurs exactly twice across the 10 blocks (e.g., the association of Treatment Levels 1 and 2 is presented in the first two blocks, whereas the association of Treatment Levels 3 and 5 is displayed in Blocks 7 and 9). Design 4A is called a *Balanced Incomplete Randomized Block Design*, with t (treatment levels) = 6, b (blocks) = 10, k (experimental units per block) = 3, r (treatment level replications per experiment) = 5, and λ (number of times each pair of treatment levels is replicated within blocks) = 2.

There are no balanced designs for certain combinations of the above parameters. When the relationship $\lambda = [r(k-1)]/(t-1)$ gives a noninteger solution for λ, one can be sure that no balanced design exists. When the solution is an integer, one can look for the corresponding design in authoritative sources (e.g., Cochran & Cox, 1957; Federer, 1955; Hinkelmann & Kempthorne, 2005, 2008; Kempthorne, 1952), in spite of knowing that even in this case not all balanced designs can be built. A less satisfactory solution is to rely on what has been called a *Partially Balanced Incomplete Randomized Block Design*, a design in which some pairwise associations between treatment levels occur λ_1 times while other associations happen λ_2 times (e.g., in Design 4C/Table 2.8, the associations 1–4 and 2–5 occur twice, whereas the associations 1–2 and 2–3 occur only once). The layouts for other alternative incomplete randomized block designs (e.g., *balanced treatment* and *extended* designs) are shown in the lower left part of Table 2.8.

Table 2.8 Treatment Levels Arrangements in Complete (Designs 2 and 3) and Incomplete (Designs 4A, 4B, 4C, 4D, and 4E) Randomized Block Designs

Complete Designs (Designs 2 and 3)		Balanced Incomplete Block Design (Design 4A)
Randomized Block	Generalized Randomized Block	
RBD (6,10)	GRBD (6,10,2)	BIBD (6,10,3,5; 2)
1 2 3 4 5 6	1 2 3 4 5 6 1 2 3 4 5 6	1 2 5
1 2 3 4 5 6	1 2 3 4 5 6 1 2 3 4 5 6	1 2 6
1 2 3 4 5 6	1 2 3 4 5 6 1 2 3 4 5 6	1 3 4
1 2 3 4 5 6	1 2 3 4 5 6 1 2 3 4 5 6	1 3 6
1 2 3 4 5 6	1 2 3 4 5 6 1 2 3 4 5 6	1 4 5
1 2 3 4 5 6	1 2 3 4 5 6 1 2 3 4 5 6	2 3 4
1 2 3 4 5 6	1 2 3 4 5 6 1 2 3 4 5 6	2 3 5
1 2 3 4 5 6	1 2 3 4 5 6 1 2 3 4 5 6	2 4 6
1 2 3 4 5 6	1 2 3 4 5 6 1 2 3 4 5 6	3 5 6
1 2 3 4 5 6	1 2 3 4 5 6 1 2 3 4 5 6	4 5 6

Balanced Treatment Incomplete Block Designs (Design 4B)			Partially Balanced Incomplete Block Design
BTIBD (4,6,3; 3,1)	BTIBD (4,7,3; 2,2)	BTIBD (4,7,3; 2,2)	PBIBD (6,3,4,2; 2,1)
0 1 2	0 1 2	0 1 3	1 4 2 5
0 1 3	0 1 4	0 1 4	2 5 3 6
0 1 4	0 2 4	0 2 3	3 6 1 4
0 2 3	0 0 3	0 2 4	(Design 4C)
0 2 4	1 2 3	1 2 3	
0 3 4	1 3 4	1 2 4	
	2 3 4	3 4 4	

Extended Block Designs (Designs 4D and 4E)					RBD (t, b)
RBD + BIBD		RBD + BTIBD			t = Treatments
			RBD + BTIBD		b = Blocks
RBD	BIBD	RBD	BTIBD		GRBD (t, b, r)
			BIBD		r = Treatment replications within a block
1 2 3 4	1 2	1 2 3 4	1 2	1	BIBD (t, b, k, r; λ)
1 2 3 4	1 3	1 2 3 4	1 3	1	k = Units per block
1 2 3 4	1 4	1 2 3 4	1 4	1	r = Treatment replications per experiment
1 2 3 4	2 3	1 2 3 4	2 3	1	BTIBD (t, b, k; λ_0, λ_1)
1 2 3 4	2 4	1 2 3 4	2 4	1	PBIBD (t, b, k, r; λ_1, λ_2)
1 2 3 4	3 4	1 2 3 4	3 4	1	*(see text for explanation of λ parameters)*

Note. Examples for incomplete and extended designs are taken from Hinkelmann and Kempthorne (2008, pp. 328–338).

Designing of incomplete block experiments is a complex matter that we cannot cover in this monograph, and therefore the main utilization of these designs is found in agricultural studies, engineering, and technological research and not in the social, behavioral, educational, or health sciences. However, the randomization and local control of these designs supply the prototype for other designs covered in this chapter. Regardless of the layout of the incomplete block design, randomization is always identical and consists of a two-step procedure: (a) random assignment of treatment level arrangements to blocks and (b) random assignment of treatment levels to experimental units within each block.

Method 8—*Two-Step Blocked Random Assignment*—is illustrated in Table 2.9 with Design 4C (six treatment levels and 12 experimental units, grouped in three blocks of 4 units). In the first step, incomplete blocks of experimental units are randomly allocated to the treatment level arrangements included in the design layout. The procedure is similar to SRA (Method 3: *Forced Equal Sizes*), with the exception that the units of assignment are the blocks themselves, instead of individual experimental units, and the single treatment levels are replaced with treatment level arrangements. In the second step, we make use of Method 7—Blocked Random Assignment—already employed in the randomization of (Complete) Randomized Block (Design 2) and Generalized Randomized Block (Design 3) designs. The final allocation of the 12 experimental units is shown at the bottom of Table 2.9.

Note that the same randomization procedure could be used with any multiple of the number of blocks. If we formed *six* blocks of four units, instead of the *three* blocks used in the illustrative example, in the first step, two homogeneous blocks of experimental units would be randomly allocated to each of the three arrangements of treatment levels included in the design.

2.3.4 Latin Square Design

Methods 7 (*Blocked Random Assignment*) and 8 (*Two-Step Blocked Random Assignment*) are applied when the strategy of elimination of the heterogeneity of experimental units is confined to a single classificatory factor (blocking variable). To pursue with the example given for the randomized block design (see Subsection 2.3.1), suppose that the researcher is manipulating *material incentives* and he or she has sound reasons to expect that, in addition to the cognitive abilities, the upper-class students' performance, as compared with the lower-class students', is less responsive to the nature of the incentives. One possible strategy is to classify the students in

Table 2.9 Randomization of a Partially Balanced Incomplete Block Design: Allocation of 12 Units (Grouped in Three Blocks of 4 Units) to Three Arrangements of Six Treatment Levels (T1 T4 T2 T5; T2 T5 T3 T6; and T3 T6 T1 T4) (Design 4C; See Table 2.8; Method 8)

Step 1: Random Assignment of Blocks to Treatment Levels Arrangements

Blocks and Random Numbers		Random Assignment of Blocks		
Block	RN	Block	RN	Arrangement
Block 1	.610	Block 3	.332	T1 T4 T2 T5
Block 2	.957	Block 1	.610	T2 T5 T3 T6
Block 3	.332	Block 2	.957	T3 T6 T1 T4

RN Step 1: Table A1.1 (Rows: 43–45; Columns: 42–44).

Step 2: Random Assignment of Units Within Blocks to Treatment Levels

Blocks, Units and Random Numbers				Random Assignment of Units Within Blocks				
Block	ID	Unit	RN	Block	ID	Unit	RN	Treatment
1	1	Alf	.846	1	2	Luke	.073	T2
1	2	Luke	.073	1	4	Willy	.545	T5
1	3	Rafe	.774	1	3	Rafe	.774	T3
1	4	Willy	.545	1	1	Alf	.846	T6
2	1	Claud	.153	2	3	Jerry	.034	T3
2	2	Derry	.398	2	1	Claud	.153	T6
2	3	Jerry	.034	2	4	Stew	.336	T1
2	4	Stew	.336	2	2	Derry	.398	T4
3	1	Aron	.408	3	4	Lance	.315	T1
3	2	Ben	.999	3	1	Aron	.408	T4
3	3	Glen	.520	3	3	Glen	.520	T2
3	4	Lance	.315	3	2	Ben	.999	T5

RN Step 2: Table A1.1 (Rows: 7–18; Columns: 34–36).

Design and Final Allocation

	Treatment					
Block	T1	T2	T3	T4	T5	T6
Block 1		2 Luke	3 Rafe		4 Willy	1 Alf
Block 2	4 Stew		3 Jerry	2 Derry		1 Claud
Block 3	4 Lance	3 Glen		1 Aron	2 Ben	

homogeneous blocks defined simultaneously by two blocking variables: *cognitive abilities* and *socioeconomic status* (SES). With the procedural constraints that the number of students should be the same in all blocks and that the number of levels of both blocking variables should equal the number of treatment levels included in the design layout, this strategy of local control gives rise to a *Latin square design* (Design 5A).

The design receives its name from an ancient Roman puzzle, which consists in finding out how many possible arrangements of the first n letters (A, B, C, etc.) in n rows and n columns could be done with the restriction that each letter appears once, and only once, in each row and in each column of the square. Square 1 in Figure 2.2 is an example of a Latin square of order 5 (an array in five rows and five columns of the first five Latin letters), having the special property that the letters in the first row and in the first column are arranged in alphabetical order (standard or normalized Latin square).

In treatment and error control design, the letters of the square represent the treatment levels, whereas the rows and the columns are filled with the

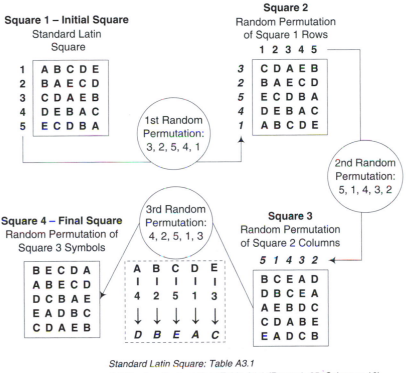

Standard Latin Square: Table A3.1
1st Random Permutation: Table A1.1 (Rows: 1–25; Columns: 16)
2nd Random Permutation: Table A1.1 (Rows: 2–16; Columns: 14)
3rd Random Permutation: Table A1.1 (Rows: 19–31; Columns: 6)

Figure 2.2   Random selection of a Latin square

blocking variables (for variations and extensions of this basic design, see the next subsection). Once the blocks (n^2 blocks; numbers of rows times number of columns) have been formed, the randomization consists in choosing at random one of the possible arrangements of letters (symbols) to assign the treatment levels to the experimental units (Method 9: *Two-Way Blocked Random Assignment*). If the experimenter had to find out all the possible arrangements (their number increases dramatically with the order of squares; see Appendix 3 for enumeration of Latin squares) for a given square, the research enterprise would be converted into a never-ending task. An easy way to obtain a random square from a relatively large collection of all available squares (see Appendix 3 for details of and simplified procedures for squares of orders 2–4) is to begin with the standard Latin square and to permute, randomly and independently, the order of the rows, the order of the columns, and the labels (letters/symbols) of the treatment levels. This procedure is illustrated in Figure 2.2 for a square of order 5 (the three random permutations were picked from Table A1.1, according to the guidelines given in Appendix 2).

Returning to our example, suppose that the experimenter has managed to form the nine blocks depicted in the allocation frame of Table 2.10 (the levels of the row variable correspond to the levels of cognitive abilities, defined by two cutoff points in IQ scores, and the levels of the column variable represent three SES-ordered categories). In the next step, adopting the aforementioned procedure (actually, with an order 3 Latin square it is sufficient to permute randomly the three rows and the last two columns of the standard Latin square in order to obtain one of the 12 possible different squares; see Appendix 3), the experimenter gets the randomized Latin square shown in the upper right side of Table 2.10 (the replacement of letters A, B, and C with T1, T2, and T3 is only a matter of consistence with the notation employed in the preceding designs). As a result, the final allocation of the 18 experimental units is the one shown in the lower portion of Table 2.10 (e.g., Daysie and Nattie, whose attributes have placed them in Block 4, would be "tested" in Treatment Level T3).

Despite its advantages in simultaneously handling two classificatory factors, the associated procedural constraints (the same number of levels needed for the experimental factor and both blocking variables and the requirement of equal numbers of experimental units per block) have made the use of Latin square designs relatively rare in the behavioral and related sciences (for a comprehensive approach, see, among others, Cochran & Cox, 1957; Federer, 1955; Fisher & Yates, 1963; Hinkelmann & Kempthorne, 2005; Kirk, 1995). The main role of Latin squares in experimental design still lies in their utilization in the randomization of within-subjects designs

Table 2.10 Randomization of a Latin Square Design: Allocation of 18 Units (Grouped in Nine Blocks of 2 Units) to Three of Treatment Levels (T1, T2, and T3) (Design 5A; Method 9)

Allocation Frame

	Vcol₁	Vcol₂	Vcol₃
Vrow₁	*Block 1* 1 Emmy 2 Tania	*Block 2* 1 Ann 2 Gina	*Block 3* 1 Hettie 2 Iris
Vrow₂	*Block 4* 1 Daysie 2 Nattie	*Block 5* 1 Clara 2 Roxie	*Block 6* 1 Amy 2 Lou
Vrow₃	*Block 7* 1 Biddy 2 Delia	*Block 8* 1 Hanna 2.Tisha	*Block 9* 1 Brita 2 Milly

Random Selected Latin Square[a]

	Vcol₁	Vcol₂	Vcol₃
Vrow₁	B	A	C
Vrow₂	C	B	A
Vrow₃	A	C	B

↓

	Vcol₁	Vcol₂	Vcol₃
Vrow₁	T2	T1	T3
Vrow₂	T3	T2	T1
Vrow₃	T1	T3	T2

[a]Square obtained by independent random permutations of rows (Permutation: 2, 3, 1; Table A1.1 [Rows: 6–12; Column: 22]) and columns (Permutation: 1, 3, 2; Table A1.1 [Rows: 28–36; Column: 6]) of the standard Latin square shown in Table A3.1 (Appendix 3).

Final Allocation

Block	Vrow	Vcol	ID	Unit	Treatment	Block	Vrow	Vcol	ID	Unit	Treatment
2	1	2	1	Ann	T1	5	2	2	2	Roxie	T2
2	1	2	2	Gina	T1	9	3	3	1	Brita	T2
6	2	3	1	Amy	T1	9	3	3	2	Milly	T2
6	2	3	2	Lou	T1	3	1	3	1	Hettie	T3
7	3	1	1	Biddy	T1	3	1	3	2	Iris	T3
7	3	1	2	Delia	T1	4	2	1	1	Daysie	T3
1	1	1	1	Emmy	T2	4	2	1	2	Nattie	T3
1	1	1	2	Tania	T2	8	3	2	1	Hanna	T3
5	2	2	1	Clara	T2	8	3	2	2	Tisha	T3

(see Chapter 3). The extension of Latin square designs to the control of more than two classificatory factors (e.g., Graeco-Latin squares) is discussed in the next subsection in conjunction with blocked random assignment in factorial designs.

2.3.5 Factorial Designs

With the randomization of the Latin square design, we have described the basic methods of blocking and randomization of the *one-factor restrictedly randomized designs*: (a) *Blocked Random Assignment* (*complete* and generalized randomized block designs: Designs 2 and 3—Method 7); (b) *Two-Step Blocked Random Assignment* (balanced, partially balanced, and extended incomplete randomized block designs: Designs 4A to 4E—Method 8); and (c) *Two-Way Blocked Random Assignment* (Latin square design: Design 5A—Method 9). In Subsection 2.2.2, we have generalized the basic SRA methods, used in the *one-factor completely randomized design* (Design 1—Methods 1 to 4), to their factorial applications (Completely Randomized Factorial Design, Completely Randomized Fractional Factorial Design, Completely Randomized Hierarchical Design, and Completely Randomized Partial Hierarchical Design—Designs 7, 14, 18, and 20). In the current subsection, Methods 7, 8, 9, and 10 (*Blocked Random Assignment via Graeco-Latin Squares*, an extension of Method 9) are applied to the remaining factorial designs classified in Figure 1.3, beginning with the factorial randomized block and related designs and concluding with variations and extensions of the Latin square design.

2.3.5.1 Factorial Randomized Block and Related Designs

Broadly stated, factorial randomized block designs are randomized designs with two or more treatments and one blocking variable. Similar to factorial completely randomized designs (see Subsection 2.2.2), factorial randomized block designs are classified into crossed versus hierarchical designs, and within the former category, the effects of treatments and their interactions may be either unambiguously estimated (designs without confounding) or confounded, as a result of some specific procedural constraint underlying the randomization plan. In the latter category, with three or more treatments, the hierarchical structure can accommodate complete crossing between two or more treatments.

2.3.5.1.1 Crossed Designs Without Confounding. The two basic factorial designs in which all treatment effects and their interactions can be unambiguously estimated are the *Randomized Block Factorial Design* (Design 8) and the *Generalized Randomized Block Factorial Design* (Design 9). From the perspective of *treatment design*, both layouts are identical to the corresponding Completely Randomized Factorial Design (Design 7; see Table 2.3). From the perspective of *error control design*, the randomization is done via Method 7 (Blocked Random Assignment) and is similar to the randomization of their one-factor counterparts (Designs 2 and 3; see Subsections 2.3.1 and 2.3.2), with the understanding that the experimental units within blocks are assigned to treatment level combinations, instead of being allocated to a single treatment level.

2.3.5.1.2 Crossed Designs With Confounding. The Completely Randomized Fractional Factorial Design (Design 14; see Table 2.3), as compared with the Completely Randomized Factorial Design (Design 7; see Table 2.3), achieves a reduction in the total number of experimental units at the cost of confounding the treatment main effects with the interaction effect. The same is true for Design 15—*Randomized Block Fractional Factorial Design*—whose randomization plan relies on Method 7 (Blocked Random Assignment—the same method used for Designs 2 and 3, assuming that we are dealing with treatment level combinations and not with treatment levels themselves).

In Design 15, the confounding is between treatments and their interaction. Two additional types of confounding can result from the procedural constraints imposed on the randomization plan. The first one gives rise to what has been called a *Randomized Block Completely Confounded Factorial Design* (Design 11). In this design (see Table 2.13), all the combinations between treatment levels are present in the global layout, but they are broken into groups of incomplete combinations that are themselves randomly assigned to homogeneous blocks of experimental units. This procedure achieves the reduction of block size with the correlative price of confounding the interaction between treatments with groups of blocks. The second additional type of confounding reduces the size of the blocks by confining the blocked random assignment to one of the treatments included in the design. More precisely, entire blocks are randomly assigned to the levels of the first treatment, and the experimental units within blocks are subsequently assigned at random to the levels of the second treatment. From a theoretical or substantive point of view, this means that the estimation of the second treatment effect is more important than the estimation of the first treatment effect (Kirk, 1995). This design, combining features of the Completely Randomized Design and the Block Randomized Design, is commonly labeled *Split-Plot Factorial Design* (Design 10; when the second treatment is a within-subjects experimental factor, the design is known as a *Mixed Design*, a somewhat misleading designation—see Subsection 3.7.2).

The randomization plan for Designs 10 (*Split-Plot Factorial Design*) and 11 (*Randomized Block Completely Confounded Factorial Design*) is an extension of the strategy described for the Incomplete Randomized Block Designs (see Subsection 2.3.3). In Design 10, the experimenter begins by randomly assigning the available blocks to the levels of the first treatment; in the second step, units within blocks are themselves assigned at random to the levels of the second treatment. For instance, in Table 2.11, Block 2 is assigned to Treatment Level A1 (Step 1); according to the intrablock randomization, Treatment Levels B2, B1, and B3 are assigned to Della, Freda, and Sally (Step 2). The randomization plan for Design 11—*Randomized Block Completely Confounded Factorial Design*—is similar, with the understanding that in the first step

Table 2.11   Randomization of a Split-Plot Design: Allocation of 12 Units (Grouped in Four Blocks of 3 Units) to Six Combinations of Treatment Levels (A1B1, A1B2, A1B3, A2B1, A2B2, and A2B3) (Design 10; Method 8)

Step 1: Random Assignment of Blocks to Treatment A

Blocks and Random Numbers		Random Assignment of Blocks		
Block	RN	Block	RN	Treatment
Block 1	.963	Block 3	.227	A1
Block 2	.684	Block 2	.684	A1
Block 3	.227	Block 4	.887	A2
Block 4	.887	Block 1	.963	A2

RN: Table A1.1 (Rows: 9–12; Columns: 2–4).

Step 2: Random Assignment of Units Within Blocks to Treatment B

Blocks, Units and Random Numbers				Random Assignment of Units Within Blocks				
Block	ID	Unit	RN	Block	ID	Unit	RN	Treatment
1	1	Donna	.505	1	2	Lottie	.388	B1
1	2	Lottie	.388	1	1	Donna	.505	B2
1	3	Tonya	.662	1	3	Tonya	.662	B3
2	1	Della	.467	2	2	Freda	.378	B1
2	2	Freda	.378	2	1	Della	.467	B2
2	3	Sally	.686	2	3	Sally	.686	B3
3	1	Julie	.900	3	2	Nina	.226	B1
3	2	Nina	.226	3	3	Suzie	.700	B2
3	3	Suzie	.700	3	1	Julie	.900	B3
4	1	Angie	.343	4	1	Angie	.343	B1
4	2	Faye	.419	4	2	Faye	.419	B2
4	3	Kate	.844	4	3	Kate	.844	B3

RN: Table A1.1 (Rows: 11–22; Columns: 16–18).

Design and Final Allocation

Treatment A	Block	Treatment B		
		B1	B2	B3
A1	Block 3	2 Nina	3 Suzie	1 Julie
	Block 2	2 Freda	1 Della	3 Sally
A2	Block 4	1 Angie	2 Faye	3 Kate
	Block 1	2 Lottie	1 Donna	3 Tonva

blocks are randomly assigned to groups of treatment level combinations instead of treatment levels of the second independent variable (see Table 2.12 for the randomization procedure and Table 2.13 for the final allocation of experimental units).

Note that there is an additional difference in the underlying layout of Designs 10 and 11. In the first design, no constraint is imposed on the number of levels of the independent variables; in the second design, the number

Table 2.12 Randomized Block Completely Confounded Factorial Design: Randomization Procedures for Allocation of 18 Units (Grouped in Six Blocks of 3 Units) to Three Groups of Treatment Level Combinations (Design 11; Method 8)

Step 1: Random Assignment of Blocks to Groups of Treatment Level Combinations

Blocks and Random Numbers		Random Assignment of Blocks		
Block	RN	Block	RN	Groups of Treatment Combinations
Block 1	.735	Block 5	.165	Group 1 (A1B1-A2B3-A3B2)
Block 2	.288	Block 2	.288	Group 1 (A1B1-A2B3-A3B2)
Block 3	.398	Block 3	.398	Group 2 (A1B2-A2B1-A3B3)
Block 4	.500	Block 4	.500	Group 2 (A1B2-A2B1-A3B3)
Block 5	.165	Block 1	.735	Group 3 (A1B3-A2B2-A3B1)
Block 6	.772	Block 6	.772	Group 3 (A1B3-A2B2-A3B1)

RN: Table A1.1 (Rows: 15–20; Columns: 24–26).

Step 2: Random Assignment of Units Within Blocks to Treatment Level Combinations

Blocks, Units and Random Numbers				Random Assignment of Units Within Blocks				
Block	ID	Unit	RN	Block	ID	Unit	RN	Treatment
1	1	Alex	.212	1	1	Alex	.212	A1B3
1	2	Jonny	.836	1	3	Sid	.281	A2B2
1	3	Sid	.281	1	2	Jonny	.836	A3B1
2	1	Barry	.956	2	3	Matt	.237	A1B1
2	2	Chet	.901	2	2	Chet	.901	A2B3
2	3	Matt	.237	2	1	Barry	.956	A3B2
3	1	Howie	.575	3	1	Howie	.575	A1B2
3	2	Kris	.931	3	3	Terry	.917	A2B1
3	3	Terry	.917	3	2	Kris	.931	A3B3
4	1	Greg	.561	4	3	Woody	.427	A1B2
4	2	Ross	.925	4	1	Greg	.561	A2B1
4	3	Woody	.427	4	2	Ross	.925	A3B3
5	1	Burt	.808	5	3	Lew	.250	A1B1
5	2	Denny	.838	5	1	Burt	.808	A2B3
5	3	Lew	.250	5	2	Denny	.838	A3B2
6	1	Benny	.773	6	2	Ossy	.074	A1B3
6	2	Ossy	.074	6	3	Ray	.267	A2B2
6	3	Ray	.267	6	1	Benny	.773	A3B1

RN: Table A1.1 (Rows: 21–38; Columns: 27–29).

46

Table 2.13 Randomized Block Completely Confounded Factorial Design: Final Allocation of 18 Units (Grouped in Six Blocks of 3 Units) to Three Groups of Treatment Level Combinations (See Table 2.12) (Design 11; Method 8)

Groups of Treatment Combinations		B1	B2	B3
Group 1	A1	Block 2: 3 Matt Block 5: 3 Lew		
	A2			Block 2: 2 Chet Block 5: 1 Burt
	A3		Block 2: 1 Barry Block 5: 2 Denny	
Group 2	A1		Block 3: 1 Howie Block 4: 3 Woody	
	A2	Block 3: 3 Terry Block 4: 1 Greg		
	A3			Block 3: 2 Kris Block 4: 2 Ross
Group 3	A1			Block 1: 1 Alex Block 6: 2 Ossy
	A2		Block 1: 3 Sid Block 6: 3 Ray	
	A3	Block 1: 2 Jonny Block 6: 1 Benny		

of levels must be equal for both treatments. This requirement also holds for Design 12—*Randomized Block Partially Confounded Factorial Design* (see Table 2.14)—in which there are at least three treatments with two levels and the confounding scheme consists in confounding different interactions with different groups of blocks (see Kirk, 1995, chaps. 12–14, for a complete discussion of crossed designs with confounding). The randomization of Design 12 is analogous to the randomization of Design 11.

2.3.5.1.3 Hierarchical Designs. The layout of randomized block factorial designs with complete or partial nesting between experimental factors

Table 2.14 Layout of a Randomized Block Partially Confounded Factorial Design With Three Two-Level Treatments ($A_2B_2C_2$) and Eight Blocks of 4 Units (Grouped in Four Groups of Treatment Level Combinations) (Design 12)

Groups of Treatment Combinations	Blocks		B_1 C_1	B_1 C_2	B_2 C_1	B_2 C_2
Group 1	Block 1	A_1	$A_1B_1C_1$	$A_1B_1C_2$		
		A_2			$A_2B_2C_1$	$A_2B_2C_2$
	Block 2	A_1			$A_1B_2C_1$	$A_1B_2C_2$
		A_2	$A_2B_1C_1$	$A_2B_1C_2$		
Group 2	Block 3	A_1	$A_1B_1C_1$		$A_1B_2C_1$	
		A_2		$A_2B_1C_2$		$A_2B_2C_2$
	Block 4	A_1		$A_1B_1C_2$		$A_1B_2C_2$
		A_2	$A_2B_1C_1$		$A_2B_2C_1$	
Group 3	Block 5	A_1	$A_1B_1C_1$			$A_1B_2C_2$
		A_2	$A_2B_1C_1$			$A_2B_2C_2$
	Block 6	A_1		$A_1B_1C_2$	$A_1B_2C_1$	
		A_2		$A_2B_1C_2$	$A_2B_2C_1$	
Group 4	Block 7	A_1	$A_1B_1C_1$			$A_1B_2C_2$
		A_2		$A_2B_1C_2$	$A_2B_2C_1$	
	Block 8	A_1		$A_1B_1C_2$	$A_1B_2C_1$	
		A_2	$A_2B_1C_1$			$A_2B_2C_2$

(Designs 19 and 21) is similar to the layout of their equivalent completely randomized designs (Designs 18 and 20; see Table 2.3), but the randomization plan, instead of Method 3, relies on Method 7—*Blocked Random Assignment* (see Subsection 2.3.1). Finally, there is also a hierarchical version of the split-plot design with more than two treatments (Design 22—*Split-Plot Partial Hierarchical Design;* see Table 2.15 for an illustrative design layout). The randomization plan for this design, based on Method 8

(Two-Step Blocked Random Assignment), is the same as what we have described for Design 10 (Split-Plot Factorial Design; see Table 2.11), with the exception that in the second step the intrablock randomization is done in reference to the treatment level combinations (in the example, combinations of Treatments B and C; see Table 2.15) and not in connection with the levels of a single treatment.

2.3.5.2 Latin Square and Related Designs

In Subsection 2.3.4, the Latin square design (Design 5A; see Table 2.10 and also the layout in Table 2.16) was introduced as the basic two-way elimination strategy of the heterogeneity of experimental units, in the sense that it allows the systematic variation of one experimental factor (whose levels are represented by the symbols or by Latin letters in the cells of the square) and the simultaneous control of two classificatory factors (whose levels are appointed to the rows and columns of the square and must be equal to the number of treatment levels). With the limitation that all factors must have the same number of levels, this basic design can be used in situations where one or two additional experimental factors (active independent variables)—or even some kind of a pseudofactor (e.g., time sequence)—replace the blocking variables in the rows and/or columns of the square.

When both rows and columns represent two experimental factors, the design becomes a special type of factorial fractional design (Design 16: *Latin Square Fractional Factorial Design*; see Table 2.16), more precisely a $1/t$ fractional replication of the corresponding completely randomized

Table 2.15   Layout of a Split-Plot Partial Hierarchical Design With Three Treatments (A, B, and C) and Four Blocks (Design 22)

Treatment A	Block		Treatments B and C			
			C1	C2	C3	C4
A1	Block 1	B1	$A_1B_1C_1$	$A_1B_1C_2$		
		B2			$A_1B_2C_3$	$A_1B_2C_4$
	Block 2	B1	$A_1B_1C_1$	$A_1B_1C_2$		
		B2			$A_1B_2C_3$	$A_1B_2C_4$
A2	Block 3	B1	$A_2B_1C_1$	$A_2B_1C_2$		
		B2			$A_2B_2C_3$	$A_2B_2C_4$
	Block 4	B1	$A_2B_1C_1$	$A_2B_1C_2$		
		B2			$A_2B_2C_3$	$A_2B_2C_4$

Table 2.16 Layout (Before Randomization) of Latin and Graeco-Latin Square Designs (Designs 5A, 5B, 13, 16, and 17)

One-Treatment Designs

Design 5A—Latin Square

	$Vcol_1$	$Vcol_2$	$Vcol_3$
$Vrow_1$	A_1	A_2	A_3
$Vrow_2$	A_2	A_3	A_1
$Vrow_3$	A_3	A_1	A_2

Two blocking variables

Design 5B—Graeco-Latin Square

	$Vcol_1$	$Vcol_2$	$Vcol_3$
$Vrow_1$	$Vcell_1A_3$	$Vcell_2A_2$	$Vcell_3A_1$
$Vrow_2$	$Vcell_2A_1$	$Vcell_3A_3$	$Vcell_1A_2$
$Vrow_3$	$Vcell_3A_2$	$Vcell_1A_1$	$Vcell_2A_3$

Three blocking variables

Factorial Designs

Design 13—Latin Square Confounded

	A_1	A_2	A_3
$Vrow_1$	B_1	B_2	B_3
$Vrow_2$	B_2	B_3	B_1
$Vrow_3$	B_3	B_1	B_2

Two treatments
One blocking variable

Design 16—Latin Square Fractional

	B_1	B_2	B_3
A_1	C_1	C_2	C_3
A_2	C_2	C_3	C_1
A_3	C_3	C_1	C_2

Three treatments
No blocking variable

Design 17—Graeco-Latin Square Fractional

	A_1	A_2	A_3
$Vrow_1$	B_1C_3	B_2C_2	B_3C_1
$Vrow_2$	B_2C_1	B_3C_3	B_1C_2
$Vrow_3$	B_3C_2	B_1C_1	B_2C_3

Three treatments
One blocking variable

A, B, C = Treatments   *Vrow, Vcol, Vcell = Blocking variables*

factorial design (e.g., Design 16 includes *nine* combinations of treatment levels, while the equivalent completely randomized design $A_3B_3C_3$ contains 27 experimental conditions). When the columns are appointed to a second experimental factor and the rows continue to represent a blocking variable, the design receives the label *Latin Square Confounded Factorial Design* (Design 13) and is structurally identical to a randomized block completely confounded factorial design (Design 11; see Table 2.12), where the number of blocks (levels of the blocking variable) is the same as the number of groups of treatment combinations included in the design layout. The randomization of Designs 13 and 16 is done with Method 9—*Two-Way Blocked Random Assignment* and is analogous to the randomization of Design 5A (see Table 2.10; in the examples in Table 2.16, a random Latin square should be selected for the assignment of the levels of Treatment B, in Design 13, and Treatment C, in Design 16).

Designs 13 and 16 modify the "logic" of local control (two-way elimination of the heterogeneity of experimental units) enclosed in the classic

Latin square design (Design 5A), by reducing the number of blocking variables to handle additional experimental factors. On the contrary, Design 5B—*Graeco-Latin Square Design* (see Table 2.16) extends this logic by accommodating a third blocking variable. This is done by juxtaposing two orthogonal Latin squares (see Table A3.2, Appendix 3) in the layout cells. The symbols of the first Latin square (Vcell$_1$, Vcell$_2$, and Vcell$_3$, in the example of Design 5B; see Table 2.16) are appointed to the third blocking variable, whereas the symbols of the juxtaposed orthogonal square (A$_1$, A$_2$, and A$_3$, in the same example) continue to represent the experimental treatment (compared with the 3×3 standard Graeco-Latin square depicted in Table A3.2, Vcell$_1$, Vcell$_2$, and Vcell$_3$ correspond to the first Latin square—defined by the letters A, B, and C—and A$_1$, A$_2$, and A$_3$ correspond to the second Latin square—defined by the numbers 1, 2, and 3). Provided that the experimenter is able to find equal-sized homogeneous blocks of experimental units categorized simultaneously by the three blocking variables (Vrow, Vcol, and Vcell) and the corresponding Graeco-Latin square, the randomization of Design 5B consists simply in taking a random permutation for the symbols of the second Latin square that represent the levels (A$_1$, A$_2$, and A$_3$) of the experimental treatment (in this example, Treatment A). This procedure is identical to the third random permutation illustrated in Figure 2.2. Note that this design should have been described in Subsection 2.3.4, since it is a one-factor design and a "natural" extension of the Latin square design. We have postponed its presentation so that we will be able to compare its structural features with the remaining factorial Latin and Graeco-Latin square designs described in this section.

Finally, Design 17—*Graeco-Latin Square Fractional Factorial Design*—is a variation of Design 5B, in which the blocking variables appointed to the columns and cells have been replaced by two experimental treatments. The randomization of Design 17 is analogous to that of Design 5A, with two exceptions: (1) the initial standard square is one of the Graeco-Latin squares shown in Table A3.2 and (2) a fourth independent random permutation must be selected for the symbols (subscripts) of the second orthogonal Latin square. In our example (see Design 17 in Table 2.16), the first and second random permutations illustrated in Figure 2.2 would apply to the rows and the columns of the Graeco-Latin square, the third random permutation would define the symbols for levels of Treatment B, and the fourth random permutation would define the symbols for levels of Treatment C. We have named this randomization method *Blocked Random Assignment via Graeco-Latin Squares* (Method 10). Note that there are no order 2 or 6 Graeco-Latin squares (see Table A3.2).

2.4 Restrictedly Randomized Designs: Stratifying

Blocking is the optimal strategy of local control and therefore must be used whenever possible. Nevertheless, as the reader has already realized, blocking methods have intrinsic procedural constraints, namely, *equal-size* homogeneous blocks and an *equal number of levels* for treatments and blocking variables in the two- and three-way blocking techniques, which inhibit their utilization in a considerable number of "real-word" randomized experiments. An alternative approach to local control of classificatory factors is the stratification of available experimental units prior to random assignment. More precisely, at the onset of the experiment the units are grouped in homogeneous groups (called *strata*) on the basis of their scores (values) in one or more *stratifying variables*.

The nature of the stratifying variables is the same as that of the blocking variables mentioned in the previous section (see also the typology of classificatory factors in Table 1.1), and their choice must be made according to the same criteria: known or expected correlations with the outcome measures. Briefly stated, stratified random assignment is a method of local control similar to blocked random assignment (in the sense that experimental units are previously assembled in homogeneous groups) but without the requirements of equal-size groups and an equal number of levels across classificatory factors, as is the case in two- and three-way blocking techniques. For example, if the researcher has sound reasons to suspect that gender (two categories), age (three age intervals), and SES (four ordered categories) can make the expected relationship between his or her experimental factor and the outcome measure disappear, he or she begins by grouping the available experimental units in 24 ($2 \times 3 \times 4$) strata and subsequently randomly assigns the units to treatment levels within each stratum. Any of the four basic SRA methods can be used (see Section 2.1), but the ideal of balanced designs recommends the forced equal sizes strategy (Method 3). Method 11 (*Stratified Random Assignment: Captive Procedure*) is simply the application of Method 3 to all of the unequal-size strata included in the randomization plan.

In the example of Tables 2.17 and 2.18, the researcher has grouped 60 experimental units (available at the onset of the experiment) in 12 strata, according to the observed scores (values) in three stratifying variables (A, B, and C). For each stratum, a series of random numbers is picked from Table A1.1 (the actual random series are shown in Table 2.17). In the next step (see Table 2.18), Method 3 (SRS—Forced Equal Sizes), coupled with the LRC, explained in Subsection 2.2.1, is applied within each stratum. More precisely, when the number of units in a stratum is not equal to or is

Table 2.17 Stratified Random Assignment (Nonsequential Procedure): Allocation Frame and Random Numbers (RN) for Allocation of 60 Units (Grouped in 12 Strata Defined by Three Stratifying Variables: A, B, and C) to Three Treatment Levels (T1, T2, and T3) (Method 11)

		B1			B2			B3		
		Stratum 1			*Stratum 3*			*Stratum 5*		
		ID	Unit	RN	ID	Unit	RN	ID	Unit	RN
		1	Erik	.921	1	Ced	.226	1	Bert	.844
	C1	2	Jeff	.111	2	Dick	.700	2	Kester	.455
		3	Rudy	.704	3	Pauly	.343			
					4	Wally	.419			
A1		*Rows: 42–44; Col.: 5–7*			*Rows: 18–21; Col.: 16–18*			*Rows: 11–12; Col.: 26–28*		
		Stratum 2			*Stratum 4*			*Stratum 6*		
		ID	Unit	RN	ID	Unit	RN	ID	Unit	RN
		1	Augie	.281	1	Baldie	.770	1	Darry	.212
		2	Clyde	.408	2	Drew	.455	2	Mitch	.906
	C2	3	Felix	.133	3	Ollie	.666	3	Norm	.483
		4	Floy	.307				4	Roddy	.932
		5	Malc	.857				5	Teddy	.374
		6	Sean	.697						
		Rows: 5–10; Col.: 10–12			*Rows: 20–22; Col.: 7–9*			*Rows: 29–33; Col.: 31–33*		
		Stratum 7			*Stratum 9*			*Stratum 11*		
		ID	Unit	RN	ID	Unit	RN	ID	Unit	RN
		1	Celia	.758	1	Cammy	.632	1	Ana	.789
		2	Cora	.262	2	Ettie	.408	2	Cesca	.865
	C1	3	Dora	.494	3	Fee	.540	3	Dotty	.005
		4	Jude	.883	4	Rose	.260	4	Edith	.269
		5	Wendy	.294	5	Sissy	.655	5	Hatty	.009
					6	Sulie	.277	6	Lola	.438
					7	Vettie	.570			
A2		*Rows: 19–23; Col.: 33–35*			*Rows: 10–16; Col.: 40–42*			*Rows: 15–20; Col.: 17–19*		
		Stratum 8			*Stratum 10*			*Stratum 12*		
		ID	Unit	RN	ID	Unit	RN	ID	Unit	RN
		1	Adela	.049	1	Lisa	.675	1	Bella	.565
		2	Brenda	.704	2	Margie	.001	2	Elsie	.027
	C2	3	Claire	.958	3	Nora	.496	3	Issy	.075
		4	Dina	.638	4	Ruth	.786	4	Lynn	.052
		5	Ina	.552				5	Mira	.240
		6	Magda	.487				6	Rori	.261
		7	Nelly	.360				7	Tonia	.742
		8	Stella	.372						
		Rows: 31–38; Col.: 25–27			*Rows: 22–25; Col.: 23–25*			*Rows: 4–10; Col.: 31–33*		

Table 2.18 Stratified Random Assignment (Nonsequential Procedure): Final Allocation of 60 Units (Grouped in 12 Strata Defined by Three Stratifying Variables: A, B, and C—See Table 2.17) to Three Treatment Levels (T1, T2, and T3) (Method 11)

		B1				B2				B3			
		Stratum 1				*Stratum 3*				*Stratum 5*			
		ID	Unit	RN	T	ID	Unit	RN	T	ID	Unit	RN	T
A1	C1	2	Jeff	.111	T1	1	Ced	.226	T1	2	Kester	.455	T2
		3	Rudy	.704	T2	3	Pauly	.343	T2	1	Bert	.844	T3
		1	Erik	.921	T3	4	Wally	.419	T3				
						2	Dick	.700	T1				
				LRC: 3, 2, 1				LRC: 1, 2, 3				LRC: 2, 3, 1	
		Stratum 2				*Stratum 4*				*Stratum 6*			
		ID	Unit	RN	T	ID	Unit	RN	T	ID	Unit	RN	T
	C2	3	Felix	.133	T1	2	Drew	.455	T1	1	Darry	.212	T1
		1	Augie	.281	T2	3	Ollie	.666	T2	5	Teddy	.374	T2
		4	Floy	.307	T3	1	Baldie	.770	T3	3	Norm	.483	T3
		2	Clyde	.408	T1					2	Mitch	.906	T2
		6	Sean	.697	T2					4	Roddy	.932	T1
		5	Malc	.857	T3								
				LRC: 3, 1, 2				LRC: 1, 3, 2				LRC: 2, 1, 3	
		Stratum 7				*Stratum 9*				*Stratum 11*			
		ID	Unit	RN	T	ID	Unit	RN	T	ID	Unit	RN	T
A2	C1	2	Cora	.262	T1	4	Rose	.260	T1	3	Dotty	.005	T1
		5	Wendy	.294	T2	6	Sulie	.277	T2	5	Hatty	.009	T2
		3	Dora	.494	T3	2	Ettie	.408	T3	4	Edith	.269	T3
		1	Celia	.758	T2	3	Fee	.540	T1	6	Lola	.438	T1
		4	Jude	.883	T3	7	Vettie	.570	T2	1	Ana	.789	T2
						1	Cammy	.632	T3	2	Cesca	.865	T3
						5	Sissy	.655	T3				
				LRC: 2, 3, 1				LRC: 3, 2, 1				LRC: 2, 1, 3	
		Stratum 8				*Stratum 10*				*Stratum 12*			
		ID	Unit	RN	T	ID	Unit	RN	T	ID	Unit	RN	T
	C2	1	Adela	.049	T1	2	Margie	.001	T1	2	Elsie	.027	T1
		7	Nelly	.360	T2	3	Nora	.496	T2	4	Lynn	.052	T2
		8	Stella	.372	T3	1	Lisa	.675	T3	3	Issy	.075	T3
		6	Magda	.487	T1	4	Ruth	.786	T3	5	Mira	.240	T1
		5	Ina	.552	T2					6	Rori	.261	T2
		4	Dina	.638	T3					1	Bella	.565	T3
		2	Brenda	.704	T1					7	Tonia	.742	T1
		3	Claire	.958	T3								
				LRC: 1, 3, 2				LRC: 3, 1, 2				LRC: 1, 2, 3	

Note. Underlined replications selected by the *last replication correction* (LRC) procedure.

not a multiple of the number of treatment levels (in the example, three treatment levels: T1, T2, and T3), the last t replications in the *systematically ordered list* of treatment levels shown in Table 2.18 are randomly selected. For instance, in Stratum 8, the systematically ordered list of treatment levels is perfectly balanced until the sixth replication (T1, T2, T3, T1, T2, T3). For the last two replications, Treatments T1 and T3 are selected, whereas Treatment T2 is excluded, on the basis of the corresponding random permutation (1, 3, 2) picked from Table A1.1 according to the guidelines given in Appendix 2. Once the systematically ordered lists of treatment replications have been established with the LRC procedure, random assignment consists simply in the association of these lists with the randomly ordered lists of units within strata (in Stratum 8, Adela, Magda, and Brenda have been assigned to Treatment Level T1; Nelly and Ina to T2; and, last, Stella, Dina, and Claire to T3). Finally, note that the application of Method 11 to factorial designs is similar to the one-factor example given in this section, with the difference that treatment level combinations, instead of the treatment levels themselves, are assigned to experimental units within strata.

With the stratified random assignment, we have concluded the description of the two broad strategies (*blocking* and *stratifying*) for local control of classificatory factors in restrictedly randomized designs. We have not yet mentioned a restrictedly randomization strategy that bears some analogy with cluster random sampling and is often described in the health sciences literature as *cluster-randomized trials*. The strategy mainly consists in having experimental units nested in higher level entities or clusters (e.g., hospitals) and randomly assigning all the units grouped in one cluster to one of the experimental conditions included in the design layout. From a practical perspective, this strategy is an application of SRA to all available clusters.

2.5 Sequential Assignment and Adaptive Randomization Methods

Until now (Section 2.2–2.4), as stated in the opening section of this chapter, all the randomization and local control procedures have been described with the understanding that the experimental units are available at the onset of the study. In technical jargon, this is called "captive" or nonsequential assignment (Underwood, 1966) and can be seen as the ideal mode of conducting randomized experiments. Unfortunately, a substantial number of experimental studies must be carried out with *virtual* allocation frames, in the sense that the experimental units are individually enrolled on successive occasions, which can be distributed for considerable time periods (months, or even years). This is the typical situation in some disciplines, namely, in the health sciences, where the experimental units are generally patients with specific diseases and prognostic characteristics and the treatment delivery must be scheduled according to the flow of participants from the beginning to the end of the study.

In any case, the sequential random assignment is analogous to the nonsequential random assignment, with some procedural adaptations to compensate for the lost "degrees of freedom." As already stated, in nonsequential assignment, it is an arbitrary and personal choice either to associate a systematically ordered list of available units to a randomly ordered list of treatment level replications or to match a randomly ordered list of units to a systematically ordered list of treatments. For the reasons mentioned in the introductory section (i.e., to give the reader a more comprehensive picture of the randomization procedure in conjunction with the design layout), we have chosen the second association procedure. The first degree of freedom we lost in the sequential assignment is the arbitrariness of this choice. Saying it in other words, *temporal allocation frames* must necessarily include a randomly ordered list of treatment level replications that is subsequently associated with a systematically ordered list of enrolled experimental units (sequential ID numbers from 1 to n).

Before proceeding with the description of sequential random assignment methods, we must address a preliminary issue concerning what is frequently called "batch" and "trickle" randomization, that is, situations where the experimental units are enrolled in small groups in successive time periods. Batch and trickle randomization can be more accurately described as special problems in the organization of temporal allocation frames (e.g., attribution of sequential ID numbers) than as randomization methods in their own right. More precisely, a temporal allocation frame is a randomly ordered list of treatment replications coupled with a systematically ordered list of ID numbers $(1–n)$, ascribed to the experimental units as they are enrolled in the experiment. If the experimental units are sequentially and individually enrolled, the attribution of ID numbers poses no problem. However, if the units come in groups, the researcher must decide which ID numbers are attributed to the units within "enrollment groups" (batches). This can be done by establishing temporal precedence based on systematic criteria (e.g., alphabetic order, date of birth) or by random determination of precedence (e.g., the experimental units draw lots), as shown in Table 2.19. In any case, the temporal precedence in the attribution of ID numbers must be independent of the randomly ordered list of treatment replications previously recorded in the temporal allocation frame. In the remaining subsections, the procedural adaptations of simple, blocked, and stratified randomization to the sequential assignment are conveniently described, as well as "minimization"—an alternative method to sequential stratified random assignment.

Table 2.19 Attribution of Sequential ID Numbers When the Order of Enrollment in the Experiment Is Unclear

	Order of Enrollment				Final ID Numbers		
ID	Unit	Date of birth	Lottery	ID	Alphabetic	Date of birth	Lottery
1	Unit 1	—	—	1	Unit 1	Unit 1	Unit 1
2	Unit 2	—	—	2	Unit 2	Unit 2	Unit 2
3	Unit 3	—	—	3	Unit 3	Unit 3	Unit 3
[?]	*Unit k*	1991-01-07	1	**4**	*Unit j*	*Unit j*	*Unit k*
[?]	*Unit j*	1990-11-22	2	**5**	*Unit k*	*Unit k*	*Unit j*
6	Unit 6	—	—	6	Unit 6	Unit 6	Unit 6
[?]	*Unit z*	1991-04-29	2	**7**	*Unit w*	*Unit y*	*Unit x*
[?]	*Unit w*	1992-11-05	3	**8**	*Unit x*	*Unit z*	*Unit z*
[?]	*Unit x*	1991-08-16	1	**9**	*Unit y*	*Unit x*	*Unit w*
[?]	*Unit y*	1990-07-23	4	**10**	*Unit z*	*Unit w*	*Unit y*
11	Unit 11	—	—	11	Unit 11	Unit 11	Unit 11
12	Unit 12	—	—	12	Unit 12	Unit 12	Unit 12

Note. Bold font identifies two groups of experimental units (Group 1: Units k and j; Group 2: Units z, w, x, and y) in which the order of enrollment is unclear (see main text for details).

2.5.1 Sequential Simple Random Assignment

With *a priori probabilities* methods (Methods 1 and 2), the application of sequential SRA in completely randomized designs is straightforward. The only task the researcher must perform is to have an adequately large series of random numbers and assign the treatment levels or treatment level combinations to the arriving experimental units (ID numbers $1-n$, ascribed by order of enrollment) according to the probabilistic scheme previously defined (see Table 2.20 and Subsection 2.2.1).

With the *forced-size* strategies, the application of Methods 3 and 4 must begin necessarily with the determination of the number of desired replications of treatment levels by means of educated guessing and formal power analysis (note that this strategy would be the standard approach routinely adopted in all randomization methods described in this monograph; see Subsection 4.1.2). Once this number has been identified, a randomly ordered list of treatment

Table 2.20 Sequential Simple Random Assignment: Assignment of 18
Experimental Units to Three Treatment Levels (T1, T2, and T3)
With Equal a Priori Probabilities (Method 1—Sequential Version)
and Forced Equal Sizes (Method 5—Time-Blocking/Two
"Randomization Fractions") Procedures (Design 1)

Method 1				Method 5: Time-Blocking							
RN	T	ID	Unit	Frame			Final Allocation				
				Time	RN	T	Time	RN	T	ID	Unit
.376	T2	1	[?]								
.566	T2	2	[?]		.307	T1		.078	T1	1	[?]
.144	T1	3	[?]		.078	T1		.149	T3	2	[?]
.502	T2	4	[?]		.538	T1		.288	T2	3	[?]
.325	T1	5	[?]		.607	T2		.307	T1	4	[?]
.948	T3	6	[?]	[1]	.760	T2	[1]	.520	T3	5	[?]
.040	T1	7	[?]		.288	T2		.538	T1	6	[?]
.163	T1	8	[?]		.149	T3		.607	T2	7	[?]
.411	T2	9	[?]		.762	T3		.760	T2	8	[?]
.884	T3	10	[?]		.520	T3		.762	T3	9	[?]
.251	T1	11	[?]								
.911	T3	12	[?]		.766	T1		.014	T1	1	[?]
.455	T2	13	[?]		.014	T1		.059	T3	2	[?]
.960	T3	14	[?]		.221	T1		.221	T1	3	[?]
.398	T2	15	[?]		.877	T2		.243	T2	4	[?]
.707	T3	16	[?]	[2]	.773	T2	[2]	.710	T3	5	[?]
.497	T2	17	[?]		.243	T2		.766	T1	6	[?]
.096	T1	18	[?]		.801	T3		.773	T2	7	[?]
[...]	[...]	[...]	[...]		.710	T3		.801	T3	8	[?]
					.059	T3		.877	T2	9	[?]
[.000, .333[→ T1				[...]	...	...	[...]	...	...	...	...
[.333, .666[→ T2				[t−1]	...	...	[t−1]	...	...	...	...
[.666, .999[→ T3				[t]	...	...	[t]	...	...	...	...

Method 1—RN: Table A1.1 (Rows: 20–37; Columns: 37–39).
Method 5 (Time 1)—RN: Table A1.1 (Rows: 2–10; Columns: 19–21).
Method 5 (Time 2)—RN: Table A1.1 (Rows: 27–35; Columns: 4–6).

replications, containing the corrected number of replications for each treatment level, is generated and associated, step by step, with the sequential ID numbers. This is an easy task when there is no temporal or budget-fixed limit for the conclusion of the experiment and the treatments can be delivered to all the "virtual" experimental units listed in the temporal allocation frame.

In situations where the study can be abruptly interrupted by previously fixed temporal limits or other external constraints, the best solution to approach the forced-size strategy is to break the total number of experimental units down into a reasonable number of *equal-size fractions* (usually *two* to *four* fractions) and to apply SRA within each fraction. This is similar to the random permuted "blocks" technique (see Appendix 1 and Table A1.3), but we avoid using the term *block* in this context, because we have been using it so far to identify homogeneous groups of experimental units formed on the basis of substantive restrictions (scores or values in classificatory factors). A more appropriate designation could be *time blocking*, with the understanding that each consecutive "randomization fraction" corresponds to a level of the "blocking variable." In the data analysis stage, the effect of this blocking variable and its interaction with the experimental factor(s) may be analyzed, hoping that (needless to say!) no interaction or main effect will be detected, or else the design will become a special type of randomized block design, and sound explanations for the impact of time of enrollment in the experiment would be required. To account for this variation of the forced-size strategy in sequential assignment, we give the designations Method 5 (*Forced Equal Sizes Sequential Assignment*) and Method 6 (*Forced Unequal Sizes Sequential Assignment*) to the basic SRA Methods 3 and 4. The illustration of Method 5 is given on the right side of Table 2.20; Method 6 is similar, with the exception that the equal number of treatment level replications within each randomization fraction is replaced with the desired pattern of unequal replications.

2.5.2 Sequential Blocked Random Assignment

The distinction between situations where there is no temporal limit for the conclusion of the study and situations where an ending point is imposed by extrinsic time schedules or any other constraints (e.g., institutional resources, research funds) is even more crucial in experimental studies relying on blocked random assignment. If there is no temporal limit, it is possible to carry out all the experimental designs and randomization methods described in Section 2.3, with two additional adaptations: (1) the allocation frames within blocks start with the randomly ordered list of treatment replications and (b) the experimenter waits until all associated (virtual) ID numbers are ascribed to the successively enrolled experimental units, with the understanding that once a block has been filled up, no more units owning the block-defining characteristic(s) are enrolled in the experiment. When the experimenter's degrees of freedom don't include the decision about the study end, sequential blocked random assignment is simply not feasible, and the alternatives are sequential simple or stratified random assignment.

Note that there is an additional restraint on blocked random assignment in the "no temporal limit" situation: When the cutoff points for continuous blocking variables are arbitrary and are chosen on the basis of the observed distribution of scores (as in the example in Subsection 2.3.1 with IQ), the blocks become undefinable at the beginning of the experiment. A way to circumvent this obstacle is to establish in advance fixed cutoff points (within "reasonable" ranges) for the blocking variable. By definition, with nominal (nonordered categories) and ordinal (ordered categories) blocking variables, no such obstacles exist. The randomization methods applying to sequential blocked random assignment are listed in Table 2.21, as well as the methods appropriate to sequential simple (previous subsection) and stratified (next subsection) random assignment.

2.5.3 Sequential Stratified Random Assignment

In the same sense that Nonsequential Stratified Random Assignment (Method 11) is the application of Method 3 (SRA with forced equal sizes, including last permutation correction) within each stratum integrated in the design layout, *Sequential Stratified Random Assignment* (Method 12) is the use of Method 5 (sequential SRA, including time-blocking strategy) in equivalent circumstances. To carry out Method 12 is an easy, but time-consuming, task. Once the strata have been defined, a randomly ordered list of treatment level replications is attributed to each randomization fraction within strata. The intrastratum randomization is identical to that with Method 5. However, in this case, the size of the randomization fractions must take account of the (intended) total number of experimental units and the expected numbers for each stratum. Usually, the size of the randomization fractions is smaller than in sequential SRA, and in some circumstances it is advisable to let the randomization fraction size vary across strata. Table 2.22 shows an example with four strata, three treatment levels, and randomization fractions (time blocking) with six experimental units.

Table 2.21 Randomization Procedures in Sequential Assignment

	End of the Study	
Randomization Methods[a]	No temporal limit[b]	Time or budget fixed
Simple Random Assignment		
A Priori Probabilities	• Methods 1 and 2	• Method 1 and 2
Forced Sizes	• Methods 3 and 4	• Methods 5 and 6
Blocked Random Assignment	• Methods 7, 8, 9, and 10	• *Not feasible*
Stratified Random Assignment	• Method 12	• Method 12

[a] See Table 1.2 for methods designations.

[b] Number of replications are previously determined by educated guessing and formal power analysis or set to an arbitrary number (not recommended). The study ends when all the prespecified allocations are done.

Table 2.22 Stratified Random Assignment (Sequential Procedure): Assignment of N Experimental Units (Grouped in Four Strata Defined by Two Stratifying Variables: A and B) to Three Treatment Levels (T1, T2, and T3) With Time Blocking Within Strata (Method 12)

		B1							B2						
		Stratum 1							*Stratum 2*						
		Frame			Final Allocation				Frame			Final Allocation			
		Time	RN	T	Time	RN	T	ID	Unit	Time	RN	T	Time	RN	T	ID	Unit
A1		[1]	.748	T1	[1]	.177	T3	1	[?]	[1]	.873	T1	[1]	.028	T1	1	[?]
			.677	T1		.406	T2	2	[?]		.028	T1		.139	T2	2	[?]
			.804	T2		.677	T1	3	[?]		.139	T2		.250	T2	3	[?]
			.406	T2		.748	T1	4	[?]		.250	T2		.677	T3	4	[?]
			.177	T3		.804	T2	5	[?]		.816	T3		.816	T3	5	[?]
			.901	T3		.901	T3	6	[?]		.677	T3		.873	T1	6	[?]
		[2]	.649	T1	[2]	.198	T2	1	[?]	[2]	.336	T1	[2]	.033	T3	1	[?]
			.325	T1		.325	T1	2	[?]		.732	T1		.336	T1	2	[?]
			.198	T2		.371	T3	3	[?]		.658	T2		.563	T3	3	[?]
			.897	T2		.649	T1	4	[?]		.761	T2		.658	T2	4	[?]
			.371	T3		.715	T3	5	[?]		.033	T3		.732	T1	5	[?]
			.715	T3		.897	T2	6	[?]		.563	T3		.761	T2	6	[?]
		[...]	...	...	[...]	...	...	...	...	[...]	...	...	[...]	...	...	...	...
		[t − 1]	...	...	[t − 1]	...	...	...	...	[t − 1]	...	...	[t − 1]	...	...	...	...
		[t]	...	...	[t]	...	...	...	...	[t]	...	...	[t]	...	...	...	...

RN: Table A1.1 (Rows: 37–42; Col.: 28–30).
RN: Table A1.1 (Rows: 3–8; Col.: 12–14).

RN: Table A1.1 (Rows: 15–20; Col.: 23–25).
RN: Table A1.1 (Rows: 24–29; Col.: 34–36).

		Stratum 3							*Stratum 4*						
		Frame			Final Allocation				Frame			Final Allocation			
		Time	RN	T	Time	RN	T	ID	Unit	Time	RN	T	Time	RN	T	ID	Unit
A2		[1]	.571	T1	[1]	.225	T2	1	[?]	[1]	.188	T1	[1]	.129	T2	1	[?]
			.996	T1		.406	T3	2	[?]		.220	T1		.188	T1	2	[?]
			.593	T2		.571	T1	3	[?]		.881	T2		.220	T1	3	[?]
			.225	T2		.572	T3	4	[?]		.129	T2		.518	T3	4	[?]
			.572	T3		.593	T2	5	[?]		.937	T3		.881	T2	5	[?]
			.406	T3		.996	T1	6	[?]		.518	T3		.937	T3	6	[?]
		[2]	.960	T1	[2]	.065	T1	1	[?]	[2]	.362	T1	[2]	.002	T3	1	[?]
			.065	T1		.201	T2	2	[?]		.770	T1		.088	T2	2	[?]
			.361	T2		.361	T2	3	[?]		.137	T2		.137	T2	3	[?]
			.201	T2		.585	T3	4	[?]		.088	T2		.362	T1	4	[?]
			.585	T3		.822	T3	5	[?]		.694	T3		.694	T3	5	[?]
			.822	T3		.960	T1	6	[?]		.002	T3		.770	T1	6	[?]
		[...]	...	...	[...]	...	...	...	...	[...]	...	...	[...]	...	...	...	...
		[t − 1]	...	...	[t − 1]	...	...	...	...	[t − 1]	...	...	[t − 1]	...	...	...	...
		[t]	...	...	[t]	...	...	...	...	[t]	...	...	[t]	...	...	...	...

RN: Table A1.1 (Rows: 26–31; Col.: 11–13).
RN: Table A1.1 (Rows: 4–9; Col.: 40–42).

RN: Table A1.1 (Rows: 15–20; Col.: 13–15).
RN: Table A1.1 (Rows: 41–46; Col.: 38–40).

2.5.4 Minimization and Related Techniques

Minimization, or more rigorously some techniques of deterministic assignment and adaptive randomization procedures, was initially proposed by Taves (1974) and Pocock and Simon (1975; for a recent review, see Scott, McPherson, Ramsay, & Campbell, 2002) as an alternative to sequential stratified random assignment, and its status among randomization methods is still a controversial issue. Even though we agree with authors who see no recommendable use for minimization (e.g., Berger, 2005; Fleiss, 1986), we will describe and illustrate the main features of the procedure in this final subsection, postponing the substantive discussion to Chapter 4.

The difficulties in achieving balanced designs with sequential stratified random assignment and related problems with "overstratification" set the stage for minimization and adaptive randomization strategies. Basically, the procedure consists in skipping the stratification phase and combining sequential SRA—Method 1 (equal a priori probabilities of assignment) either with deterministic (nonrandom) assignment or with sequential SRA—Method 2 (unequal a priori probabilities of assignment). The final goal is to have a balanced design in which the levels of classificatory or prognostic factors are homogeneously distributed across the experimental conditions included in the design layout, hence the expression "minimizing treatment imbalance." The main steps of *Minimization* (Method 13) are summarized in Table 2.23, and the procedure is illustrated in Table 2.24.

Table 2.23   Major Steps in the Minimization Method (Method 13)

Step 1—Specification of randomization procedures

First unit

- Simple Random Assignment (Method 1: Equal Probabilities of Assignment)

Subsequent units

Treatments are balanced

- Simple Random Assignment (Method 1: Equal Probabilities of Assignment)

Treatments are imbalanced

- Deterministic Assignment
- Simple Random Assignment (Method 2: Unequal Probabilities of Assignment)

Step 2—Specification of the criteria for assessing treatment imbalance and the "maximum tolerate imbalance"

- The number of units previously assigned to at least one treatment is different from the number of units assigned to the remaining treatment(s)

(Continued)

Table 2.23 (Continued)

- Taves's methods
- Pocock & Simon's methods
- Other methods and algorithms

Step 3—Determination of the values on classificatory factors for the n-th unit to be assigned

Step 4—Assessment of treatment imbalance if the n-th unit is assigned to the t-th treatment

- Counting the number of units previously assigned to each treatment within each classificatory factor level and adding the n-th unit
- Decision about whether or not treatment imbalance exists based on the application of the formulas and criteria specified in *Step 2*

Step 5—Assignment of the n-th unit according to the randomization procedure specified in *Step 1*

Suppose that the researcher is carrying out a randomized experiment with three treatment levels and 50 units have already been assigned. When the 51st unit joins the experiment, it must be previously classified according to the relevant prognostic factors (in the example, the structural characteristic of the 51st unit puts it on Levels 1, 2, and 2 of the 3 prognostic factors considered by the researcher). Treatment imbalance—*if the unit is assigned to each of the treatment levels included in the design*—is then assessed on the basis of the previously chosen measure of "treatment imbalance" (calculus with *range* and *variance* measures is illustrated in Section B of Table 2.24). Finally, if the observed imbalance is greater than the "maximum tolerate imbalance," also defined in advance at the beginning of the study, the unit is assigned to the treatment level that minimizes the overall imbalance (in the example, the 51st unit is assigned to Treatment 3, for which the range or the variance measure gives the smallest value: range = 4; variance = 1.66). This is a deterministic (nonrandom) assignment. A variation of the procedure uses the *biased coin method* (Efron, 1971), our Method 2 (unequal a priori probabilities of assignment), with probabilities of assignment inversely proportional to the amount of imbalance for each treatment.

Please note that the unit is *not* assigned to the treatment level with the lowest number of experimental units, as a less attentive inspection of the data in Section A of Table 2.24 would suggest (our example is the

Table 2.24 Minimization: Assessment Treatment Imbalance Within the Levels of Classificatory (Prognostic) Factors (Method 13)

A. 50 Patients distributed by treatment and factor levels					Observations
	Treatment 1	Treatment 2	Treatment 3	*Marginals*	• The data for this example are taken from Pocock and Simon (1975, p. 108).
Factor 1					
Level 1	9	10	9	*28*	
Level 2	8	7	7	*22*	• There are 50 patients already assigned and the experimenter wants to assess treatment imbalance (within prognostic factor levels) before the 51st patient (whose intrinsic characteristics place him/her in Levels 1, 2, and 2 of Factors 1, 2, and 3—see shaded cells) is assigned to one of the three treatments.
Marginals	*17*	*17*	*16*	*50*	
Factor 2					
Level 1	8	6	7	*21*	
Level 2	9	11	9	*29*	
Marginals	*17*	*17*	*16*	*50*	
Factor 3					
Level 1	8	8	8	*24*	
Level 2	4	5	3	*12*	
Level 3	5	4	5	*14*	
Marginals	*17*	*17*	*16*	*50*	

B. Imbalance assessment: Measure = Range

		Units per treatment					Imbalance if treatment t is assigned to the *51st* unit		
		Units assigned			Next unit assigned		If T1 is assigned: max(uT1,T2,T3) − min(uT1,T2,T3)	If T2 is assigned: max(T1,uT2,T3) − min(T1,uT2,T3)	If T3 is assigned: max(T1,T2,uT3) − min(T1,T2,uT3)
F	L	T1	T2	T3	uT1	uT2 uT3			
1	1	9	10	9	*10*	*11 10*	10 − 9 = 1	11 − 9 = 2	10 − 9 = 1
2	2	9	11	9	*10*	*12 10*	11 − 9 = 2	12 − 9 = 3	11 − 9 = 2
3	2	4	5	3	*5*	*6 4*	5 − 3 = 2	6 − 3 = 3	5 − 4 = 1
*Total amount of imbalance (**G**)*							1 + 2 + 2 = **5**	2 + 3 + 3 = **8**	1 + 2 + 1 = **4**

C. Imbalance assessment: Measure = Variance

		Units per treatment					Imbalance if treatment t is assigned to the *51st* unit		
		Units assigned			Next unit assigned		If T1 is assigned: Variance (uT1,T2,T3)	If T2 is assigned: Variance (T1,uT2,T3)	If T3 is assigned: Variance (T1,T2,uT3)
F	L	T1	T2	T3	uT1	uT2 uT3			
1	1	9	10	9	*10*	*11 10*	Var (10,10, 9) = 0.33	Var (9,11, 9) = 1.33	Var (9,10, 10) = 0.33
2	2	9	11	9	*10*	*12 10*	Var (10,11,9) = 1.00	Var (9,12,9) = 3.00	Var (9,11,10) = 1.00
3	2	4	5	3	*5*	*6 4*	Var (5,5,3) = 1.33	Var (4,6,3) = 2.33	Var (4,5,4) = 0.33
*Total amount of imbalance (**G**)*							0.33+1.00+1.33=**2.66**	1.33+3.00+2.33=**6.66**	0.33+1.00+0.33=**1.66**

original example of Pocock & Simon, 1975). For instance, if the levels of prognostic factors for the 51st unit were Level 2 (Factor 1), Level 1 (Factor 2), and Level 1 (Factor 3), the range measures (6, 3, and 4, respectively) or the variance measures (4.00, 1.00, and 2.00, respectively) would imply the assignment of Treatment T2, in the case of deterministic assignment, or greater probabilities of assignment to Treatment T2, in the case of the application of Method 2. We have also assumed that all prognostic factors were equally important; therefore, no weighting scheme has been applied to the calculus of the amounts of imbalance. Finally, note that when the probabilistic scheme used in Method 2 approaches the equal probabilities of assignment procedure, minimization becomes SRA and "then the baby is lost with the bath water; . . . minimization no longer does what it purports to do" (Berger, 2010, p. 406).

CHAPTER 3. WITHIN-SUBJECTS
DESIGNS RANDOMIZATION

3.1 Basic Assumptions and Specific Threats to Validity

A within-subjects design is an experimental design in which *two or more* units (subjects) are exposed to *two or more* treatment levels (or treatment level combinations) over *two or more* periods and outcome measures are recorded after each exposure. As such, within-subjects designs contrast with between-subjects designs, wherein each experimental unit is only exposed to *one* treatment level (or treatment level combination). Figure 3.1 outlines a within-subjects design in which every experimental unit receives three treatment levels (A, B, and C, not necessarily in this order) in three con- secutive periods (Periods 1, 2, and 3). Briefly stated, within-subjects designs concern experimental situations "where a number of subjects . . . receive a sequence of treatments over a number of time periods" (Bate & Jones, 2006, p. 3249).

In methodological and statistical literature, within-subjects designs are also labeled *repeated measures designs* or *repeated measurement designs*, emphasizing the idea that several measures are taken on the same subjects. However, it is convenient to make a clear distinction between what has

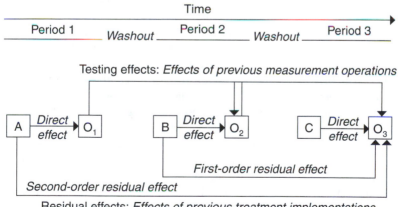

Figure 3.1 Direct and carryover effects in within-subjects designs (the first-order residual effect of A on O_2 is omitted)

been called a *longitudinal data structure* (i.e., collecting one or more measures on the same units over successive periods) and an *experimental repeated measures design*. In a longitudinal data structure, the interval between the first and the last period of measurement can vary from a few seconds to months or even years, and the intervals between adjacent periods can have the same or different durations. The same is true in relation to a repeated measures design, given that from a measurement perspective the design is a special kind of longitudinal data structure. However, what makes the specificity of within-subjects or repeated measures experimental designs is the administration of different treatment levels to the same units and the recording of outcome measures immediately after each administration, not the longitudinal data structure in itself. Longitudinal data structures can arise from experimental, quasi-experimental, and nonexperimental studies (see Figure 1.1). More specifically, they can take the form of either *before- and after-treatment measures* in interrupted time series quasi-experimental designs or *single/multiple pretest–posttest measures* in between-subjects experimental (pretest–posttest designs and longitudinal designs) and quasi-experimental (regression discontinuity designs and nonequivalent comparison group designs; see Shadish et al., 2002) designs. Finally, longitudinal data structures can be obtained in nonexperimetal research, as it is the typical case of panel surveys. An additional distinction must also be made between repeated measures designs and designs with "multiple measures," these being true between-subjects designs in which two or more different outcome measures have been collected after the treatment administration (multivariate analysis of variance designs).

Moreover, in some disciplines (e.g., experimental psychology) the expression *within-subjects designs* applies to completely different situations: "subjects-by-trials" and "subjects-by-treatments" designs (see Kirk, 1995). The first situation corresponds to studies in which the same participants are submitted to several trials to quantify learning progress in specific tasks. Rigorously speaking, these are not randomized experiments, since all participants are measured in the same series of ordered trials, and the aim of the study is to establish a functional relationship (learning curve) between the amount of training (number of trials) and the quality of the performance (indexed by the number of errors or the time required for accomplishing the learning task). Subjects-by-trials experiments will not be covered in this monograph, but we should note that comparing the learning curves of two or more groups of participants tested under different learning conditions could be an example of a between-subjects design if the participants had been randomly assigned to distinct learning groups. The second situation, subjects-by-treatments designs, corresponds exactly to our initial definition of within-subjects experimental designs and is the main topic of this chapter. When moving from one period to the next, subjects are exposed to a different treatment level; thus, they are said to cross over treatments, hence the designation *cross-over designs*, under which these designs are also known.

As compared with between-subjects designs, within-subjects designs have two main advantages. First, for the same number of observations, they require fewer experimental units ($N_W = N_B/t$; compare the structural features of basic one-factor designs in Table 4.2, Chapter 4). Second, as each experimental unit acts as its own control by being observed in different experimental conditions, *error variability* is expected to be substantially reduced. Taken together, these advantages add up to make within-subjects designs more powerful than between-subjects designs. Unfortunately, the advantages can be overcome by serious drawbacks.

First of all, there are research problems and theoretical hypotheses that by their very nature and content don't allow the use of cross-over designs. For example, when social or educational programs are known for having lasting and nonreversible effects (hopefully!), it makes no sense to deliver alternative programs to the same subjects (e.g., assessing the differential effectiveness of two methods of teaching reading skills to the same subjects in two consecutive periods). By the same token, when manipulations rely on the cognitive definition of situations, as in the case of many experiments in social and cognitive psychology, once a *cover story* is created to allow the implementation of a treatment, there is no possibility of constructing a plausible scenario to introduce an alternative treatment. In brief, before proceeding with a cross-over design, the researcher must always take into account the possibility that his or her manipulations may be meaningless to the study participants. This is basically a problem of construct validity of the presumed causes (see Subsection 4.1.1).

Second, in a cross-over experiment there is always the very possibility that the effect of a treatment level will be confounded with the effects of the treatment levels and the measurement operations that took place in the previous periods (see Figure 3.1). This kind of confounding is in essence a matter of internal and statistical conclusion validity of local causal inferences that is known under several designations in methodological textbooks and the experimental design literature.

By definition, the measurement operations—that is, the operationalization of the dependent variable but not, as it is obvious, the outcome actually recorded—are identical for all subjects in all periods. As a result, no matter which treatment level has been administered in the previous period, the potential confounding effect of the associated measurement operation is indistinguishable from the confounding effects of the measurement operations associated with the remaining treatment levels. In other words, the confounding effects of previous measurement operations are intrinsically *position effects*: How many measurement operations have preceded the current observation?

Also by definition, treatment levels are always distinct operationalizations of the independent variable, therefore the potential confounding effect of the treatment level administrated in the previous period is unlikely to be identical to the confounding effects of the other treatment levels. In other words, these effects are essentially *sequence effects*: Which is precisely the treatment level administered in the previous period, or more generally, which is the sequence of treatment levels administered in all previous periods?

Position effects and sequence effects in cross-over designs have been contrasted under different labels: *rank order effects* versus *sequence effects* (Lindquist, 1953); *practice, order, time-related,* or *progressive-error effects* versus *treatment-carryover* or *treatment-transfer effects* (Kiess & Bloomquist, 1985); *practice* or *testing position effects* versus *carryover effects* (Keppel, 1991); *testing position effects* versus *sequence effects* (Reese, 1997); and *order main effects* versus *carryover effects* (Maxwell & Delaney, 2004)—the list is not exhaustive. Generic labels for both effects (some of them rather ambiguous as *order effects*) have also been used, such as *multiple-treatment effects* (Kiess & Bloomquist, 1985) or *context effects* (Greenwald, 1976). In specialized cross-over designs literature (e.g., Bose & Dey, 2009; Jones & Kenward, 2003), sequence effects are interchangeably named *carryover effects* or *residual effects* and are distinguished from treatment *direct effects* (see Figure 3.1).

Taken all together, the effects of previous treatments and the effects of previous measurement operations can be conceptualized as external events or situational nuisance variables, and in this sense, they can be thought of as a threat to internal validity called *history*. Taken alone, the effects of previous measurement operations correspond exactly to the Campbellian definition of *testing*. In practice, given that each treatment is always coupled with the corresponding outcome measure, we cannot disentangle the *testing effects of previous measurement operations* from the *residual effects of previous treatments*. So we think that the *carryover effects of previous periods* can be best described as *additive and interactive effects of history and testing*. From a substantive point of view, these effects can be explained by perceptive (e.g., assimilation/contrast), learning (e.g., transfer, fatigue, boredom), motivational, and more general cognitive and affective processes involved in the definition/interpretation of the experimental situation.

In a very clear presentation of Rubin's causal model, Holland (1986) puts into words the *fundamental problem of causal inference*—"It is impossible to observe the value of $Y_t(u)$ and $Y_c(u)$ on the same unit, and, therefore, it is impossible to observe the effect of t on u" (p. 947)—and elaborates on two general solutions, which he calls the "scientific solution" and the "statistical solution." The latter solution is the one adopted in between-subjects designs and relies on the randomization methods described in the preceding chapter, on Rubin's SUTVA, and on the estimation of average causal effects; the former solution is the solution achieved by cross-over designs if the strong assumption of homogeneity or invariance is tenable. To be more precise, an ideal cross-over design is carried out by presupposing that the units' general behavior is constant across experimental conditions (*temporal stability*) and there are no lasting carryover effects of previous periods (*causal transience*).

In practice, there are two basic and complementary strategies to approach this ideal: (1) to insert sufficiently wide time intervals (*washout* or *rest* periods; see Figure 3.1) between adjacent experimental periods, hoping that potential carryover effects will dissipate, and (2) to compensate for carryover effects by *counterbalancing* the order of presentation of the different treatments. The first strategy is always recommendable, despite knowing that the longer the duration of the experiment is, the lower the probability of ensuring the constancy of units' general behavior across experimental conditions. The implementation of the second strategy is the main subject of Sections 3.3 through 3.7. However, before proceeding with the description and the illustration of counterbalancing schemes, we must classify the different kinds of cross-over designs and summarize their structural properties. This will be done in the next section.

3.2 Treatment Design and Methods of Randomization

Formally speaking, a cross-over design—denoted by $CO(t, n, p)$—is an array of n rows and p columns, defining np experimental sites (cells), coupled with a plan for the random assignment of t treatment levels (or treatment level combinations) to the np experimental sites. By convention, each *row* corresponds to one experimental unit (subject) that receives two or more treatment levels in successive periods (columns). Also by convention, the different treatment levels assigned to the np experimental sites are denoted by Latin letters (A, B, C, . . .).

There are two basic structural properties of cross-over designs: uniformity and balance. *Uniformity* concerns the number of replications of treatment levels within rows (subjects) and columns (periods). *Balance* relates to the sequence of treatment levels across the rows.

A cross-over design is said to be *uniform on rows* when, for each experimental unit (subject), the same number of periods is assigned to each treatment level; likewise, a design is said to be *uniform on columns* when, in each period, the same number of experimental units (subjects) is assigned to each treatment level. For example, Designs 6B2p (see Table 3.1) and 6N4 (see

70

Table 3.2) are uniform on rows but not on columns; similarly, Designs 6D2e (see Table 3.1) and 6R4 (see Table 3.2) are uniform on columns but not on rows. It is evident that the necessary condition for uniformity on rows is that $p = \mu_r t$ and the necessary condition for uniformity on columns is that $n = \mu_c t$, where μ_r and μ_c are integers greater than or equal to 1.

Table 3.1 Uniformity and Balance in One-Treatment Cross-Over Designs: Examples for Two Treatment Levels ($t = 2$)

Design 6A: $n = 2, p = 2$		Designs 6C: $n > 2, p = 2$		
6A2		6C2a	6C2b	6C2c
AB		AA	*AA*	*AB*
BA		AB	*AB*	*BA*
$\lambda_1 = 1$		BA	*BA*	*BB*
2 × 2 Cross-Over Design		BB	—	—
		$\lambda_2 = 1$		
		Ballam's Design		

Designs 6B: $n = 2, p > 2$				Designs 6D: $n > 2, p > 2$				
6B2a	6B2e	6B2i	6B2n	6D2a	6D2d	6D2g	6D2i	6D2k
ABB	AABB	ABAA	ABBAA	ABA	AAB	AABB	AABB	AABBBA
BAA	BBAA	BABB	BAABB	ABB	ABB	ABBA	ABAA	ABBAAB
$\lambda_2 = 1$	$\lambda_1 = 1$	$\lambda_1 = 2$	$\lambda_2 = 2$	BAA	BAA	ABBB	ABBB	BAABBA
6B2b	6B2f	6B2j	6B2o	BAB	BBA	BAAA	BAAA	BBAAAB
ABA	ABAB	ABBB	*AABBA*	$\lambda_1 = 3$	$\lambda_2 = 2$	BAAB	BABB	$\lambda_2 = 5$
BAB	BABA	BAAA	*BAABB*	6D2b	6D2e	BBAA	BBAA	6D2l
$\lambda_1 = 2$	$\lambda_1 = 3$	$\lambda_1 = 1$	$\lambda_2 = 2$	AAB	AAB	$\lambda_1 = 4$	$\lambda_1 = 4$	AAA AAA
6B2c	6B2g	6B2k	6B2p	ABA	ABA	6D2h	6D2j	AAA BBB
AAB	ABBA	AAAB	*ABAB*	BAB	ABB	AABB	*ABAB*	BBB AAA
BBA	BAAB	BBBA	*AABB*	BBA	BAA	ABBA	*ABBA*	BBB BBB
$\lambda_2 = 1$	$\lambda_1 = 2$	$\lambda_1 = 1$	—	$\lambda_1 = 3$	BAB	BAAB	*BAAB*	$\lambda_1 = 1$
6B2d	6Bh		6B2l	6D2c	BBA	BBAA	—	
ABB	AABA	*AAAA BBB AA B*		*AAB*	$\lambda_1 = 4$	$\lambda_2 = 3$		
BAB	BBAB	*BBB AAAA B AA*		*ABA*	6D2f			
—	$\lambda_1 = 2$	$\lambda_1 = 3$		*BAB*	*AAA*			
		6B2m		$\lambda_1 = 2$	*AAB*			
		AAA BBB AAA BBB			*ABB*			
		BBB AAA BBB AAA			—			
		$\lambda_1 = 3$						

Notes. All designs are shown in their standard form before randomization. Solid horizontal lines denote *uniformity on subjects*; dashed horizontal lines denote *nonuniformity on subjects*; solid vertical lines denote *uniformity on periods*; dashed vertical lines denote *nonuniformity on periods*. *Nonbalanced designs* are shown in italic type and *balanced designs* in regular type. *Strongly balanced designs* are shaded (see main text for explanation of λ parameters).

Table 3.2 Uniformity and Balance (First-Order Carryover Effects) in One-Treatment Cross-Over Designs: Examples for Three and Four Treatment Levels ($t = 3$ and $t = 4$)

	Nonbalanced		Balanced	Strongly Balanced
Nonutilizable Designs	Random Counterbalanc.	Standard Latin Squares	Williams's Latin Squares	Extra-Period Designs

$t = 3$

	Design 6N3	Design 6M3	Design 6H3	Design 6R3
$n = 3, p = 4$	$n = 3, p = 3$	$n = 3, p = 3$	$n = 6, p = 3$	$n = 6, p = 4$
A B B C	B A C	A B C	A B C ⎫	A B C C ⎫
B D D A	C A B	B C A	B C A ⎬ Square 1	B C A A ⎬ Rectang. 1
C A A D	A B C	C A B	C A B ⎭	C A B B ⎭
			A C B ⎫	A C B B ⎫
			B A C ⎬ Square 2	B A C C ⎬ Rectang. 2
			C B A ⎭	C B A A ⎭
			$\lambda_1 = 2$	$\lambda_2 = 2$

$t = 4$

	Design 6N4	Design 6M4	Design 6G4	Design 6R4
$n = 4, p = 5$	$n = 4, p = 4$	$n = 4, p = 4$	$n = 4, p = 4$	$n = 4, p = 5$
A B C D D	C A D B	A B C D	A B C D	A B C D D
B D A C C	A D C B	B A D C	B D A C	B D A C C
C A D B B	C B D A	C D B A	C A D B	C A D B B
D C B A A	B A D C	D C A B	D C B A	D C B A A
			$\lambda_1 = 1$	$\lambda_2 = 1$

Notes. With the exception of *Designs 6N3* and *6N4*, which are possible final designs obtained from random counterbalancing, all designs are shown in their standard form before randomization. Solid horizontal lines denote *uniformity on subjects*; dashed horizontal lines denote *nonuniformity on subjects*; solid vertical lines denote *uniformity on periods*; dashed vertical lines denote *nonuniformity on periods* (see main text for explanation of λ parameters). The relationship between balanced designs and extra-period strongly balanced designs is explained in Subsection 3.5.3.

A cross-over design is said to be a *uniform design* when it is simultaneously uniform on rows and columns (i.e., $p = \mu_r t$ and $n = \mu_c t$). For example, Designs 6A2 ($\mu_r = 1$, $\mu_c = 1$), 6B2e ($\mu_r = 2$, $\mu_c = 1$), 6H3 ($\mu_r = 1$, $\mu_c = 2$), and 6M4 ($\mu_r = 1$, $\mu_c = 1$) are uniform designs (see Tables 3.1 and 3.2).

A cross-over design is said to be *balanced* with respect to the *first-order carryover effects* when each treatment level is not immediately preceded by itself but is immediately preceded by all the remaining treatment levels the same number of times. For example, in Design 6G4, Treatment Level A is immediately preceded once (and only once) by Treatment Levels B, C, and D; the same is true for B, C, and D regarding the remaining treatments. This pattern doesn't occur in Design 6M4, wherein A is immediately preceded twice by B, once by C, and never by D (see Table 3.2).

The necessary condition to achieve balance for the first-order carryover effects is that the equation $[n(p - 1)]/[t(t - 1)] = \lambda_1$ gives an integer value (≥ 1) for λ_1. In this case—and when all additional conditions are fulfilled—the parameter λ_1 can be read as the number of times a treatment level is immediately preceded by each of the remaining treatment levels in balanced designs (see Tables 3.1 and 3.2).

A cross-over design is said to be *strongly balanced* with respect to the first-order carryover effects when each treatment level is immediately preceded by all treatment levels (including the *treatment level itself*) the same number of times. For example, in Design 6R4, A is immediately preceded by A, B, C, and D only once; the same is true for B, C, and D (see Table 3.2).

The necessary condition to have a strongly balanced design for the first-order carryover effects is that the equation $[n(p - 1)]/[t^2] = \lambda_2$ gives an integer value (≥ 1) for λ_2. If this is true—and if all additional conditions are satisfied—the parameter λ_2 is the number of times a treatment level is immediately preceded by all treatment levels (including the *treatment level itself*) in strongly balanced designs (see Tables 3.1 and 3.2).

For a given number of treatment levels and periods and an anticipated degree of balance and/or uniformity, a *standard design* is the design that accomplishes the intended structural properties with the minimum possible number of experimental units. By convention and to avoid misidentification or giving different names to the same design, standard designs are always written with the first row and the first column in alphabetical order (*standard form*). So a standard design is a *minimal design in its standard form*. With the exception of nonutilizable designs and Designs 6N3 and 6N4, all designs presented in Tables 3.1 and 3.2 are in their standard form (please note that in a standard design there are no duplicated sequences). In Section 3.5, we illustrate the procedure for reducing a given design to its standard form (see Table 3.11, Steps 2 and 3).

Cross-over designs can be classified on the basis of the following criteria: (a) the *number of treatment* and *treatment levels* (*one* vs. *two or more treatments*, *two* vs. *three or more treatment levels*); (b) the combination of *within-subjects treatments* with *between-subjects treatments* (designs involving *only within-subjects treatments* vs. designs including *at least one between-subjects treatment*); (c) the relationship between the *number of periods* and the *number of treatment levels*—or treatment level combinations—included in the study (*complete, incomplete,* and *extended* sequences); (d) the structural properties of the standard design, namely, *uniformity* (*nonuniform* vs. *uniform designs*) and *balance* (*nonbalanced, partially balanced, nearly balanced, balanced, nearly strongly balanced,* and *strongly balanced designs*); (e) the number of *admissible partitions* of the standard design (designs consisting of a *single set of sequences* vs. designs organized into different subsets of sequences; *one-brick* designs vs.

multiple-bricks designs); and (f) the number of *replications* of the standard design (*one* vs. *two or more* replications).

Table 3.3 shows a classification of cross-over designs based on the first four criteria. Please note that criterion (c) and criterion (d) are not strictly independent, since the extension of sequences (i.e., the number of periods) is directly related to the structural properties of the intended design. The last two criteria are especially relevant when within-subjects treatments are combined with between-subjects treatments and/or between-subjects blocking structures. In addition to power-related issues, the replication of standard designs creates the conditions to give identical sets of sequences to groups of experimental units either defined by between-subjects blocking structures or generated by between-subjects randomization. Standard designs consisting of multiple bricks can also be broken into different but structurally equivalent subsets of sequences, which can be randomly assigned to distinct groups of experimental units.

The randomization methods relevant to cross-over designs can be categorized in terms of the intended structural properties and the presence/absence

Table 3.3   Classification of Cross-Over Experimental Designs

---

One treatment

Two levels ($t = 2$)

Two sequences and two periods ($n = 2, p = 2$) (Design 6A)

Higher-order designs

Two sequences and more than two periods ($n = 2, p > 2$) (Design 6B)

More than two sequences and two periods ($n > 2, p = 2$) (Design 6C)

More than two sequences and more than two periods ($n > 2, p > 2$) (Design 6D)

Three or more levels ($t > 2$)

Complete sequences ($p = t$)

Balanced designs

All possible sequences ($n = t!$) (Design 6E)

Complete sets of mutually orthogonal Latin squares ($n = t(t - 1)$) (Design 6F)

Williams's designs: t even ($n = t$) (Design 6G)

Williams's designs: t odd ($n = 2t$) (Design 6H)

Hedayat's and Afsarinejad's Designs ($n = t$; for $t = 9, 15, 21, 27$) (Design 6I)

Newcombe's and Prescott's "Triples" ($n = 3t$) (Design 6J)

Locally Balanced Designs ($n = t(t - 1)$, t odd) (Design 6K)

(Continued)

Table 3.3 (Continued)

Nearly balanced designs

Russel's Designs ($n = t$, for $t = 5$, 7) (Design 6L)

Nonbalanced designs

Uniform designs (Repeated Measures Latin Square) ($n = t$) (Design 6M)

Non uniform designs (Repeated Measures Randomized Block) (Design 6N)

Incomplete sequences ($p < t$)

Balanced designs (Designs 6O)

Strongly balanced designs (extra-period designs) (Designs 6P)

Partially balanced designs (Designs 6Q)

Extended sequences ($p > t$)

Strongly balanced designs

Extra-period designs ($p = t + 1$) (Designs 6R)

Many periods designs (Designs 6S)

Nearly strongly balanced designs (Designs 6T)

Two or more treatments

Only within-subjects treatments (Designs 6U)

At least one between-subjects treatment (Designs 6V)

Notes. This classification is based on Jones and Kenward's (2003) detailed presentation of cross-over designs. For each design, n is the *minimum number* of experimental units required and can be read as the *number of different sequences of treatments* included in the standard design. The number of *treatment levels* is denoted by t and the number of *periods* of observation by p.

of restrictions imposed by concomitant consideration of between-subjects treatments or blocking structures. In other words, if neither uniformity nor balance is wanted for the design, the proper method is to randomly order the treatment levels separately for each unit (Method 14: *Random Counterbalancing*); if uniformity, but not balance, is a requisite, randomly selected Latin squares are the suitable choice (Method 15: *Positional Counterbalancing*). Finally, if some degree of balance is required, the researcher must select the appropriate standard design and proceed to the randomization following the major steps for *Sequential Counterbalancing* (Methods 16–18) described in Table 3.4. The choice of the sequential counterbalancing method depends on the restrictions imposed by between-subjects blocking structures and/or between-subjects randomization.

Having in mind that in practice it is impossible to disentangle the *testing effects* of previous measurement operations and the *residual effects* of previous treatments (see Section 3.1), the main *theoretical* assumptions about carryover effects and the distinctive features of counterbalancing methods are summarized in Table 3.5. The reader should be careful about the clear delimitation between the so-called symmetrical and asymmetrical residual effects of previous treatments. As we noted in Section 3.1, by definition the residual effects of different treatment levels are expected to be dissimilar. Yet, depending on the very nature of the treatment and the magnitude of the differential features of treatment levels (i.e., experimental conditions), it can be conceivable to handle all carryover effects as "symmetrical effects." These matters are not consensual, and they are intertwined with the general approaches to cross-over

Table 3.4   Major Steps in the Randomization of Cross-Over Experimental Designs

---

Nonsequential Counterbalancing

Method 14: Random Counterbalancing (RC-ro)

- The order of treatment levels is randomized separately for each experimental unit

Method 15: Positional Counterbalancing (PC-Ls)

- Random selection of a $t \times t$ Latin square for each consecutive group of t experimental units

Sequential Counterbalancing

Method 16: Nonrestricted Sequential Counterbalancing (SC-nr)

- Random assignment of treatment levels to the letters (symbols) of the standard design
- Random assignment of sequences of treatment levels to the experimental units (regardless of the number of constitutive bricks and the number of replications of the standard design, all the sequences included in the whole design are seen as a single set of sequences; the number of experimental units equals the number of sequences)

Method 17: Restricted Sequential Counterbalancing:
The Same Sequences per Group (SC-rs)

- Random assignment of treatment levels to the letters (symbols) of the standard design
- Replication of the standard design (*two or more* replications)

(Continued)

76

Table 3.4 (Continued)

- Random assignment of sequences of treatment levels to experimental units within the groups of experimental units[a] (*one or more* replications per group; the size of the groups equals or is a multiple of the number of sequences per replication)

Method 18: Restricted Sequential Counterbalancing: Different Sequences per Group (SC-rd)

- Random assignment of treatment levels to the letters (symbols) of the standard design
- *One or more* replications of a standard design consisting of *two or more* bricks. Partition of the whole design into k different subsets of sequences. The subsets may be defined either by the different bricks (e.g. Latin squares) of the standard design (one replication) or by the interactive classificatory variable *replication × brick* (two or more replications of multiple-bricks standard designs)
- Random assignment of k subsets of sequences to the groups of experimental units[a] (the number of groups equals the number of subsets of sequences)
- Random assignment of sequences of treatment levels to the experimental units within the groups (the size of the groups equals the number of sequences per subset)

---

[a] *Groups of experimental units* can be defined either by *between-subjects blocking structures* (e.g., gender of patients, hospital, or gender × hospital) or by *between-subjects randomization* (cross-over designs including at least one between-subjects treatment—Design 6V; see Table 3.3). Groups of experimental units can also result from the combination of between-subjects blocking structures with between-subjects randomization.

designs. In broad terms, we can identify two main approaches. The first one remains on theoretical ground, and in the presence of asymmetrical residual effects, the researcher is recommended to leave out cross-over designs and opt for between-subjects designs (e.g., Maxwell & Delaney, 2004). When no asymmetrical residual effects are expected, random or positional counterbalancing could be employed, depending on the assumptions about testing effects: Random counterbalancing is sufficient when no testing effects are expected, and positional counterbalancing is the suitable strategy for control cumulative testing effects. The second approach takes a more practical point of view and considers that the issue is essentially an empirical one (e.g., Jones & Kenward, 2003). Sequential counterbalancing could and should be used as a device to control asymmetrical effects. In any case, carryover effects must be assessed and statistically modeled in conjunction with direct effects in the data analysis stage. It should also be noted that there are studies in which the assessment of carryover effects is the experimenter's main goal.

Table 3.5   Assumptions About Carryover Effects of Previous Periods and
Distinctive Control Features of Counterbalancing Methods

Carryover Effects of Previous Periods	Control Features of Counterbalancing Method				
	Random (RC-ro) *Met. 14*	Positional (PC-Ls) *Met. 15*	Sequential (SC-nr) *Met. 16*	Sequential (SC-rs) *Met. 17*	Sequential (SC-rd) *Met. 18*
Assumptions about the effects of previous treatments					
No residual effects	Yes	Yes	Yes	Yes	Yes
Symmetrical residual effects	Yes	Yes	Yes	Yes	Yes
Asymmetrical residual effects	*No*	*No*	Yes	Yes	Yes[a]
Assumptions about the effects of previous measurements					
No testing effects	Yes	Yes	Yes	Yes	Yes
Cumulative testing effects	*No*	Yes	Yes	Yes	Yes

Note. Met. = Method; for the complete designations of counterbalancing methods, see Table 3.4.
[a] Control of asymmetrical residual effects is assumed for the design as a whole and not for the k different partitions (subsets of sequences).

In Sections 3.3 to 3.6, the five randomization methods of cross-over designs are described and illustrated with one-treatment designs (Designs 6A–6T; see Table 3.3). The standard designs used for the illustration of randomization methods are identified with the labels given in Table 3.3, followed by the number of treatment levels included in the design; for example, *Design 6G4* in Table 3.15 means that we have used a balanced Williams's square for an even number of treatment levels (Design 6G; see Table 3.3) with *four* treatment levels.

To make the text less cumbersome, we will use the term *treatment(s)* instead of *treatment level(s)*, with the understanding that we are referring to the different levels of a treatment and not to the treatment itself (i.e., the within-subjects experimental factor; see Table 1.5 for the notational system used throughout the book). Please note that this is the current practice in the within-subjects designs literature.

The final section deals with the adjustment of counterbalancing schemes to factorial cross-over designs (Designs 6U and 6V; see Table 3.3). As we did in Chapter 2, instead of presenting randomization methods as stand-alone tools, emphasis is placed on the interdependence between counterbalancing strategies and the structural features of cross-over experimental designs. This is particularly relevant for the construction and selection of appropriate standard designs in the case of sequential counterbalancing.

3.3 Random Counterbalancing

When no asymmetrical residual effects of previous treatments are expected and the testing effects of previous measurement operations can be dismissed, the only requisite for the cross-over design is *uniformity on rows* (i.e., all treatments are assigned to each subject the same number of times), and the counterbalancing strategy consists in randomly ordering the treatments separately for each subject (Method 14: *Random Counterbalancing*). This is easily done by taking as many random permutations of t integers (t = number of treatments) as are necessary to randomize the order of the treatments for all participants in the study. In Table 3.6, the procedure is illustrated with seven subjects and four treatments: Seven random permutations of the first four integers were drawn from Table A1.1 according to the procedure explained in Appendix 2. The treatments are ordered in consonance with the random permutations adopting the system of correspondence, previously established by the researcher, between integer numbers and treatment labels (e.g., the random permutation taken for Brent—4, 3, 1, 2—leads to the sequence D, C, A, B; see Table 3.6).

The design produced by this method of counterbalancing is called a *Repeated Measures Randomized Block Design* (Design 6N; see Table 3.3) and is structurally equivalent to the between-subjects *Randomized Block Design* (Design 2; see Subsection 2.3.1). In the within-subjects version, subjects are thought of as distinct blocks, and the p experimental sites within each row act as units of randomization. So Method 14—*Random Counterbalancing*—is a simple variation of Method 7—*Blocked Random Assignment With One Blocking Variable*.

3.4 Positional Counterbalancing

If no asymmetrical residual effects of previous treatments are anticipated but the cumulative testing effects of previous measurement operations are a matter of concern, the cross-over design should guarantee, in addition to uniformity on rows, that each treatment occurs equally often in all periods

Table 3.6   Random Counterbalancing: Independent Random Ordering of Four
Treatments (A, B, C, and D) for Seven Units (Design 6N4; Method 14)

ID	Unit	Random Permutations[a]				Correspondence Between Random Digits and Treatments	Treatments			
1	Arch	2	1	4	3		B	A	D	C
2	Brent	4	3	1	2		D	C	A	B
3	Cal	3	2	1	4	$1 \rightarrow A$	C	B	A	D
4	Dusty	2	1	3	4	$2 \rightarrow B$	B	A	C	D
5	Gerry	4	2	1	3	$3 \rightarrow C$	D	B	A	C
6	Milt	1	4	3	2	$4 \rightarrow D$	A	D	C	B
7	Vick	4	2	1	3		D	B	A	C

[a] *Random permutations—Table A1.1*: 1st (*Rows*: 16–28; *Col.*: 13); 2nd (*Rows*: 30–42; *Col.*: 31); 3rd (*Rows*: 14–36; *Col.*: 24); 4th (*Rows*: 2–8; *Col.*: 24); 5th (*Rows*: 12–28; *Col.*: 36); 6th (*Rows*: 18–38; *Col.*: 2); 7th (*Rows*: 11–24; *Col.*: 26).

(*uniformity on columns*). This is done by selecting a standard Latin square (see Table A3.1, Appendix 3) and by permuting, randomly and independently, the order of the rows, the order of the columns, and the labels (letters/symbols) of the treatments.

The procedure of selection and randomization of the Latin square is the same as the one we illustrated in Chapter 2 (see Figure 2.2) along with the randomization of the *Between-Subjects Latin Square Design* (Design 5A). However, although in the between-subjects design the randomization is limited to a single Latin square, in the case of the *Repeated Measures Latin Square Design* (Design 6M; see Table 3.3) a new randomized Latin square is required for each consecutive group of n experimental units. Thus, Method 15—*Positional Counterbalancing*—can be seen as a variation of Method 9—*Two-Way Blocked Random Assignment: Latin Squares* (see Subsection 2.3.4). More precisely, for each group of n ($n = p = t$) experimental units, the double-blocking structure of Latin squares defines n^2 experimental sites (units of randomization), and the random assignment of treatments to experimental sites is done by the randomization of the proper standard Latin square.

Method 15 is illustrated in Table 3.7 with a five-treatment design and 15 experimental units. Please note that in captive assignment situations the

Table 3.7 Positional Counterbalancing: Random Assignment of Sequences of Five Treatments (A, B, C, D, and E) to 15 Units (Three Latin Squares) (Design 6M5; Method 15)

ID	Unit	Treatments					Comments
1	Adie	A	E	B	D	C	First Latin square
2	Bab	E	B	D	C	A	Square obtained by independent random permutations of rows, columns, and symbols of the standard Latin square
3	Candy	C	D	E	A	B	shown in Table A3.1 (Appendix 3):
4	Daph	D	C	A	B	E	Permutation rows: *3, 2, 4, 1, 5* (Rows: 23–39; Col: 32)
							Permutation columns: *4, 1, 5, 2, 3* (Rows: 20–37; Col: 11)
5	Elvie	B	A	C	E	D	Permutation symbols: *3, 2, 5, 4, 1* (Rows: 4–40; Col: 40)
6	Fanny	E	A	B	D	C	Second Latin square
7	Fel	A	C	D	E	B	Square obtained by independent random permutations of rows, columns, and symbols of the standard Latin square
8	Jill	B	D	E	C	A	shown in Table A3.1 (Appendix 3):
9	Kim	C	E	A	B	D	Permutation rows: *3, 2, 1, 4, 5* (Rows: 12–26; Col: 35)
							Permutation columns: *1, 5, 3, 4, 2* (Rows: 15–29; Col: 3)
10	Lin	D	B	C	A	E	Permutation symbols: *2, 1, 5, 3, 4* (Rows: 17–50; Col: 9)
11	Mandy	D	B	C	A	E	Third Latin square
12	Mary	C	A	B	E	D	Square obtained by independent random permutations of rows, columns, and symbols of the standard Latin square
13	Normie	E	D	A	B	C	shown in Table A3.1 (Appendix 3):
14	Ronnie	B	C	E	D	A	Permutation rows: *5, 4, 2, 3, 1* (Rows: 12–21; Col: 28)
							Permutation columns: *3, 5, 4, 2, 1* (Rows: 7–25; Col: 16)
15	Tiff	A	E	D	C	B	Permutation symbols: *2, 3, 1, 4, 5* (Rows: 4–24; Col: 7)

Note. Permutations for rows, columns, and symbols were taken from Table A1.1 (Appendix 1). The complete procedure is illustrated in Figure 2.2.

names of experimental units should be listed in a systematic order (alphabetical or other) before the randomization. In noncaptive assignment circumstances, the names are replaced with sequential ID numbers ($1-n$), which are ascribed to experimental units as long as they are enrolled in the experiment. In any case, the number of experimental units must be a multiple of the number of treatments. Standard Latin squares of orders 2 to 12 are given in Table A3.1 (Appendix 3). For orders higher than 5, the randomization is the very same as that given in Table 3.7. For orders 2 to 4, short-cuts and details are given in Appendix 3.

In introductory methodological textbooks, *positional counterbalancing* is frequently called *partial counterbalancing* and is contrasted with situations where all possible sequences of *t* treatments are included in the design (*complete counterbalancing*). Both designations are somehow ambiguous and should be avoided. Partial counterbalancing can be confused with partially balanced designs, in which a precise degree of balance is achieved (see Subsection 3.5.2). This is not the case with repeated measures Latin square designs: With the exception of the *2 × 2 Cross-Over Design* (Design 6A2; see Table 3.1), which is a balanced design (position and sequence are redundant terms), all designs including three or more treatments are nonbalanced designs (e.g., in the first square of Table 3.7, Treatment A is preceded twice by C, once by B and E, and never by D; in the whole design, Treatment A is preceded once by B, twice by D, three times by E, and six times by C).

What is achieved by repeated measures Latin square designs is that all treatments are administered the same number of times (in the example of Table 3.7, $\mu_c = 3$) in all positions (periods); that is the reason why we adopt the designation *positional counterbalancing*, instead of *partial counterbalancing* (for misunderstandings underlying the use of the expression *complete counterbalancing*, see Subsection 3.5.1).

3.5 Nonrestricted Sequential Counterbalancing

When the potential occurrence of asymmetrical carryover effects of previous periods is a matter of concern, the selection of a balanced design achieves an ideal sequencing of treatments and, more important, allows the simultaneous assessment of direct and carryover effects. In the analysis stage, statistical adjustment for carryover effects provides the researcher with a more accurate estimation of direct effects.

In sequential counterbalancing, the critical feature is the selection of a standard design with the desired structural properties. Once the design has been chosen, the randomization is straightforward and consists in simple variations of the methods described in Chapter 2, with the understanding that sequences of treatments, instead of the treatments themselves, are randomly assigned to experimental units.

The major steps of sequential counterbalancing methods are summarized in Table 3.4. This section deals with Method 16—*Nonrestricted Sequential Counterbalancing*—that is, with situations where the random assignment of sequences is done at once for all experimental units, not being restricted by between-subjects blocking structures and/or random assignment of units to the levels of between-subjects treatments included in the design, as is the case with Methods 17 and 18, discussed in the next section.

Since the implementation of Method 16 is identical for all designs described in this section, we will give the details in one case (Design 6F: *Complete Sets of Mutually Orthogonal Latin Squares*), devoting the bulk of the text to the selection and construction of the standard designs to be randomized, with special emphasis on uniform balanced designs. In consonance with the classification of cross-over designs presented in Table 3.3, designs consisting of *complete* ($p = t$), *incomplete* ($p < t$), and *extended* ($p > t$) sequences are presented in the three main subsections. Within each subsection, designs are organized according to their degree of balance.

3.5.1 Complete Sequences (p = t)

In complete-sequences designs, the number of periods equals the number of treatments ($p = t$), and all standard designs are uniform designs; that is, the number of replications per row (subject) and per column (period) is the same for all treatments.

3.5.1.1 Balanced Designs

The most basic cross-over design is the design with two treatments (A and B) and two periods involving only two possible sequences: AB and BA (Design 6A2; see Table 3.1). With this design, both positional and sequential counterbalancing produce a balanced design, hence the researcher can adopt either Method 15 or Method 16.

3.5.1.1.1 All Possible Sequences. At first glance, the inclusion of all possible sequences of treatments would be the ideal procedure for all cross-over designs. However, the minimum number ($n = t!$) of experimental units required for the standard design precludes its use in experimental studies with a high number of treatments. For example, with 2, 3, 4, 5, and 6 treatments, the numbers of different sequences of the standard designs are 2, 6, 24, 120, and 720, respectively (see Table 3.12).

When applying Method 16—*Nonrestricted Sequential Counterbalancing*— to cross-over designs including all possible sequences of treatments (Designs 6A and 6E), Step 1 (*random assignment of treatments to symbols of the standard design*; see Table 3.9) is unnecessary, because changing the symbols of treatments would result in the same set of sequences.

One important structural property of cross-over designs including all possible sequences of treatments is that they are balanced not only for the first-order carryover effects but also for higher order carryover effects (see Table A2.1, Appendix 2, where the entire set of sequences for two up to five treatments is given). This is the reason why sequential counterbalancing with all possible sequences is frequently called *complete counterbalancing*. As we have already noted, this is an ambiguous designation, because in cross-over designs literature *complete balance* is synonymous with *strong balance* (Jones & Kenward, 2003), as is the case with Designs 6P, 6R, and 6S (see Table 3.3 and Subsections 3.5.2 and 3.5.3).

3.5.1.1.2 Sets of Mutually Orthogonal Latin Squares. A realistic alternative to "all possible sequences" designs, which preserves balance for the first- and higher order carryover effects and requires a substantially smaller number of experimental units (see Table 3.12), is the use of complete sets of mutually orthogonal Latin squares (MOLS). Two Latin squares of the same order are said to be orthogonal if, when superimposed, each symbol (e.g., Latin letter) of the first square occurs once and only once in conjunction with each symbol (e.g., Greek letter or number) of the second square. For a given number of t treatments, complete sets of $t - 1$ MOLS can be constructed when t is a prime or a power of a prime number; that is, we can have complete sets of $t - 1$ MOLS for 3, 4 (=2^2), 5, 7, 8 (=2^3), 9 (=3^2), 11, 13, (. . .) treatments.

When a complete set of MOLS exists and the squares are *odd sided*, the $t - 1$ squares can be easily constructed by cyclically moving the rows or the columns of the initial square (see illustrations in Table 3.8 for 3- and 5-sided squares). For *even-sided* squares, the procedure is a little more complicated and is not illustrated here (see Fisher & Yates, 1963). However, standard forms of complete sets of 4- and 8-sided MOLS, as well as odd-sided squares up to 11, are shown in Tables A3.3 and A3.4 (Appendix 3).

Once the complete set of MOLS (standard form) has been chosen, the researcher can proceed to *Nonrestricted Sequential Counterbalancing* (Method 16) according to the steps summarized in Table 3.4 and illustrated in Table 3.9 for the case of four treatments (A, B, C, and D). Given that the

Table 3.8 Construction of Complete Sets of Mutually Orthogonal Latin Squares (MOLS): Procedure and Examples for Odd-Sided Squares

3 × 3			
One step up		Two steps up	Write the first column of the $t - 1$ squares in alphabetical order. The following columns are obtained by cyclically moving up the preceding column: *one step* for the first square, *two steps* for the second square, *three steps* for the third square, and so on, until $t - 1$ *steps* for the last square in the complete set.
A B C↑		A C↑ B	
B C↑ A		B A C↑	
C↑ A B		C↑ B A	

5 × 5			
One step up	Two steps up	Three steps up	Four steps up
A B C D E↑	A C E↑ B D	A D B E↑ C	A E↑ D C B
B C D E↑ A	B D A C E↑	B E↑ C A D	B A E↑ D C
C D E↑ A B	C E↑ B D A	C A D B E↑	C B A E↑ D
D E↑ A B C	D A C E↑ B	D B E↑ C A	D C B A E↑
E↑ A B C D	E↑ B D A C	E↑ C A D B	E↑ D C B A

Table 3.9 Nonrestricted Sequential Counterbalancing: Random Assignment of Sequences of Four Treatments (A, B, C, and D; Three Mutually Orthogonal Latin Squares—MOLS 4; See Table A3.3) to 12 Units (Design 6F4; Method 16)

Step 1: Random Assignment of Treatments to the Symbols of the Standard Design

MOLS 4 Standard Form					Randomly Selected Sequences				
Square 1						Square 1			SN
A	B	C	D	Random Permutation:		C	B	D	A	s1r1
B	A	D	C	3, 2, 4, 1		B	C	A	D	s1r2
C	D	A	B	*(Table A1.1: Rows 42–49; Column 3)*		D	A	C	B	s1r3
D	C	B	A			A	D	B	C	s1r4
Square 2						Square 2			
A	C	D	B	A − 3 → C		C	D	A	B	s2r1
B	D	C	A	B − 2 → B		B	A	D	C	s2r2
C	A	B	D	C − 4 → D		D	C	B	A	s2r3
D	B	A	C	D − 1 → A		A	B	C	D	s2r4
Square 3						Square 3			
A	D	B	C			C	A	B	D	s3r1
B	C	A	D			B	D	C	A	s3r2
C	B	D	A			D	B	A	C	s3r3
D	A	C	B			A	C	D	B	s3r4

Step 2: Random Assignment of Sequences of Treatments to Experimental Units

Sequences and Random Numbers						Random Assignment of Sequences to Units						
SN	Sequence				RN	SN	Sequence				RN	ID	Unit
s1r1	C	B	D	A	.937	s1r4	A	D	B	C	.032	1	Allie
s1r2	B	C	A	D	.518	s2r3	D	C	B	A	.102	2	Beth
s1r3	D	A	C	B	.484	s2r4	A	B	C	D	.197	3	Cath
s1r4	A	D	B	C	.032	s3r4	A	C	D	B	.205	4	Debbie
s2r1	C	D	A	B	.517	s3r2	B	D	C	A	.388	5	Ellie
s2r2	B	A	D	C	.879	s1r3	D	A	C	B	.484	6	Flora
s2r3	D	C	B	A	.102	s2r1	C	D	A	B	.517	7	Gwen
s2r4	A	B	C	D	.197	s1r2	B	C	A	D	.518	8	Jenny
s3r1	C	A	B	D	.621	s3r3	D	B	A	C	.546	9	Moll
s3r2	B	D	C	A	.388	s3r1	C	A	B	D	.621	10	Prissy
s3r3	D	B	A	C	.546	s2r2	B	A	D	C	.879	11	Val
s3r4	A	C	D	B	.205	s1r1	C	B	D	A	.937	12	Willa

RN: Table A1.1 (Rows: 19–30; Columns: 13–15).

standard form of MOLS doesn't constitute all possible sequences of treatments, Step 1 ensures that the sequences to be included in the cross-over design are randomly selected within the range of possibilities allowed by the combinatorial structure of the design. In Step 2, selected sequences are randomly assigned to experimental units. Please note that Step 2 is a simple variation of Method 3—*Simple Random Assignment With Forced Equal Sizes*—described in Subsection 2.2.1, in which sequences of treatments, instead of the treatments themselves, are assigned to experimental units.

In Table 3.9, we have associated a randomly ordered list of sequences to a systematically ordered list of experimental units. As we noted in Chapter 2, it is formally equivalent to associate a randomly ordered list of experimental units to a systematically ordered list of sequences. We have chosen the first procedure because it applies to both captive and noncaptive assignment circumstances. In the captive assignment, subjects' names are listed in some systematic order (e.g., alphabetical) prior to the randomization; in the noncaptive assignment, the names are replaced with sequential ID numbers (1–n), which are ascribed to experimental units as they are enrolled in the experiment. In the example of Table 3.9, there is only one replication of Design 6F4; therefore, the number of experimental units is equal to the number of sequences; if the final design comprises two or more replications of the standard design, the number of experimental units must be a multiple of the number of sequences.

As stated in Table 3.4, regardless of the number of constitutive bricks (in the example, three squares) and the number of replications of the standard design, all the sequences included in the final design are seen as a single set of sequences, and the only procedural constraint is the assignment of the same number of experimental units to each sequence. It is always a good practice to keep track of the location of sequences in the standard design (e.g., ascribing them a sequence number–SN in Table 3.9). In case of experimental attrition in multiple-bricks designs, this will allow an accurate statistical analysis of intact subsets of the whole design.

3.5.1.1.3 Williams's Designs. All possible sequences designs and MOLS designs achieve structural balance for first- and higher order carryover effects by using a considerable number of experimental units per treatment. In the former designs, this number quickly becomes unreasonable, whereas in the latter ones it is kept in acceptable sizes. However, there are situations where a limited number of available subjects and/or a restrictive budget force the experimenter to work with fewer subjects than those required to implement a MOLS design. In these situations, it would be highly desirable to know what is the minimum number of subjects required to achieve a given degree of balance. With respect to the first-order carryover effects, the answer to this question was given by Williams (1949, 1950) about 60 years ago: For an *even* number of treatments, it is possible to have a balanced design in that the number of experimental units equals the number of treatments; for an *odd* number of treatments, the number of subjects should double the number of treatments. Williams's designs are special cases of Latin squares in which each treatment is immediately preceded equally often by all the remaining treatments (see Designs 6H3 and 6G4 in Table 3.2 and Designs 6G4 and 6H5 in Table 3.11).

There are several procedures for constructing Williams's designs (see, Namboodiri, 1972), including the original ones given by Williams (1949). In Table 3.10, we illustrate the procedure devised by Sheehe and Bross (1961), which applies to both even and odd treatments and has the advantage of being easy to remember. Williams's Latin squares are the most frequently used designs in sequential counterbalancing and are also known under the names *single carryover design* (even number of treatments) and *double carryover design* (odd number of treatments).

Like any other cross-over design, the designs obtained by the procedure explained in Table 3.10 can and should be reduced to their standard form. In Table 3.11, we show how this is done by renaming the treatments so that the first row is written in alphabetical order and by reordering the rows so that the first column is also written in alphabetical order. Standard forms of Williams's squares of 2 up to 12 orders are given in Table A3.5 (Appendix 3). Starting with these standard forms, the sequential counterbalancing of William's designs is the same as what we have illustrated in Table 3.9 with MOLS. Please note that the Williams's design for two treatments is the 2-sided standard Latin square (see Table A3.1) and the Williams's design for three treatments is identical to the MOLS design (see Table A3.3).

3.5.1.1.4 Other Balanced Designs. For some cross-over designs with an odd number of treatments, Williams's designs are no longer *minimal designs*, since Hedayat and Afsarinejad (1975, 1978) have devised balanced squares with $n = t$ for 9, 15, 21, and 27 treatments (the standard design for $t = 9$ is given in Table 3.13, Design 6I9).

3.5.1.2 Nearly Balanced Designs

In the cases of three, five, and seven treatments, Williams's designs (i.e., double carryover designs requiring 6, 10, and 14 experimental units, respectively) remain the minimal balanced designs. When the number of available experimental units is not enough to comply with the requirements of Williams's designs, alternative *nearly balanced designs* (with $n = t$) can

Table 3.10 Construction of Balanced Latin Squares for the First-Order
Carryover Effects in Cross-Over Designs (Williams's Squares)

Even-order squares (Design 6G4)	Odd-order squares (Design 6H5)

Step 1: Numbering the treatments sequentially $(1-n)$ in the first row of the Latin square.

1, 2, 3, 4   1, 2, 3, 4, 5

Step 2: Starting with *one cyclic $n \times n$* Latin square by moving the rows one step to the left.

```
1 2 3 4          1 2 3 4 5
2 3 4 1          2 3 4 5 1
3 4 1 2          3 4 5 1 2
4 1 2 3          4 5 1 2 3
                 5 1 2 3 4
```

Step 3: Constructing a mirror square by reversing the rows of the first square.

```
1 2 3 4   4 3 2 1      1 2 3 4 5   5 4 3 2 1
2 3 4 1   1 4 3 2      2 3 4 5 1   1 5 4 3 2
3 4 1 2   2 1 4 3      3 4 5 1 2   2 1 5 4 3
4 1 2 3   3 2 1 4      4 5 1 2 3   3 2 1 5 4
                       5 1 2 3 4   4 3 2 1 5
```

Step 4: Interlacing the columns of the two squares obtained in Step 3.

```
1 4 2 3 3 2 4 1        1 5 2 4 3 3 4 2 5 1
2 1 3 4 4 3 1 2        2 1 3 5 4 4 5 3 1 2
3 2 4 1 1 4 2 3        3 2 4 1 5 5 1 4 2 3
4 3 1 2 2 1 3 4        4 3 5 2 1 1 2 5 3 4
                       5 4 1 3 2 2 3 1 4 5
```

Step 5: Slicing down the second square obtained in Step 4.

```
1 4 2 3    Retaining only       1 5 2 4 3
2 1 3 4    the first square      2 1 3 5 4
3 2 4 1    Single carryover      3 2 4 1 5
4 3 1 2    design (Form 1)       4 3 5 2 1                 Retaining
3 2 4 1                          5 4 1 3 2                 both squares
4 3 1 2                          3 4 2 5 1            Double carryover
1 4 2 3                          4 5 3 1 2            design (Form 1)
2 1 3 4                          5 1 4 2 3
                                 1 2 5 3 4
                                 2 3 1 4 5
```

be used with five and seven treatments. These designs, developed by
Russell (1991), approach the combinatorial properties of balanced designs
in the sense that all treatments are equally often immediately preceded by
the remaining treatments, with the exception of two of them. For example,
in Design 6L7 (see Table 3.13), Treatment A is immediately preceded once

Table 3.11 Reduction of Williams's Squares to the Standard Form

Even-order squares (Design 6G4)	Odd-order squares (Design 6H5)

Step 1: Replacing the numbers with the letters in the squares retained from Table 3.10.

$1 \rightarrow A$ $2 \rightarrow B$ $3 \rightarrow C$ $4 \rightarrow D$

1 4 2 3	A D B C
2 1 3 4	B A C D
3 2 4 1	C B D A
4 3 1 2	D C A B
Form 1	*Form 2*

$1 \rightarrow A$ $2 \rightarrow B$ $3 \rightarrow C$ $4 \rightarrow D$ $5 \rightarrow E$

1 5 2 4 3	A E B D C
2 1 3 5 4	B A C E D
3 2 4 1 5	C B D A E
4 3 5 2 1	D C E B A
5 4 1 3 2	E D A C B
3 4 2 5 1	C D B E A
4 5 3 1 2	D E C A B
5 1 4 2 3	E A D B C
1 2 5 3 4	A B E C D
2 3 1 4 5	B C A D E
Form 1	*Form 2*

Step 2: Relabeling the treatments so that the first row appears in alphabetical order.

$A \rightarrow A$ $D \rightarrow B$ $B \rightarrow C$ $C \rightarrow D$

A D B C	A B C D
B A C D	C A D B
C B D A	D C B A
D C A B	B D A C
Form 2	*Form 3*

$A \rightarrow A$ $E \rightarrow B$ $B \rightarrow C$ $D \rightarrow D$ $C \rightarrow E$

A E B D C	A B C D E
B A C E D	C A E B D
C B D A E	E C D A B
D C E B A	D E B C A
E D A C B	B D A E C
C D B E A	E D C B A
D E C A B	D B E A C
E A D B C	B A D C E
A B E C D	A C B E D
B C A D E	C E A D B
Form 2	*Form 3*

Step 3: Sorting the rows (within each square) so that the treatments in the first column appear in alphabetical order.

A B C D	A B C D
C A D B	B D A C
D C B A	C A D B
B D A C	D C B A
Form 3	*Form 4 (Standard)*

A B C D E	A B C D E
C A E B D	B D A E C
E C D A B	C A E B D
D E B C A	D E B C A
B D A E C	E C D A B
E D C B A	A C B E D
D B E A C	B A D C E
B A D C E	C E A D B
A C B E D	D B E A C
C E A D B	E D C B A
Form 3	*Form 4 (Standard)*

by Treatments B, C, D, and G, but it is preceded twice by E and never by F (a similar pattern occurs for treatments B, C, D, E, F, and G).

3.5.1.3 Choosing a Uniform Balanced Design

Putting aside "all possible sequences" designs, the choice of a uniform balanced standard design in sequential counterbalancing is between MOLS (Designs 6F) and minimal designs (Designs 6G, 6H, and 6I). As Jones and Kenward (2003) remarked, when the main concern is balance with respect to the first-order carryover effects, which is often the case, minimal designs are the obvious choice, having the practical advantage of making the experimental *mise en place* less expensive and less prone to procedural errors, given that a smaller number of distinct sequences is involved in the research protocol. On the other hand, MOLS designs allow, in the analysis stage, the assessment and modeling of higher order carryover effects that, in certain circumstances, can be, in their own right, the aim of the experiment. Please note that in this choice we are not talking about power: Either standard MOLS or standard minimal designs can be replicated to meet the power requirements. Needless to say, with a limited number of available experimental units, minimal designs are the obvious choice.

In Table 3.12, we give the minimum number of experimental units required for the sequential counterbalancing with the uniform balanced designs reviewed in this subsection. In Table 3.13, we show Newcombe and Prescott's "Triples" (Designs 6J5 and 6J7), which are balanced designs requiring $n = 3t$ subjects and can be used when a complete replication of a double carryover design, calling for $n = 4t$ subjects, is not feasible. For a thorough review of uniform balanced designs, see Bate and Jones (2008). For more advanced topics in the choice of designs when few subjects are available and the implementation of complex algorithms for the construction of cyclic cross-over designs, see Bate, Godolphin, and Godolphin (2008).

3.5.2 Incomplete Sequences (p < t)

There are situations in which researchers carry out designs with a relatively high number of treatments, but because of the time needed for the implementation of each treatment and/or for some technical feature of the design, it is not recommended that the subjects be observed in all the experimental conditions. In these situations, one possible strategy is the administration of incomplete sequences of treatments with a prespecified pattern. When the number of p periods ($p < t$) is equal for all subjects and all treatments are equally replicated within each period (*uniformity on periods*),

Table 3.12 Sequential Counterbalancing: Minimum Number of Experimental Units Required in Uniform Balanced Cross-Over Designs

	Design 6E All Sequences	Design 6F MOLS	Design 6G $WD_{t\ even}$	Design 6H $WD_{t\ odd}$	Design 6I $HA_{t\ odd}$	Design 6J $NP_{t\ odd}$	Design 6K $AP_{t\ odd}$
t	$n = t!$	$n = t(t-1)$	$n = t$	$n = 2t$	$n = t$	$n = 3t$	$n = t(t-1)$
2	2	—	2	—	—	—	—
3	6	6	—	6	—	—	6
4	24	12	4	—	—	—	—
5	120	20	—	10	—	15	20
6	720	—	6	—	—	—	—
7	5040	42	—	14	—	21	42
8	40320	56	8	—	—	—	—
9	362880	72	—	18	9	27	72
10	3628800	—	10	—	—	—	—
11	39916800	110	—	22	—	33	110
12	479001600	—	12	—	—	—	—

Note. For a given number of treatments (t), the *minimal design* is shaded. With two treatments, Designs 6E and 6G are identical. The same is true for Designs 6E, 6F, 6H, and 6K, in the case of three treatments. The nonabbreviated designations for all designs are given in Table 3.3.

the resulting design is called an *incomplete cross-over design*. Depending on the pattern of treatment replication, the design can be *balanced, strongly balanced,* or *partially balanced.*

3.5.2.1 Balanced Designs

There are several ways to build an incomplete balanced design, but here we only give two of them, referring the reader to the text of Jones and Kenward (2003) for a systematic presentation. The first and the easiest way to get an incomplete balanced design for t treatments and $p < t$ periods is to rely on MOLS designs and to delete one or more periods of the whole design. For example, if an incomplete design with $t = 5$ and $p = 3$ is needed, the researcher may go to Table A3.3 (Appendix 3), select the 5×5 standard MOLS, and delete the last two columns. The resulting design (Design 6O5), with five treatments and 20 sequences of three different treatments (ABC, BCD, CDE, DEA, EAB, ACE, BDA, CEB, DAC, EBD, ADB, BEC, CAD, DBE, ECA, AED, BAE, CBA, DCB, and EDC),

Table 3.13 Sequential Counterbalancing: Complementary Balanced (Designs 6I9, 6J5, and 6J7) and Nearly Balanced (Designs 6L5 and 6L7) Cross-Over Designs

Hedayat and Afsarinejad's Design 6I9									Newcombe and Prescott's "Triples"									
									Design 6J5					**Design 6J7**				
A	B	C	D	E	F	G	H	I	*Square 1*					*Square 1*				
B	H	D	F	A	G	I	E	C	A	B	C	D	E	A	B	C	D	E	F	G
C	A	E	B	I	D	H	G	F	B	D	E	C	A	B	F	E	G	D	C	A
D	G	A	I	F	H	C	B	E	C	E	B	A	D	C	E	G	B	A	D	F
E	D	I	H	B	A	F	C	G	D	C	A	E	B	D	G	B	C	F	A	E
F	I	G	C	H	E	A	D	B	E	A	D	B	C	E	D	A	F	B	G	C
G	E	H	A	C	I	B	F	D	*Square 2*					F	C	D	A	G	E	B
H	F	B	G	D	C	E	I	A	A	D	C	B	E	G	A	F	E	C	B	D
I	C	F	E	G	B	D	A	H	B	C	E	D	A	*Square 2*				

Russell's Designs

Design 6L5

A	B	C	D	E
B	D	E	C	A
C	E	B	A	D
D	C	A	E	B
E	A	D	B	C

Design 6L7

A	B	C	D	E	F	G
B	F	G	A	D	C	E
C	G	D	F	B	E	A
D	A	F	E	G	B	C
E	D	B	G	C	A	F
F	C	E	B	A	G	D
G	E	A	C	F	D	B

Design 6J5 (continued)

Square 2
C A B E D
D E A C B
E B D A C

Square 3
A E C B D
B A E D C
C D B E A
D B A C E
E C D A B

Design 6J7 (continued)

Square 2
A F B E D C G
B C F D G E A
C D E A B G F
D A G F C B E
E G D B F A C
F E C G A D B
G B A C E F D

Square 3
A C E B G D F
B E D F A G C
C G A E F B D
D B F G E C A
E A B D C F G
F D G C B A E
G F C A D E B

Notes. Newcombe and Prescott's "Triples" have been built with one step cyclically moving, beginning with the first rows given by Newcombe (1996, pp. 2144–2145). The noncyclic Hedayat and Afsarinejad's square is the design given by the authors (Hedayat & Afsarinejad, 1978, p. 625). Designs 6I9, 6J5, and 6J7 have been reduced to their standard form using the procedure illustrated in Table 3.11. Russell's Designs are given in their standard form by Jones and Kenward (2003, pp. 162–163).

requiring a minimum of 20 subjects, includes four replications of each treatment per period, and, as the reader could easily verify, is a balanced design for the first-order carryover effects: All treatments are immediately preceded equally often by the remaining treatments ($\lambda_1 = 2$). Note that the designs obtained by this procedure are also balanced for higher order carryover effects.

The second way to obtain an incomplete balanced design is to pick the corresponding between-subjects *balanced incomplete block design* and replace each row with the possible permutations of the treatments involved. For example, if Design 4A (6 treatments, 10 blocks, and 3 units per block; see Table 2.8) is used as a template, each of the 10 rows would give rise to 6 permutations of 3 treatments. In the case of the first row, the set of Treatments 1, 2, and 5 would generate the following permutations: 1, 2, 5; 1, 5, 2; 2, 1, 5; 2, 5, 1; 5, 1, 2; and 5, 2, 1. Repeating the procedure for the remaining rows and replacing treatment numbers with letters, to be consonant with the notation adopted for cross-over designs, the final design (Design 6O6) would consist of 60 sequences (the last 6 sequences would be DEF, DFE, EDF, EFD, FDE, and FED). Like designs based on MOLS, designs based on balanced incomplete block designs are balanced for carryover effects of all orders.

3.5.2.2 Strongly Balanced Designs (Extra-Period Designs)

If the reader adds an extra period to a balanced incomplete cross-over design containing $p < t - 1$ periods and the treatments in the last period of the original design are exactly replicated in the extra period, he or she gets a *strongly balanced design* (see Section 3.2 for the formal definition of strong balance), in which the number of periods remains smaller than the number of treatments ($p < t$). For example, if the design described in the previous paragraph (Design 6O6) is converted into an extra-period design (Design 6P6) with four periods, the last six sequences would be read as DEFF, DFEE, EDFF, EFDD, FDEE, and FEDD.

3.5.2.3 Partially Balanced Designs

When the number of available experimental units and/or the values of t and p wanted by the researcher don't permit a balanced incomplete cross-over design, he or she can adopt a special type of incomplete-sequences designs ($p < t$) in which all treatments are equally replicated in each period (uniformity on periods) but not immediately preceded by the remaining treatments the same number of times. More specifically, in a *partially balanced design* (Design 6Q), a treatment is immediately preceded α_1 times by some treatments and α_2 times by the remaining different treatments. For example, in Design 6Q4 ($t = 4$, $n = 8$, $p = 3$), including the sequences ABC, ABD, BAC, BAD, CDA, CDB, DCA, and DCB, Treatment C is immediately preceded twice by Treatment D and only once by Treatments A and B (please note that all treatments are replicated twice within each of the three periods).

There is an abundant literature on partially balanced cross-over designs and a great diversity of methods of design construction, including cyclic designs (e.g., Davis & Hall, 1969; Iqbal & Jones, 1994) and the partially balanced designs of Patterson and Lucas (1962). These and other methods, along with an extensive enumeration of designs, are systematically presented in Jones and Kenward's (2003) book, to which the reader is referred. From the randomization perspective, both partially balanced designs and balanced and strongly balanced designs with incomplete sequences ($p < t$) are handled in the same way as the complete-sequences designs ($p = t$) described at length in Subsection 3.5.1. The same is true for the extended-sequences designs ($p > t$), briefly presented in the next subsection.

3.5.3 Extended Sequences ($p > t$)

When the number of treatments is relatively low, it is possible to replicate one or more treatments within the same sequence. Designs 6B and 6D, depicted in Table 3.1, are special cases of extended sequences with two treatments (A and B), and some of them are known under different labels: *reversal*, *switch-back*, or *alternating-treatment* designs (e.g., Designs 6B2f, 6B2m, and 6B2l); *switching treatments in blocks* designs (e.g., Design 6D2l); and *multiple baseline* designs (e.g., Design 6D2f; see Cotton, 1998, for designs historically focused on the point at which treatment change is introduced). Multiple baseline designs and some *unique sequences* of treatments (e.g., ABA, ABAB) have also been used in the so-called single-case (quasi)experimental studies (see Anderson, 2002; Barlow & Hersen, 1984). However, from the standpoint of treatment design, the main aim of extended sequences ($p > t$) with two or more treatments is to obtain strongly balanced designs.

3.5.3.1 Extra-Period Strongly Balanced Designs

The easiest way to have a strongly balanced design is to add an extra period to a uniform balanced design, as illustrated in the right columns of Table 3.2 with Williams's Designs: Design 6H3 is converted into Design 6R3, and Design 6G4 gives rise to Design 6R4. However, adding an extra period (identical to the last one of the original design) breaks the uniformity of the $p = t + 1$ *Extra-Period Strongly Balanced Designs* (Designs 6R). The choice between the two designs lies in theoretical grounds and statistical trade-offs in the estimation of direct and first-order carryover effects: In uniform balanced designs (e.g., Designs 6H3 and 6G4), the direct effects of treatments are orthogonal to the subjects (rows) and to the periods (columns) but not to the first-order carryover effects; in nonuniform extra-period strongly balanced designs (e.g., Designs 6R3 and 6R4), the direct effects of treatments are orthogonal to the first-order carryover effects and also to the periods (columns), but the orthogonality relative to the subjects (rows) is lost.

3.5.3.2 Many-Periods Strongly Balanced Designs

A second type of extended-sequences design, known as *Many-Periods Designs* (Design 6S), makes use of more periods than the extra-period designs and can simultaneously achieve uniformity and strong balance, making the direct effects of treatments orthogonal to the first-order carryover effects, to the subjects (rows), and to the periods (columns). An example for two treatments is given in Table 3.1 (see Design 6D2k). For examples of designs with more than two treatments (e.g., Quenouille's designs, Berenblut's designs) and for bibliographic sources on the methods of construction, as well as for the illustration of *Nearly Strongly Balanced Designs* (Designs 6T), we refer the reader to Jones and Kenward (2003) once again.

3.6 Restricted Sequential Counterbalancing

Method 16—*Nonrestricted Sequential Counterbalancing*—is applicable to all designs reviewed in the previous section, regardless of their structural properties or the relationship between the number of treatments and the number of periods per sequence. In Table 3.9, we used a single replication of a standard design with three bricks (MOLS for four treatments) to illustrate Method 16. Method 16 could also be applied to single-brick designs or to several replications of the same standard design consisting of either one or multiple bricks, with the understanding that each different sequence included in the whole design is assigned to the same number of subjects. Method 16 is the default method for sequential counterbalancing in cross-over designs, and its distinctive feature is that all sequences are considered a unique set of sequences. There is no place to create groups of experimental units on the basis of their structural characteristics (i.e., classificatory factors; see Table 1.1), and the only procedural constraint is that the number of experimental units equals the number of sequences in the whole design. It is for this reason—the absence of restrictions to the randomization imposed by between-subjects blocking structures—that we call Method 16 *Nonrestricted Sequential Counterbalancing*.

In some circumstances, either for theoretical reasons (e.g., studying the moderator effects of classificatory factors) or for local constraints (e.g., patients coming from different hospitals), it is advisable or even required to split the available experimental units into groups defined by one or more structural characteristics (e.g., gender, educational level, personality traits, diagnostic categories, etc.). In these circumstances, the random assignment of sequences of treatments is done within each group of experimental units, that is, the randomization is restricted by between-subjects blocking structures. Ideally, the same sequences of treatments should be administered to all groups (Method 17: *Restricted Sequential Counterbalancing: The Same Sequences per Group*). This is easily done by replicating the standard design and giving one or more replications to each group of experimental units. When this is not feasible, different subsets of sequences can be randomly assigned to different groups of experimental units (Method 18: *Restricted Sequential Counterbalancing: Different Sequences per Group*), keeping the desired structural properties in the whole design but missing these properties within each subset of sequences. In any case, the number of groups must be consonant with the admissible partitions of the whole cross-over design, and the number of experimental units in each group must equal the number of sequences per partition. Table 3.14 summarizes the acceptable methods of sequential counterbalancing according to the number of replications and the possible partitions of the standard design.

3.6.1 The Same Sequences per Group

As the reader must have already realized, Method 17— *Restricted Sequential Counterbalancing: The Same Sequences per Group*—is a simple extension of Method 16 intended to accommodate between-subjects blocking structures introduced by some meaningful classifica-tory factor (see Table 1.1). Method 17 is fully illustrated in Table 3.15, in which a four-sided Williams's square is replicated three times (Step 2), and the random assignment of sequences is done within each group of four experimental units (Step 3). The randomly selected sequences in Step 1 are identical for the three groups (Step 3), and the whole design is a

Table 3.14 Replications and Partitions of Cross-Over Standard Designs: Acceptable Methods of Sequential Counterbalancing

Partitions of the standard design	Replications of the standard design	
	One	Two or more
Single set of sequences (One-brick designs)	• Method 16^a	• Method 16^a • Method 17^b (*Replications*)
K different subsets of sequences (Multiple-bricks designs)	• Method 16^a • Method 18^c (*Bricks*)	• Method 16^a • Method 17^b (*Replications*) • Method 18^c (*Replications* × *Bricks*)

Note. See Table 3.4 for a short description of the three methods of sequential counterbalancing.

[a] Nonrestricted Sequential Counterbalancing: *One* group of experimental units.

[b] Restricted Sequential Counterbalancing: *Two or more* groups of experimental units (*the same* sequences per group).

[c] Restricted Sequential Counterbalancing: *Two or more* groups of experimental units (*different* sequences per group).

96

Table 3.15 Restricted Sequential Counterbalancing—The Same Sequences per Group: Random Assignment of Sequences of Four Treatments (A, B, C, and D; Three Replications of the Williams's Design; See Table A3.5) to Three Groups of Four Units (Design 6G4; Method 17)

Step 1: Random Assignment of Treatments to the Symbols of the Standard Design

Williams's Square Standard Form	Random Permutation: 4, 1, 3, 2 (*Table A1.1: Rows 2–11; Column 25*)	Randomly Selected Sequences	
A B C D	A – 4 → D	D A C B	r1
B D A C	B – 1 → A	A B D C	r2
C A D B	C – 3 → C	C D B A	r3
D C B A	D – 2 → B	B C A D	r4

Step 2: Replication of the Standard Design

The standard design has been replicated three times: *Replication 1*, *Replication 2*, and *Replication 3*. One replication for each group of four experimental units.

Step 3: Random Assignment of Sequences to Experimental Units Within Groups

SN	Sequence	RN	SN	Sequence	RN	ID Unit
Group 1—Replication 1						
g1r1	D A C B	.674	g1r2	A B D C	.067	1 Bart
g1r2	A B D C	.067	g1r3	C D B A	.204	2 Clay
g1r3	C D B A	.204	g1r4	B C A D	.328	3 Herb
g1r4	B C A D	.328	g1r1	D A C B	.674	4 Max
Group 2—Replication 2						
g2r1	D A C B	.374	g2r2	A B D C	.011	1 Abe
g2r2	A B D C	.011	g2r4	B C A D	.182	2 Dex
g2r3	C D B A	.861	g2r1	D A C B	.374	3 Gary
g2r4	B C A D	.182	g2r3	C D B A	.861	4 Rand
Group 3—Replication 3						
g3r1	D A C B	.139	g3r1	D A C B	.139	1 Aleck
g3r2	A B D C	.250	g3r2	A B D C	.250	2 Eddie
g3r3	C D B A	.816	g3r4	B C A D	.677	3 Lee
g3r4	B C A D	.677	g3r3	C D B A	.816	4 Sam

Sequences and Random Numbers | Random Assignment of Sequences to Units

---

RN: Table A1.1 (Group 1 — Rows: 3–6; Columns: 7–9), (Group 2 — Rows: 10–13; Columns: 30–32), (Group 3 — Rows: 17–20; Columns: 23–25).

balanced design (Design 6G4) with $\lambda_1 = 3$. For each group taken alone, the design remains a balanced design with $\lambda_1 = 1$. This is particularly relevant when experimental attrition or some unexpected technical mistake prevents the experimenter from obtaining complete data for one or

Table 3.16   Restricted Sequential Counterbalancing—Different Sequences per Group: Random Assignment of Sequences of Four Treatments (A, B, C, and D; Three Mutually Orthogonal Latin Squares— MOLS 4; See Table A3.3) to Three Groups of Four Units (Design 6F4; Method 18)

Step 1: Random Assignment of Treatments to the Symbols of the Standard Design
Step 1 is identical to Method 16: *Nonrestricted Counterbalancing*. To save space, we assume that the same random permutation (3, 2, 4, 1) has been obtained (see Table 3.9).

Step 2: (Replication and) Partition of the Standard Design
In this example, there is only one replication of the standard design, which has been broken into three subsets of four sequences: Brick 1 (Square 1), Brick 2 (Square 2), and Brick 3 (Square 3) (see the squares on the right of the upper panel of Table 3.9).

Step 3: Random Assignment of Subsets of Sequences to Groups of Experimental Units
Three groups of four units are required: *Group 1*, *Group 2*, and *Group 3*.

Bricks and Random Numbers		Random Assignment of Bricks to Groups		
Brick	RN	Brick	RN	Group
Brick 1 (Square 1)	.959	Brick 2 (Square 2)	.097	Group 1
Brick 2 (Square 2)	.097	Brick 3 (Square 3)	.534	Group 2
Brick 3 (Square 3)	.534	Brick 1 (Square 1)	.959	Group 3

RN: Table A1.1 (Rows: 11–13; Columns: 19–21).

Step 4: Random Assignment of Sequences to Experimental Units Within Groups

Sequences and Random Numbers			Random Assignment of Sequences to Units			
SN	Sequence	RN	SN	Sequence	RN	ID Unit
Group 1—Brick 2 (Square 2)						
s2r1	C D A B	.628	s2r2	B A D C	.538	1 Annie
s2r2	B A D C	.538	s2r4	A B C D	.578	2 Gracie
s2r3	D C B A	.783	s2r1	C D A B	.628	3 Liz
s2r4	A B C D	.578	s2r3	D C B A	.783	4 Tess
Group 2—Brick 3 (Square 3)						
s3r1	C A B D	.484	s3r4	A C D B	.207	1 Bev
s3r2	B D C A	.820	s3r1	C A B D	.484	2 Elsa
s3r3	D B A C	.739	s3r3	D B A C	.739	3 Jan
s3r4	A C D B	.207	s3r2	B D C A	.820	4 Zoey
Group 3—Brick 1 (Square 1)						
s1r1	C B D A	.452	s1r2	B C A D	.135	1 Cynth
s1r2	B C A D	.135	s1r1	C B D A	.452	2 Dori
s1r3	D A C B	.938	s1r4	A D B C	.710	3 Penny
s1r4	A D B C	.710	s1r3	D A C B	.938	4 Vicky

RN: Table A1.1 (Group 1 — Rows: 26–29; Columns: 19–21), (Group 2 — Rows: 10–13; Columns: 7–9), (Group 3 — Rows: 13–16; Columns: 21–23).

more groups. In these cases, the data of intact groups can be analyzed separately, ensuring the degree of balance initially intended.

3.6.2 Different Sequences per Group

Contrary to Method 17, which requires at least two replications of a single-brick or a multiple-bricks standard design (see Table 3.14), Method 18—*Restricted Sequential Counterbalancing: Different Sequences per Group*—applies only to standard designs consisting of two or more distinct subsets of sequences (bricks) and can be used with a single replication of the selected design. In this case, as illustrated in Table 3.16 with a standard design with three bricks (MOLS for four treatments), each different brick is randomly assigned to a different group of experimental units categorized by some important classificatory factor. The whole design, with 12 sequences, is a balanced design ($\lambda_1 = 3$), but no balance is achieved within each brick (e.g., in Brick 3, randomly assigned to Group 2, Treatment A is immediately preceded twice by C, once by B, and never by D; see Table 3.16). The best one can say is that each brick (Latin square) taken by itself is a uniform design that could be obtained by Method 15—*Positional Counterbalancing* (see Section 3.4).

In practice, the main difference between Methods 17 and 18 (see Tables 3.4, 3.15, and 3.16) is that Method 18 includes a specific step (Step 3 in Table 3.16) to randomly assign the different subsets of sequences to the different groups defined by the between-subjects blocking structures. Note that Method 18 could also be applied to several replications of multiple-bricks standard designs. In any case, once the user specifies the number of replications of the standard design, the *number of admissible partitions* in Step 2 of Table 3.16 as well as the number of groups of experimental units required for the whole design are automatically defined: (a) they equal the number of bricks in the case of a single replication and (b) they correspond to the product *number of replications* times *number of bricks* in the case of two or more replications (in this case, some groups are administered identical subsets of sequences). Obviously, the number of experimental units per group must equal the number of sequences per partition of the whole design.

As we have already stated, when the procedural constraints (number of groups created by blocking variables and number of experimental units per group) are compatible with the whole design structure (number of subsets of sequences resulting from replications and/or partitions of the standard design and number of sequences per subset), Method 17 is always the best choice, and Method 18 should be used parsimoniously in restricted sequential counterbalancing. Nevertheless, there are some important balanced designs whose randomization requires the *mise en place* of Method 18. To be more specific, when the number of treatments is an odd number and some additional procedural constraints and randomization restrictions are assembled (i.e., the total number of available experimental units is $n = t(t - 1)$), and these units can be meaningfully categorized by some classificatory factor into $(t - 1)/2$ equal-size groups), *locally balanced designs* (Anderson & Preece, 2002) are particularly useful.

Locally balanced designs are built by adding vertically $(t - 1)/2$ different pairs of Williams's squares (double carryover designs; see Subsection 3.5.1). In the randomization phase (Step 3 of Method 18; see Table 3.16), each pair of Williams's squares is randomly assigned to one of the previously formed groups of homogeneous experimental units. Besides the achieved *local* balance within each pair of Williams's squares and, obviously, on the whole design, locally balanced designs have the additional structural properties summarized in Table 3.17, in which the standard forms of designs with five (Design 6K5) and seven (Design 6K7) treatments are depicted. Property (b) is specially relevant in the situations where subjects unexpectedly drop out from the experiment in the last period(s), because the data for the first $(t + 1)/2$ periods can be analyzed as if they had been obtained in an Incomplete Balanced Design (Design 6O; see Subsection 3.5.2). Please note that the locally balanced design for $t = 3$ is simply the Williams's design shown in Table 3.2 (Design 6H3). For an odd number of treatments higher than seven and for details on the construction of locally balanced designs, refer to the original work of Anderson and Preece (2002).

3.7 Factorial Designs

From Section 3.3 to Section 3.6, we explained and illustrated randomization methods applied to cross-over designs in which only *one* experimental factor is manipulated (Designs 6A–6T, according to the classification scheme presented in Table 3.3). As the reader has been warned at the end of Section 3.2, for the sake of simplicity and in consonance with the current practice in cross-over designs literature, we have used the term *treatment(s)* instead of *treatment level(s)*, with the understanding that we have been referring to the different levels of a treatment and not to the treatment itself. In this final section, the randomization of true factorial cross-over designs (Designs 6U and 6V in Table 3.3) is discussed, and we return to the terminology used throughout Chapter 2 and Sections 3.1 and 3.2. Designs consisting of multiple within-subjects factors (*treatments*), each with two or more *treatment levels*, are covered in the first subsection; designs containing simultaneously between-subjects and within-subjects treatments are addressed in the second subsection.

Table 3.17 Standard Forms of Locally Balanced Designs for Five and Seven Treatments

Design 6K5
$t = 5, n = 20, p = 5$

Williams's Squares 1

Square 1:

A	B	C	D	E
B	D	A	E	C
C	A	E	B	D
D	E	B	C	A
E	C	D	A	B

Square 2:

A	C	B	E	D
B	A	D	C	E
C	E	A	D	B
D	B	E	A	C
E	D	C	B	A

Williams's Squares 2

Square 1:

A	D	E	C	B
B	E	C	A	D
C	B	D	E	A
D	C	A	B	E
E	A	B	D	C

Square 2:

A	E	D	B	C
B	C	E	D	A
C	D	B	A	E
D	A	C	E	B
E	B	A	C	D

Design 6K7
$t = 7, n = 42, p = 7$

Williams's Squares 1

Square 1:

A	B	C	D	E	F	G
B	E	F	A	C	G	D
C	F	D	E	G	A	B
D	A	E	G	B	C	F
E	C	G	B	F	D	A
F	G	A	C	D	B	E
G	D	B	F	A	E	C

Square 2:

A	D	F	B	G	C	E
B	A	G	E	D	F	C
C	E	A	F	B	D	G
D	G	C	A	F	E	B
E	B	D	C	A	G	F
F	C	B	G	E	A	D
G	F	E	D	C	B	A

Williams's Squares 2

Square 1:

A	E	D	G	F	B	C
B	C	A	D	G	E	F
C	G	E	B	A	F	D
D	B	G	F	C	A	E
E	F	B	A	D	C	G
F	D	C	E	B	G	A
G	A	F	C	E	D	B

Square 2:

A	G	B	E	C	D	F
B	D	E	C	F	A	G
C	B	F	G	D	E	A
D	F	A	B	E	G	C
E	A	C	F	G	B	D
F	E	G	D	A	C	B
G	C	D	A	B	F	E

Williams's Squares 3

Square 1:

A	C	E	F	D	G	B
B	F	C	G	A	D	E
C	D	G	A	E	B	F
D	E	B	C	G	F	A
E	G	F	D	B	A	C
F	A	D	B	C	E	G
G	B	A	E	F	C	D

Square 2:

A	F	G	C	B	E	D
B	G	D	F	E	C	A
C	A	B	D	F	G	E
D	C	F	E	A	B	G
E	D	A	G	C	F	B
F	B	E	A	G	D	C
G	E	C	B	D	A	F

Additional Proprieties of Locally Balanced Designs:

(a) In the whole design, each pair of two different treatments occurs once in all the possible associations of two consecutive periods. This is illustrated with the pair *CE* in the two designs (see shaded cells). For example, in Design 6K5, the pair *CE* occurs in the 1st and the 2nd periods (Sequence 8), in the 2nd and the 3rd periods (Sequence 17), in the 3rd and the 4th periods (Sequence 19), and in the 4th and the 5th periods (Sequence 7).

(b) In the $(t + 1)/2$ first periods (i.e., the first three periods for Design 6K5 and the first five periods for Design 6K7), each treatment is immediately preceded by the remaining treatments within each different pair of Williams's squares. This is illustrated with reference to Treatment *B* in the two designs (see underlined treatments).

3.7.1 Only Within-Subjects Treatments

In some disciplines, it is not uncommon to see researchers manipulating simultaneously two or more within-subjects experimental factors. For example, in classical experimental psychology, subjects can be faced with stimuli differing consistently in *two independent dimensions*; in cognitive social psychology, manipulations of *physiological arousal* can be coupled with distinct *instructional definitions* of situations or social stimuli; in the health and pharmacological sciences, the conjoint effects of *two drugs*, each one given at different doses, can be the main aim of the experiment; finally and among other possible examples, in market research, consumers may be asked to evaluate similar products coming from different *brands* with alternative *forms*.

The examples given above are focused on the simplest case of factorial cross-over designs, that is, a design including only *two* treatments: W (e.g., Drug A in the third example and *Brand Name* in the fourth example) and X (e.g., Drug B in the third example and *Form of Product* in the fourth example). If each treatment has only two treatment levels (e.g., *low* and *high* doses for Drugs A and B in the third example, *established* vs. *new* for Brand Name, and *solid* vs. *liquid* for Form of Product in the fourth example), we get a factorial cross-over design with four experimental conditions or treatment level combinations: W_1X_1, W_1X_2, W_2X_1, and W_2X_2 (see Table 1.5 for the notational system used throughout this book). In this situation, it is tempting to rely on one of the *four periods designs* presented in the previous sections and, according to the assumptions about carryover effects, choose a suitable design for Random (Method 14), Positional (Method 15), or Sequential (Methods 16, 17, or 18) Counterbalancing, depending on the characteristics of the selected design and/or the absence/presence of between-subjects blocking structures (see Table 3.14). Randomization could be easily done by replacing the symbols A, B, C, and D of the final design with treatment level combinations W_1X_1, W_1X_2, W_2X_1, and W_2X_2, respectively. This procedure can actually be done, and it is absolutely correct (see, e.g., Fletcher & John's, 1985, utilization of 8×8 Latin squares in the construction of a 2×4 factorial cross-over design). However, as the number of treatments or the number of levels per treatment increases, the number of required periods (extension of sequences) for accommodating all the possible treatment level combinations quickly becomes excessive. At this point, the best solution is to skip complete-sequences designs and rely on designs with fewer periods than treatment level combinations but having a well-known factorial structure and a specific degree of balance.

Generalized cyclic designs (GC/n), introduced by John (1973) and developed in subsequent articles (e.g., Fletcher, 1987; Fletcher & John, 1985), are special cases of incomplete block designs (see Chapter 2, Subsection 2.3.3) exhibiting what has been called a *factorial (cross-over) structure*: The different treatments (factors) are orthogonal to each other and each treatment (factor) is orthogonal to the carryover effects belonging to the remaining treatments (factors) (see Fletcher & John, 1985, for a more formal definition of factorial structure, and Jones & Kenward, 2003, for a brief review of the literature on GC/n and similar designs). In Table 3.18, a simple procedure for the construction of a generalized cyclic design is illustrated with the original example given by John (1973) for a 4×3 factorial design, using $p = 4$ periods (Design 6U12). In this design, there are two within-subjects treatments (W and X), the first one with four levels (W_1, W_2, W_3, and W_4) and the second with three levels (X_1, X_2, and X_3), giving rise to 12 treatment level combinations (W_1X_1, W_1X_2, W_1X_3, . . ., W_4X_1, W_4X_2, and W_4X_3). Each different combination is administered in all periods (uniformity on periods), and a block of four treatment level combinations is given to each subject (see Form B of Design 6U12 in Table 3.18).

For design construction purposes, it is more convenient to rely on a slightly different notational system (see Form A of Design 6U12 in Table 3.18), in which the sequences of treatment level combinations are denoted by series of p pairs of digits (in each pair, the first digit indicates the levels of the first treatment, varying from 0 to t_{W-1}, and the second digit represents the levels of the second treatment, varying from 0 to t_{X-1}). Beginning with a predefined generating sequence (in the example, the generating sequence is the sequence 00, 10, 21, and 32 in the first block), in each period the levels for Treatment W are obtained by cycling the *first digit* of the corresponding pair of digits in the generating sequence one step (i.e., adding 1 to the previous treatment level and reducing modulus $t_W = 4$ when necessary). Also in each period, the levels for Treatment X are obtained by repeating t_W times the *second digit* of the pair and by cycling this digit one step the next t_W times, reducing modulus $t_X = 3$ when necessary. Adopting our notational system, the 0 to t_{W-1} levels for Treatment W are converted into 1 to t_W levels ($0 = W_1$, $1 = W_2$, $2 = W_3$, and $3 = W_4$), and the 0 to t_{X-1} levels for Treatment X are converted into 1 to t_X levels ($0 = X_1$, $1 = X_2$, and $2 = X_3$). As the reader could verify by himself, the design obtained has a factorial structure, in which (a) Treatments W and X are orthogonal, (b) Treatment W is orthogonal to the carryover effects of Treatment X, and (c) Treatment X is orthogonal to the carryover effects of Treatment W (see Table 3.18).

Once Design 6U12 has been generated, 12 experimental units are required, and the randomization is done via Method 16—*Nonrestricted Sequential Counterbalancing*. If the whole design is replicated and there are meaningful between-subjects blocking structures, Method 17—*Restricted Sequential Counterbalancing: The Same Sequences per Group*—could also

Table 3.18 Construction of Generalized Cyclic Designs With Two Treatments and Four Periods: Examples of One-Brick (Design 6U12) and Two-Bricks (Design 6U6) Designs

Design 6U12 (4 × 3 Cross-Over Design)									Design 6U6 (2 × 3 Cross-Over Design)					
Form A					Form B						Form A			
Block	P1	P2	P3	P4	P1	P2	P3	P4	Brick	Block	P1	P2	P3	P4
1	**00**	**10**	**21**	**32**	W_1X_1	W_2X_1	W_3X_2	W_4X_3	1	1	**00**	**12**	**01**	**10**
2	10	20	31	02	W_2X_1	W_3X_1	W_4X_2	W_1X_3	1	2	10	02	11	00
3	20	30	01	12	W_3X_1	W_4X_1	W_1X_2	W_2X_3	1	3	01	10	02	11
4	30	00	11	22	W_4X_1	W_1X_1	W_2X_2	W_3X_3	1	4	11	00	12	01
5	01	11	22	30	W_1X_2	W_2X_2	W_3X_3	W_4X_1	1	5	02	11	00	12
6	11	21	32	00	W_2X_2	W_3X_2	W_4X_3	W_1X_1	1	6	12	01	10	02
7	21	31	02	10	W_3X_2	W_4X_2	W_1X_3	W_2X_1	2	7	**00**	**02**	**11**	**10**
8	31	01	12	20	W_4X_2	W_1X_2	W_2X_3	W_3X_1	2	8	10	12	01	00
9	02	12	20	31	W_1X_3	W_2X_3	W_3X_1	W_4X_2	2	9	01	00	12	11
10	12	22	30	01	W_2X_3	W_3X_3	W_4X_1	W_1X_2	2	10	11	10	02	01
11	22	32	00	11	W_3X_3	W_4X_3	W_1X_1	W_2X_2	2	11	02	01	10	12
12	32	02	10	21	W_4X_3	W_1X_3	W_2X_1	W_3X_2	2	12	12	11	00	02

Notes. The one-brick design (Design 6U12), given by John (1973, p. 55), is generated by the initial sequence 00, 10, 21, and 32 (depicted in bold type; nonshaded numbers are obtained from the first digit of each pair of digits and shaded numbers from the second one—for details, see main text). The two-bricks design (Design 6U6), given by Fletcher (1987, p. 650), is obtained from two different generating sequences: 00, 12, 01, and 10 (first brick), and 00, 02, 11, and 10 (second brick).

be applied. When the whole design includes multiple bricks (as in the case of Design 6U6, whose Form A is also depicted in Table 3.18) and a between-subjects blocking structure is present, the researcher must apply Method 18—*Restricted Sequential Counterbalancing*: *Different Sequences per Group* (see Tables 3.4 and 3.14).

Fletcher (1987, pp. 653–654) gives an extended list of *generating sequences* for *two* (2 × 2, 2 × 3, 2 × 4, 3 × 3, and 4 × 4) and *three* (2 × 2 × 2 and 3 × 3 × 3) treatments generalized cyclic designs, including, for each design, variants with different numbers of periods (*p*) and experimental units (*n*). The reader can take these generating sequences to build a specific design, relying on the procedure explained in the previous paragraphs and illustrated in Table 3.18 with two treatments generalized cyclic designs. In the case of the three treatments (e.g., W, X, and Y) designs, the procedure for design construction can be easily extended. For example, suppose you have a $3 \times 2 \times 2$ design, with $p = 6$ and $n = 12$, and the generating sequence is 001, 201, 010, 100, 110, and 211. Taking the 3-tuple in the second period (201), the treatment level combinations for the 12 blocks in this period would be obtained: (a) for Treatment W levels, by cycling the *first digit* one step (reducing modulus $t_W = 3$ when necessary); (b) for Treatment X levels, by repeating $t_W = 3$ times the *second digit* and cycling this digit one step the next t_W times (reducing modulus $t_X = 2$ when necessary); and (c) for Treatment Y levels, by repeating $t_W t_X = 6$ times the third digit and cycling this digit one step the next $t_W t_X$ times (reducing modulus $t_Y = 2$ when necessary). The 12 treatment level combinations for the second period would be 201, 001, 101, 211, 011, 111, 200, 000, 100, 210, 010, and 110. Replacing this notation with our notational system, these combinations would be read as $W_3X_1Y_2$, $W_1X_1Y_2$, $W_2X_1Y_2$, . . ., $W_3X_2Y_1$, $W_1X_2Y_1$, and $W_2X_2Y_1$. Of course, the procedure should be applied to the generating 3-tuples for the remaining five periods.

Generalized cyclic designs can be used in studies that have treatments with either an equal or a different number of treatment levels. When the number of treatment levels is the same for all the treatments involved in the study and the number of periods equals the number of treatment levels, factorial cross-over designs can be alternatively built on the basis of special types of MOLS, consisting of pairs of nearly column-complete Latin squares. Bate and Boxall (2008), using Williams's (1949) approach to MOLS construction, give a catalog of factorial cross-over designs for three up to nine treatment levels per experimental factor, including the particular case of six treatment levels for which no MOLS exist. In Table 3.19, we give an example of a 5×5 design (Design 6U25), referring the reader to the original source for theoretical and technical details on the construction and utilization of these and other designs.

3.7.2 At Least One Between-Subjects Treatment

To conclude our presentation on randomization methods in experimental design, we must consider designs having both between and within-subjects manipulations. The simplest design of this kind would be a design with two treatments: one between-subjects factor (T_A) and one within-subjects factor (W). Design randomization would be a two-step procedure. In the first step, the available experimental units would be randomly assigned to the levels of T_A (T_{A1}, T_{A2}, T_{A3}, . . .) using one of the simple random assignment (SRA) methods described in Subsection 2.2.1, even though Method 3—*Forced Equal Sizes*—would be the most appropriate choice. In the second step, a counterbalancing scheme would be applied for determination of the order in which the levels of W (W_1, W_2, W_3, . . .) would be administered to each experimental unit. This design has been popularized under the name of

Table 3.19 Construction of Factorial Cross-Over Designs From NC MOLS and Random Assignment of Treatment Levels to Experimental Conditions: Example of a Design (Design 6U25) With Two Treatments (W and X) and Five Levels per Treatment

Standard NC Squares (Form 1)[a]				Transposed Standard NC Squares (Form 2)[b]			
Square A	Square B	Square C	Square D	Square A	Square B	Square C	Square D
0 1 2 3 4	0 1 2 3 4	0 1 2 3 4	0 1 2 3 4	0 1 3 2 4	0 4 2 3 1	0 3 4 1 2	0 2 1 4 3
1 2 3 4 0	4 0 1 2 3	3 4 0 1 2	2 3 4 0 1	1 2 4 3 0	1 0 3 4 2	1 4 0 2 3	1 3 2 0 4
3 4 0 1 2	2 3 4 0 1	4 0 1 2 3	1 2 3 4 0	2 3 0 4 1	2 1 4 0 3	2 0 1 3 4	2 4 3 1 0
2 3 4 0 1	3 4 0 1 2	1 2 3 4 0	4 0 1 2 3	3 4 1 0 2	3 2 0 1 4	3 1 2 4 0	3 0 4 2 1
4 0 1 2 3	1 2 3 4 0	2 3 4 0 1	3 4 0 1 2	4 0 2 1 3	4 3 1 2 0	4 2 3 0 1	4 1 0 3 2

Numbers Replaced With Symbols (Form 3)[c]		Randomly Changed Symbols (Form 4)[d]		Symbols Replaced With Numbers (Form 5)[e]		Final Design (Form 6)[f] $t_W = t_X = 5,\ n = 2t = 10,\ p = 5$				
Square A	Square C	Square A	Square C	Square A	Square C	P1	P2	P3	P4	P5
ABDCE	ADEBC	EABCD	EBDAC	51234	52413	W_5X_5	W_1X_2	W_2X_4	W_3X_1	W_4X_3
BCEDA	BEACD	ACDBE	ADECB	13425	14532	W_1X_1	W_3X_4	W_4X_5	W_2X_3	W_5X_2
CDAEB	CABDE	CBEDA	CEABD	32541	35124	W_3X_3	W_2X_5	W_5X_1	W_4X_2	W_1X_4
DEBAC	DBCEA	BDAEC	BACDE	24153	21345	W_2X_2	W_4X_1	W_1X_3	W_5X_4	W_3X_5
EACBD	ECDAB	DECAB	DCBEA	45312	43251	W_4X_4	W_5X_3	W_3X_2	W_1X_5	W_2X_1
Square B	Square D	Square B	Square D	Square B	Square D					
AECDB	ACBED	EDCBA	ECADB	54321	53142	W_5X_5	W_4X_3	W_3X_1	W_2X_4	W_1X_2
BADEC	BDCAE	AEBDC	ABCED	15243	12354	W_1X_1	W_5X_2	W_2X_3	W_4X_5	W_3X_4
CBEAD	CEDBA	CADEB	CDBAE	31452	34215	W_3X_3	W_1X_4	W_4X_2	W_5X_1	W_2X_5
DCABE	DAECB	BCEAD	BEDCA	23514	25431	W_2X_2	W_3X_5	W_5X_4	W_1X_3	W_4X_1
EDBCA	EBADC	DBACE	DAEBC	42135	41523	W_4X_4	W_2X_1	W_1X_5	W_3X_2	W_5X_3

[a] *Form 1*—Standard *nearly column-complete* (NC) Latin squares given by Bate and Boxall (2008, p. 191). Squares *A* and *B* form a first pair of *quasi-complete* (QC) Latin squares; Squares *C* and *D* compose a second pair of *quasi-complete* (QC) Latin squares. Taken together, the four Latin squares form a complete set of MOLS.

[b] *Form 1 to Form 2*—The columns of Squares A, B, C, and D in Form 1 become the rows of Squares A, B, C, and D in Form 2.

[c] *Form 2 to Form 3*—Natural order: 0 → A; 1 → B; 2 → C; 3 → D; 4 → E.

[d] *Form 3 to Form 4*—Taking a random permutation of five integers (5, 1, 3, 2, 4) from Appendix 1/Table A1.1 (Rows 22–37; Column 13) and changing the symbols: A – 5 → E; B – 1 → A; C – 3 → C; D – 2 → B; E – 4 → D.

[e] *Form 4 to Form 5*—Natural order: A → 1; B → 2; C → 3; D → 4; E → 5.

[f] *Form 5 to Form 6* (Final design)—Numbers of *Squares A* and *B* become the levels of Treatment *W*; numbers of *Squares C* and *D* (shaded numbers) become the levels of Treatment *X*.

mixed design (e.g., Lindquist, 1953), but we avoid this designation because in statistics the term *mixed design* refers specifically to any design that includes "both random- and fixed-effects factors, regardless of whether they are between-subjects or within-subjects" (Maxwell & Delaney, 2004, p. 593). From a structural perspective, the design is similar to the *Split-Plot Factorial Design* (Design 10) discussed in Chapter 2 (see Table 2.11), with the understanding that each block is formed by a single experimental unit. Theoretically it is possible to combine the structural features of many between-subjects designs classified in Figure 1.3 with counterbalancing schemes for one or more within-subjects factors (a very early systematization of these designs is given by Lindquist, 1953). However, with the increase in the number of factors and factor levels, the designs quickly become statistically "intractable," not to mention the procedural constraints imposed on randomization.

Except for the combination of Random Counterbalancing (Method 14) with one of the four SRA methods (Methods 1–4), the two-step procedure described above must be reversed; that is, the optimal randomization strategy has to begin by choosing the counterbalancing scheme (positional or sequential counterbalancing) for the within-subjects factor and to replicate the standard design one or more times within each level (or treatment level combination) of the between-subjects factor(s). On the understanding that Method 3 is used to randomly assign the participants to the experimental conditions defined by the between-subjects treatment design, the number of experimental units required for the whole design must equal *the number of sequences in the standard cross-over design* times *the number of replications of this design per between-subjects experimental condition* times *the number of between-subjects experimental conditions*. If *Positional Counterbalancing* (Method 15) is chosen for the within-subjects factor, *the number of sequences in the standard cross-over design* will equal the order of the selected standard Latin square. If sequential counterbalancing is the researcher's option, what we said about between-subjects blocking structures in Section 3.6 can then be applied, mutatis mutandis, to the experimental groups created via Method 3. To be more precise, the randomization of designs with both between- and within-subjects factors is a special case of Methods 17 and 18, bearing in mind that the restrictive features of these methods apply to randomized groups of participants and not to groups defined by the intrinsic characteristics of available experimental units. Whenever possible, Method 17 must be used instead of Method 18, which is to say that the sequences for the levels of the within-subjects factor are the same in all randomized groups.

CHAPTER 4. VALIDITY ISSUES, ANALYSIS GUIDELINES, AND REPORTING STANDARDS

In the previous chapters, the methods of randomization in between-subjects and within-subjects designs were intentionally presented without any mention of statistical software for random assignment or counterbalancing procedures. As the reader was informed in the Preface, the 18 methods described and illustrated throughout Chapters 2 and 3 could be rigorously implemented by relying on the materials given in the appendices and using the common features (e.g., copy and paste, replace, tables, and sort commands) included in any word processor software. This deliberate pedagogical strategy was planned to be in agreement with the user-friendly "philosophy" underlying the SAGE Quantitative Applications in the Social Sciences Series since the very first title in the mid-1970s, as Lewis-Beck (2008) has recently reminded us.

However, once the reader has mastered the critical features of local control and randomization procedures (i.e., the error control design) and their intrinsic relationships with the associated design layout (i.e., the treatment design), either the use of basic random number generators or the adoption of specialized software is, obviously, the ideal approach to randomization in "real-world" experimental research. Therefore, in this final chapter and whenever it is convenient, references to particular programs, computational routines, and randomization tools will be given to the reader. Needless to say, statistical software is being continuously updated, and exact citations of program releases are condemned to perish in a few months. So we invite the reader to regularly consult the software providers' websites. A good place to begin with is the *directory of statistical software providers* offered by STATA (www.stata.com/links/stat_software.html). For an excellent overview of free online software, we recommend John C. Pezzullo's *Interactive Statistics Pages* (http://statpages.org/). Finally, in the *companion website* of this monograph (www.sagepub.com/alferes), we will try to keep the reader informed about both *specific random assignment software* and the *randomization features* included in general-use statistical packages (e.g., BMDP, GenStat, IBM SPSS, R, SAS, STATA, STATISTICA, SYSTAT). As mentioned in the Preface, IBM SPSS and R versions of the author's SCRAED program are free and available from the companion website of this monograph, in which catalogs (e.g., TEXT and EXCEL files) of between-subjects and within-subjects designs and statistical code for running the associated analysis in different statistical packages (e.g., IBM SPSS) and computing environments (e.g., R) are also available.

In addition to these potentially useful tips on the selection and use of computer programs, this final chapter has three main objectives: (1) to restate the crucial role of randomization procedures in the broader context of the validity of scientific claims, (2) to establish the relevant connections between design and data analysis issues, and (3) to give the reader a clear picture of the standards required for truthful communication of research findings, with special emphasis on randomized experiments. A guide to the chapter contents is given in Figure 4.1, where the main features of randomized experiments, from the planning stage to the final report, are summarized. Figure 4.1 could be misread as a tentative plan for writing a comprehensive book on experimental design and data analysis. Yet there are excellent and authoritative reference works in this field, so that the reader will be referred to them whenever it is opportune. Our goal is obviously more modest, and this chapter is focused on the links between the core contents of the previous chapters and the practice of conducting randomized experiments, with special attention to the inescapable connections between local and generalized causal inferences and to the intersection points between experimental design features and data analysis strategies. More specifically, Chapters 2 and 3 were centered in *error control design* (randomization plans) and its interface with *treatment design* (design layouts), leaving out the interface with *sampling and observational design* (see Figure 4.1). This interface is the main concern of Section 4.1. On the other hand, some theoretical and technical details of randomization methods omitted in the two previous chapters are discussed in Section 4.2 along with general guidelines for data analysis. The concluding section is a brief guide for reporting randomized experiments.

4.1 Planning and Monitoring Randomized Experiments

As it was asserted in Section 1.2, scientific hypotheses are conjectural statements about the relationships between theoretical constructs, empirically represented by particular events or realizations. At the most abstract level, constructs can be thought of as the main nodes in the nomological network specified by theoretical conjectures. The translation of theoretical constructs into particular events (manipulations and measurement operations) is the first task an experimenter must deal with by clearly formulating the *research hypothesis*. In the methodological literature, there are some nuances in the use of the term *hypothesis*, ranging from an abstract proposition to a statistical hypothesis statement, as it can be read in Kirk's (1995) definition of experimental design, quoted in Section 1.1. A good strategy to formulate a research hypothesis is the *perspectivist approach* suggested by McGuire (2004b), in which the researcher begins to express the hypothesis in six different modes: (1) *natural language* (e.g., frustration, operationalized by [. . .], leads to aggression, measured by [. . .]); (2) *abstract symbolic*

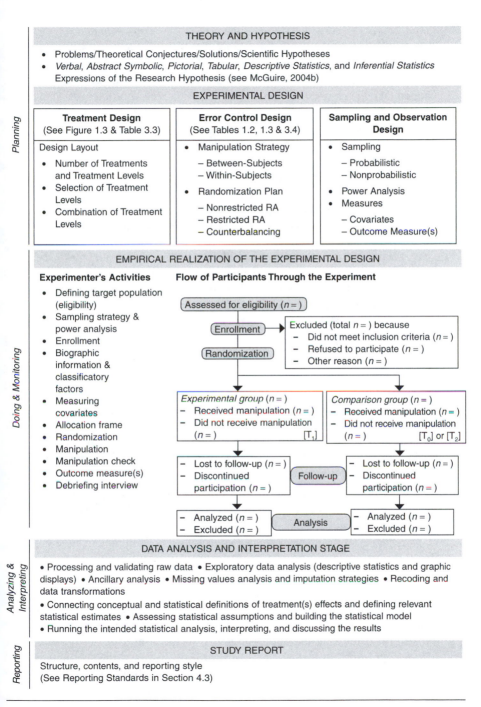

Figure 4.1   Conducting and reporting a randomized experiment

language (e.g., DV = f (IV_1, IV_2, IV_1*IV_2); DV = dependent variable, IV = independent variable); (3) *pictorial representation* (e.g., graphical anticipation of the expected main results); (4) *tabular depiction* (e.g., the planned layout, *cases/rows* by *variables/columns* in a statistical package data editor); (5) *descriptive statistics* (e.g., means, mean differences, standardized effect sizes); and (6) *inferential statistics* (e.g., t tests, F tests, confidence intervals). The *worksheets for generating a program of research* given in McGuire (2004a) can be an invaluable tool for beginners and even for experienced researchers.

Once the research hypothesis has been formulated, the next step is to build the research design connecting the three main components shown in Figure 4.1 and to anticipate all possible drawbacks in the empirical realization of the study by a tentative answer to the following questions:

a. Who (*the experimenter*) will deliver the treatments and make the observations and/or collect the self-reports (*measurement operations*), and which exactly will be the *treatment levels* or *treatment level combinations* to be administered and the behavioral responses to be recorded (*outcome measures*)?

b. Where (*laboratory* or *field* settings), when (*study temporal structure*), and under what conditions (previous *local control* and *randomization, constancy of pseudofactors, treatment implementation,* and *manipulation check*) will these responses be recorded?

c. How many participants will be involved in the study (*power analysis* and *study size*), how will they be recruited and enrolled (*sampling strategy*), and how will their intrinsic characteristics (*classificatory factors/blocking structures/dispositional moderators/covariates*) be identified and/or measured?

d. How will participants be informed of the study objectives in advance (*informed consent*), and what will be the *protocol* and the *timing* for the covariates measurement, local control, randomization, follow-up of treatments implementation, data collection, and debriefing interview?

e. What *theoretical* and *practical implications* of the study can be anticipated?

In the next two subsections, we give the reader an overview of the "interrelated activities" involved in planning and monitoring a randomized experiment addressing the questions above in the context of Campbell's "threats approach" to the validity of causal inferences and the substantive assumptions underlying Rubin's causal model. Obviously, this is a selective overview centered on the interfaces of error control design—the main subject of this monograph—and cannot be read as an "art of experimentation" exposition. In the social sciences, one of the pioneering efforts to write essays on this subject is documented by the chapters on *field experiments* (French, 1953) and *laboratory experiments* (Festinger, 1953) included in the remarkable edited volume *Research Methods in the Behavioral Sciences* (Festinger & Katz, 1953), associated with the creation of the Institute for Social Research at the University of Michigan in 1949. Aronson, one the most prominent students of Festinger, has continued this tradition in his contributions to the "Experimental Method" chapters (e.g., Aronson & Carlsmith, 1968; Wilson, Aronson, & Carlsmith, 2010) included in the successive editions of the *Handbook of Social Psychology*, to which the reader is referred. An outstanding presentation and discussion of 28 "classic" social psychology experiments—published between 1959 and 2001—is given in Abelson, Frey, and Gregg (2004).

4.1.1 External and Construct Validity Issues

Although Chapters 2 and 3 were essentially focused on strategies to ensure valid local inferences, in the introductory chapter, we have conveniently highlighted the connections between the experimental and statistical components of causality and the extrapolation (external validity) and representation (construct validity) features underlying generalized causal inferences (see Figure 1.2). This subsection gives a brief review of these connections, with special emphasis on the sampling strategies behind randomized experiments and some specific threats to the construct validity of experimental treatments.

4.1.1.1 Sampling Strategies and External Validity

If there were no budgetary constraints or practical limitations in recruiting participants and obtaining their informed consent and if the experimenter's goal is to simultaneously ensure the optimal conditions for both local inferences of causality and generalization of causal relationships, randomized experiments would always be preceded by probabilistic sampling from target populations. The structural characteristics of the target population would be synonymous with the eligibility criteria for the randomized experiment, and the preliminary sampling procedure would be done by trying to minimize coverage, sampling, and nonresponse errors (Groves, 1989; Groves et al., 2004).

4.1.1.1.1 The Ideal Model for Generalized Causal Inferences. This "ideal model" of generalized causal inference (see Figure 4.2) has been applied in some areas of research (e.g., "split-ballot" experiments in cross-sectional

survey research, some of them focusing on the study of question formats and the cognitive processes underlying response editing, or repeated measures designs embedded in longitudinal survey research), but it is far from being the norm in social and behavioral experimental studies. In addition to financial matters and practical reasons, there are other sound arguments in favor of experimentation without previous probabilistic sampling. One extreme position defending "external invalidity" was taken by Mook (1983) on the grounds that the bulk of experimental research is centered on the identification of causal processes and the appraisal of competing theories, and therefore "generalization to the real world" is not the main concern. A classic example is Harlow's (1958) study on the "nature of love," in which psychoanalytic and behaviorist hypotheses about the secondary nature of the infant–mother attachment were experimentally disconfirmed. Harlow's subjects were rhesus monkeys, and the experimental settings comprised, among other devices, wire and cloth surrogate mothers and artificial living cages. There was no formal sampling of the "participants," and we could not easily imagine a situation more distant from the daily existence of normal savage monkeys.

This lack of "ecological" validity is frequently a source of misunderstandings about randomized experiments among the general public and even in some academic forums. As Aronson, Wilson, and Brewer (1998) consistently argue, the basic requirements for an experiment are *experimental realism* (i.e., an impact and meaningful manipulation) and *psychological realism* (i.e., a manipulation that triggers the relevant psychological processes) and not naive or *mundane realism* (i.e., a true but nonpertinent similarity with people's everyday life).

4.1.1.1.2 "Realistic" Models for Generalized Causal Inferences. Having said this, we are not suggesting that external validity issues can be dismissed. On the contrary, the generalization of causal relationships can and must be the central aim of the scientific enterprise. However, there are more "realistic" ways to achieve this desideratum by circumventing the difficulties inherent to probabilistic sampling strategies. This is not the place to describe these alternative ways, but we refer the reader to Shadish et al. (2002), where Cook's (1993, 2000) model of generalized causal inference is fully explained. This approach, relying on special strategies of purposive or intentional sampling (e.g., deliberately heterogeneous sampling, modal instance sampling), makes simultaneous use of different principles of generalization (e.g., assessing superficial and deep similarities, making discriminations, interpolations, and extrapolations) and is applied to both external and construct validity issues. In brief, "realistic" models for generalized causal inference encapsulate the often quoted reply of Sir Ronald

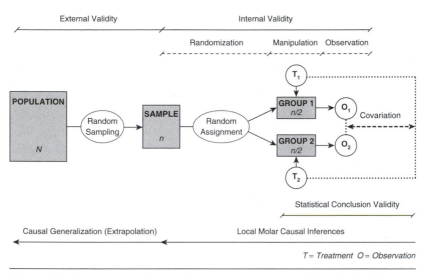

Figure 4.2   Random sampling, random assignment, and validity of scientific inferences

Fisher when asked how many experiments would be necessary to make a certain point: "Elaborate!" was the elliptic answer.

4.1.1.1.3 Specific Threats to External Validity and the "No Different Versions of Treatments" Assumption.
In the last update of Campbell's "threats approach" to the validity of scientific inferences (Shadish et al., 2002), external validity is equated not just with the extrapolation of causal relationships to target populations but also with the extrapolation of these relationships to other operationalizations of treatments and outcome measures, as well as to different physical and social settings (see Figure 2.1). Among the potential threats to external validity (interactions of the causal relationship with *units*, *treatment variations*, *outcomes*, and *settings*, and *context-dependent mediation*), the second one is particularly relevant in the context of this monograph given that the *variations in treatment implementation* or *partial implementation of treatments* encompass to some extent the first component of Rubin's SUTVA, which is the "no different versions of treatments" assumption. We will return to this point in the discussion of construct validity issues.

4.1.1.1.4 Assessing Eligibility and Participants' Enrollment.
With non-probabilistic intentional or convenience sampling, the first activity an experimenter is obliged to do is to clearly define and check the eligibility criteria for the available participants. This is also the initial step in the flowchart embedded in Figure 4.1, which is an adaptation of the diagrams

inserted in the successive versions of the *Consort Statement* (see Section 4.3). This chart will be used in Subsection 4.1.2 to organize the review of statistical conclusion and internal validity issues. The panel regarding classificatory factors in Table 1.1 can be seen as a reminder of the typical eligibility criteria used in experimental research. Informed consent matters will be briefly discussed in connection with the postexperimental interview in the final paragraph of Subsection 4.1.2.

4.1.1.1.5 Random Assignment and Random Sampling. We should conclude these short notes on external validity issues by noting that SRA can be thought of as a special case of *simple random sampling*, wherein *multiple random samples* (e.g., groups of experimental units assigned to different treatments) are drawn *without reposition* from a *population* consisting of *all available experimental units*. The number of samples equals the number of treatment levels (or treatment level combinations), and the sampling procedure ends when there are no more units to sample. In "forced-size methods" (Methods 3 and 4), the sample size (i.e., the number of experimental units per treatment) is fixed by the researcher; in "a priori probabilities methods" (Methods 1 and 2), the sample size varies around the theoretical probabilities of assignment previously specified by the experimenter. By the same token, blocked random assignment (Methods 7–10 and the two variants of SRA—Methods 5 and 6) and stratified random assignment (Methods 11 and 12) are special cases of *stratified random sampling*, in which multiple random samples are drawn without reposition within each stratum of the population (i.e., all the available experimental units). To extend the analogy, the so-called cluster assignment—where entire groups of subjects are randomly assigned to experimental conditions—is a special case of *cluster sampling*, in which all the identified clusters are assigned to experimental treatments. A very readable introduction to random sampling is Kalton (1983). Dattalo (2010) gives an overview of the methodological and statistical alternatives to random sampling and random assignment. For reference works on sampling strategies, the reader may consult the classics of Cochran (1977) and Kish (1965) or more recent sources, such as Lohr (2010) or Thompson (2002).

4.1.1.2 Treatments, Outcome Measures, and Construct Validity

Ensuring the construct validity of causal inferences is perhaps the most demanding task a researcher must deal with. In a certain sense, definitions of constructs can be always replaced with "definitions of definitions," in a never-ending regressive process. Putting aside the neo-positivist illusion of single and unequivocal operational definitions, Cook and Campbell (1979; see also Campbell & Fiske, 1959; Cook, 1985) defend the path of multiple operationalizations and the assessment of convergent and discriminant validity of the different measures and manipulations of scientific constructs. In the systematization presented by Shadish et al. (2002), the threats to construct validity can be divided into two broad categories: (1) *general threats*, which affect simultaneously all the structural elements of a research design (see Threats 1–5 in Figure 4.3), and (2) *specific threats*, which can be more directly related to treatments, settings, units, or observations (see Threats 6–14 in Figure 4.3).

In Figure 4.3, we also sketch out the main contributions of Rosenthal (1976) to the study of "experimental artifacts," with particular emphasis on experimenter effects and the psychological processes underlying participants' behavior in an experimental situation. It is not our intention to make a detailed explanation of the very nature of all these artifacts, and for that the reader is referred to the classic volumes edited by Rosenthal and Rosnow (1969) and Miller (1972) and to the more recent synthesis by Rosnow and Rosenthal (1997). However, some specific threats and artifacts strictly concerning the main subject of this monograph will be considered in the next few paragraphs.

4.1.1.2.1 Specific Threats to Construct Validity and the "No Different Versions of Treatments" Assumption. First, the "no different versions of treatments" component of Rubin's SUTVA can be more clearly understood in the context of the multiple events that may introduce some kind of confounding in the treatment implementation. More precisely, and particularly in the social and behavioral sciences, in which the treatments may consist of complex and prolonged manipulations, the experimenter's expectancies, as well as his or her more or less unconscious actions intended to compensate for the less desirable effects, can result in different operationalizations of the same treatment. This is the reason why "blind studies" and "randomization concealment" are highly recommended standards in all "best practices" sources (see Section 4.3). The first expression refers to the practice of masking the research hypothesis and the very nature of the experimental conditions from those who administer the treatments and/or collect the outcome measures, and obviously also from the participants. The second one concerns the procedure of keeping the actual random assignment unknown until the moment of treatment implementation.

4.1.1.2.2 Specific Threats to Construct Validity and the "No Interference Between Units" Assumption. Second, and as explicitly shown in Figure 4.3, participants' behavior in a randomized experiment must be conceived as a special instance of general behavior, in which the outcome responses are also determined by situational "demand characteristics" and the participants can

116

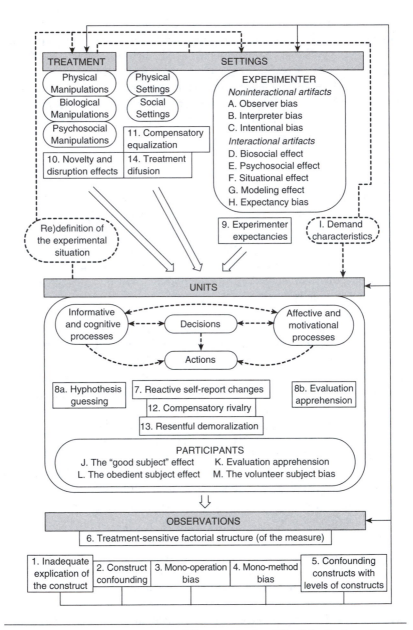

Figure 4.3   Threats to construct validity: Synthesis of Shadish, Cook, and
Campbell's (2002) approach (Threats 1–14; Threats 8a and 8b are
generically named *reactivity to the experimental situation*) and
Rosnow and Rosenthal's (1997) framework (Artifacts A–M)

actively (re)define the experimental situations in a manner that is not coincident with the intended operational definition of the focal treatment. In addition to the cognitive and affective processes underlying participants' decisions and actions in a randomized experiment, the possibility of social interactions between participants assigned to different treatments should also be taken into account, especially when the settings, the nature, and the duration of the manipulation favor the occurrence of these interactions, as is the case with social and educational programs and prolonged medical or psychological interventions. The component of Rubin's SUTVA labeled "no interference between experimental units" is a general assumption that encompasses some of the threats to construct validity, namely, *treatment diffusion* and the opposite behaviors encapsulated in the Campbellian expressions *compensatory rivalry* and *resentful demoralization* (see Threats 12–14 in Figure 4.3; for a detailed explanation of the many procedures to prevent artifacts and potential threats to the construct validity of causes and effects in experimental research, the reader is referred to Rosnow & Rosenthal, 1997; Shadish et al., 2002).

4.1.2 Statistical Conclusion and Internal Validity Issues

Given that local control and randomization procedures were conceptualized as the essential devices to ensure statistical conclusion and internal validity of causal inferences, we have thoroughly presented their rationale in the introductory sections of Chapters 2 and 3. Consequently, here we will be very briefly focusing on some issues omitted in Sections 2.1 and 3.1. In passing, it should be noted that in the very first systematizations of the Cambpellian approach (Campbell, 1957, 1969; Campbell & Stanley, 1966), statistical conclusion and internal validity were subsumed under the label *internal validity*, and the main threats to internal validity could be broadly defined as the shortcomings ruled out by a proper randomization. We echoed this initial conceptualization when representing the complementarity of the statistical and experimental components of valid local molar causal inferences in Figure 1.2.

4.1.2.1 Power Analysis, Covariance Assessment and Testing, and Statistical Conclusion Validity

Demonstrating covariance between treatments and outcome measures is the preliminary condition to infer causality. Besides the unreliability of measures or treatment implementations and the random variance associated with settings and experimental units, covariance estimation and testing could be affected by the "group" of threats to statistical conclusion validity depicted at the top of Figure 2.1. Here, we will resume these threats with a special emphasis on power issues and the strategies for "study size" planning.

4.1.2.1.1 Study Size and Power Analysis. A recurring question among students and novice researchers is the famous "*N* question": Now that the experimental design has been built and the variables operationalized, how many participants do I need to test my research hypothesis? To frame the question more correctly, *how many participants (or observations) per experimental condition are needed?* Unfortunately, this question cannot be answered directly, since the solution requires that the researcher is able to give the response to three preliminary questions: (1) What is the maximum risk or margin of error that he or she is willing to incur by rejecting the null hypothesis when it is true? (2) What is the admissible margin of error if he or she does not reject the null hypothesis when it is false? (3) Is he or she competent enough to provide an estimate of the expected experimental effect?

With the help of relatively simple formulas and tables (Cohen, 1988), an adequate answer to these preliminary questions allows the researcher to determine the required number of participants (or observations) per experimental condition. The answer to Question 1 is to establish the probability for the so-called Type I error (α), which is the highest margin of error that the research can accept when declaring that the statistical hypothesis under investigation (i.e., the null hypothesis) has been rejected. Please note that in statistical terms, the "hypothesis under investigation" is the null hypothesis (there is no covariation between the treatment and the outcome response, which is to say that there are no differences between the outcome means of different experimental conditions). Stating things this way may confuse the less informed researchers, who have come to believe that their aim is to "prove" the alternative hypothesis (i.e., there are differences between the outcome means of different experimental conditions) and not to reject the null hypothesis. A substantive response to Question 1 can be given by setting α at the conventional level of .05.

The answer to Question 2 connects directly with the so-called Type II error (β): the probability of declaring that there are no differences between the outcome means of experimental conditions, when actually these differences exist (not rejecting the null hypothesis when it is false). The complementary probability $(1 - \beta)$ of Type II error is called *power* or *sensibility* and corresponds to the correct decision of rejecting the null hypothesis when it is false. In other words, power is the probability of detecting differences between conditions if such differences really exist. In a similar way to what is done with Type I error, Cohen (1988) proposes to set β at the conventional level of .20 as the highest margin for Type II error, which would mean that the researcher has at least 80 chances in 100 $(1 - \beta \geq .80)$ to obtain "significant results" if they actually exist.

Finally, to answer correctly Question 3, the researcher must rely on the results of previously published studies or define in advance what is the minimal acceptable difference between experimental conditions (i.e., the magnitude or size of the experimental effect), based on criteria of theoretical or practical relevance. However, the absence of studies involving the same variables or insufficient information to clearly define those criteria makes the answer to Question 3 problematic.

We are not giving here the formulas to carry out prospective or a priori power analysis, but the reader can consult the classic source already cited (Cohen, 1988) or some more recent reviews of power issues in experimental design (e.g., Kelley & Rausch, 2006; Murphy, 2002). The main general-use statistical packages (e.g., R, SAS, STATISTICA, SYSTAT) include specific modules and routines for doing prospective power analysis for t tests, and ANOVA and ANCOVA designs. A very recommendable stand-alone commercial package is BioStat's Power and Precision (a similar version, named Sample Power, is sold in conjunction with the IBM SPSS statistical program). Among the free software, our choice goes to G*Power (Faul, Erdfelder, Lang, & Buchner, 2007) and to the Java Applets offered by Lenth (2006–2009).

Using these packages and statistical tools to calculate the number of experimental units per experimental condition in advance is a relatively simple task, particularly with regard to the specification of α and $1 - \beta$ values. For the specification of effect sizes, the user typically has at his disposal two main options: (1) to provide independent values for expected means (or mean differences) and residual variability or (2) to directly introduce the expected standardized effect size (e.g., Cohen's d for t tests or Cohen's f for effects in ANOVA and ANCOVA designs).

We conclude these notes on power with three final remarks. First, we side with Lenth (2001) when he advocates that in prospective power analysis it is better to gather sound information from pilot studies than to specify more or less arbitrary "small," "medium," or "large" effect sizes (i.e., values of .20, .50, and .80 for the d statistic or values of .10, .25, and .40 for the f statistic). Second, when using prospective power analysis in conjunction with Methods 7 to 10 (see Table 1.2) or with Methods 15 to 18 (see Tables 1.3 and 3.4), the number of experimental units (or observations) per experimental condition resulting from the formal analysis should be replaced with the next integer compatible with the procedural constraints of the error control design (e.g., the number of participants per block must equal or be a multiple of the number of experimental conditions) or with the intended structural properties of the chosen cross-over design. Finally, although we recommend the regular use of prospective power analysis, we warn the reader against a posteriori or retrospective analysis (some statistical packages routinely give values for observed power) and against the practice of relying on observed power values to make substantive interpretations of the study results. As Maxwell and Delaney (2004) note, "Saying $p > .05$ is tantamount to saying that observed power is less than .5" (p. 125).

4.1.2.1.2 Effect Size, Statistical Testing, and Confidence Intervals Estimation. In the preceding discussion of prospective power analysis, we implicitly relied on the "traditional" hybrid formulation of the *null hypothesis significance testing* (NHST). In spite of its ubiquity in published research, the NHST has always been the subject of strong controversies, with sound arguments for and against (see the volume edited by Harlow, Mulaik, & Steiger, 1997, and the review of Nickerson, 2000).

This matter is outside the scope of this monograph, but we should advise the reader to be critical with regard to common misunderstandings (e.g., p values don't inform the researcher about the probability of the null hypothesis being true given the obtained data, but on the contrary they correspond to the conditional probability of obtaining these or more extreme data given that the null hypothesis is true) and to take into account the more informative procedure of calculating confidence limits for mean differences. This shift from the NHST to the confidence intervals estimation for theoretically relevant statistical contrasts and to the appraisal of effect sizes is more visible in the health sciences than in the social and behavioral sciences (Fidler, 2011), despite the institutional or quasi-institutional recommendations (e.g., Wilkinson & Task Force on Statistical Inference, 1999). By saying this, we are not proposing that NHST should be banned, but we are rather endorsing its proper use (see Abelson, 1997; Jones & Tukey, 2000) in conjunction with the substantive evaluation of effect sizes.

4.1.2.2 Flow of Participants Through the Experiment and Internal Validity

In the middle panel of Figure 4.1, on the left of the chart showing the flow of participants, we listed the main activities of researchers when conducting a randomized experiment. Eligibility matters and sampling strategies were briefly discussed in Subsection 4.1.1, and prospective power analysis was approached in the opening paragraphs of this subsection. Here, we resume our selective overview of researchers' activities, beginning with the collection of biographic information about enrolled participants and ending with the ethical issues underlying randomized experiments.

4.1.2.2.1 Biographic Information, Classificatory Factors, and Covariates Measurement. Collecting all relevant biographic information and recording the values of major classificatory factors (e.g., age, gender, and ethnicity) are tasks intertwined with the assessment of participants' eligibility for a randomized experiment. Depending on the specifications in the error control design, once the participants meeting the eligibility criteria are enrolled and their informed consent obtained, the experimenters may have to get additional data about classificatory factors and to proceed with covariates measurement. These covariates could be either used as blocking/stratifying variables in the context of local control procedures or statistically handled in the data analysis stage.

From a substantive point of view, we refer the reader to Lazarsfeld (1959) on the conceptualization and classification of dispositional variables (generality vs. specificity, degree of directiveness/dynamics, and time perspective) in social and behavioral research and also to the discussion given in Rosenberg (1979); another important classic is Campbell's (1963) systematic review of acquired behavioral dispositions. For more contemporary approaches to dispositional variables in personality psychology, the reader may consult the synthesis presented in McCrae and Costa (1999).

4.1.2.2.2 Allocation Frames, Local Control, and Randomization. The next step is to build the allocation frame and to implement one of the methods of randomization or counterbalancing fully described and illustrated in Chapters 2 and 3. As already stated, this can be done with the same resources we have used throughout this monograph or with the help of RGN and specialized software.

A Google search with the expression "random number generator" gives more than 4,250,000 results, so the reader has certainly many accessible choices. The vast majority of RGN, either available on the Internet or incorporated in statistical spreadsheets and statistical software, produce pseudo-random numbers on the basis of some existing algorithm (see Appendix 1). Provided that a *uniform probability distribution* is chosen, the *starting point* is arbitrarily set (e.g., current date and time expressed in milliseconds), and the *algorithm* is accurate, these pseudo-RNG are good enough for experimental design purposes. If the reader wants true random numbers, he or she can obtain them from websites such as RANDOM.ORG (www.random .org/), from which we got the series included in Table A1.1. As RANDOM .ORG states, the randomness of these numbers comes from atmospheric noise, and no predictable pattern can be identified in the obtained series.

Virtually all statistical packages include RNG, and most of them also include the so-called design of experiments module accessible from their graphic interfaces (e.g., SAS, STATISTICA, SYSTAT). One problem with these modules is that they allow the randomization of many complex designs employed in engineering, industry, and technological research (e.g., fractional factorial designs with a high number of treatments, such as Taguchi designs, or response surface models, such as Box-Behnken designs), but some basic designs used in the social, behavioral, and health sciences are not available, as is the case with many restrictedly randomized between-subjects designs or counterbalancing schemes for cross-over designs. A very recommendable choice that allows the implementation of most of the between-subjects and within-subjects randomization methods described in this monograph is the Design module of GenStat. However, for some designs the best solution is to rely on the programming features of available software and to build specific routines for the intended randomization procedure. In fact, this is the solution we have adopted in SCRAED, a program that includes the 18 randomization methods explained in Chapters 2 and 3 and whose IBM SPSS and R versions can be freely downloaded from the companion website of this monograph.

4.1.2.2.3 Treatment Implementation, Manipulation Check, and Compliance.
As stated in all "reporting standards" (see Section 4.3), information about the settings, contents, and duration of experimental manipulations is a crucial feature in the assessment of the internal validity of causal inferences. From a practical point of view, it is convenient to make a clear distinction between randomized experiments in which the time elapsed between the beginning of treatment delivery and the measurement of the dependent variable(s) is relatively short (i.e., about 30–40 minutes to 2–3 hours) and randomized experiments in which the modus operandi is extended over several days or even months or years. Although not necessarily so, experiments of the first type are generally conducted in "laboratory" settings, and the researchers have a high degree of control over participants and nuisance situational variables (pseudofactors). In these circumstances, pseudofactors are controlled by holding them constant in all experimental conditions, and a relatively brief *manipulation check* (i.e., collecting a measure that is known to be sensitive to the focal treatment) can be done immediately after the treatment delivery. Even in the absence of manipulation checks, researchers can easily verify to what extent participants comply with the assigned experimental condition.

Experiments of the second type, that is, long-duration experiments, are typically (yet not inevitably) conducted in "field" settings, and in many instances treatment exposition occurs without the researchers' supervision, as is the case with medical prescriptions or some important components of social and educational interventions. In these situations, a well-planned follow-up is a critical device to evaluate whether participants comply with the assigned treatment. Treatment noncompliance or compliance with an unassigned treatment breaks the very nature of a randomized experiment. It is also a violation of Rubin's SUTVA and must be directly addressed in the data analysis stage (see Section 4.2).

4.1.2.2.4 Attrition, Measurement Operations, and Internal Validity. In the Campbellian framework, "experimental mortality" or *attrition* is a threat to the internal validity of causal inferences and is broadly defined as "differential loss of respondents from the comparison groups" (Campbell & Stanley, 1966, p. 5) or "loss of respondents to treatment or to measurement" (Shadish et al., 2002, p. 55). In Section 2.1, we explicitly associated attrition with the "Units" box (see Figure 2.1), but it could as well be simultaneously associated with the "Treatment" and the "Observations" boxes, implying both treatment noncompliance and the absence of outcome measures from randomly assigned participants. It is also theoretically conceivable that a participant has fully complied with the treatment, although he or she has been absent from the "measurement session" (see the hypothetical example in Table 4.1, in which the reverse situation is also shown: collecting outcome measures from noncompliers). In practice, given that there is no record of the outcome measure, the information about compliance with treatment becomes irrelevant (i.e., the participant must necessarily be ignored in the analysis stage).

A rather important issue is that attrition artifacts can more seriously affect between-subjects designs than within-subjects or cross-over designs. In the first case, the comparability between experimental conditions introduced by random assignment is derogated; in the second one, the worst scenario is the breaking of the intended degree of balance for the chosen design.

4.1.2.2.5 Debriefing Interview and Ethical Issues. Ethical issues must be a major concern in all randomized experiments, beginning with obtaining participants' informed consent and ending with a warm and elucidative postexperimental or debriefing interview. In addition to the informative features related to the current experiment, the postexperimental interview can be an excellent occasion to improve participants' knowledge about scientific methods of inquiry, with potential benefits to their personal lives. In the past four decades, we have observed the emergence and consolidation of a powerful movement condemning all experiments involving deceptive features. Providing that these features are really required for the appraisal of the research hypotheses and don't cause irreversible damage to the participants, we don't side with this "politically correct" movement. *Technical illusions*, to borrow Milgram's terminology (Evans, 1976, as cited in Korn, 1997, p. 104), are often irreplaceable devices, and their use can be fully justified in the debriefing session. As a marginal note, we refer the reader to one of the rare moments of self-disclosure in Festinger's (1980) writings, where he confesses that "in many years of doing experiments involving elaborate deceptions, I have never encountered an instance in which a subject felt harmed or ill used" (p. 250). For a well-informed history and appraisal of deceptive experimentation in social psychology, see Korn (1997).

As is obvious, ethical issues are not confined to deceptive experiments, and they are a matter of concern to all types of scientific inquiry. For an extensive examination of the ethical aspects of quantitative research, we refer the reader to the handbook recently edited by Panter and Sterba (2011), especially to the chapters focusing on randomized experiments (Mark & Lenz-Watson, 2011), sample size planning (Maxwell & Kelley, 2011), and data analysis (Rosnow & Rosenthal, 2011). For a well-articulated defense of randomization procedures in scientific inquiry and a systematic discussion of ethical and substantive objections to random assignment, the reader is referred to Cook and Payne (2002).

4.2 Analyzing Randomized Experiments

In a wonderful book about the proper use of statistics in scientific research, Abelson (1995) remarks that data analysis is best described by the detective work, the narrative devices, and the rhetorical principles needed "to organize a useful argument from quantitative evidence" (p. xiii). Relying on Tukey's (1977) "philosophy" of data analysis, Abelson elaborates on the fundamental criteria for producing sound statistical arguments: indexing the *magnitude* (e.g., effect sizes) of qualitative claims, *articulating* theoretically relevant comparisons (e.g., formulating specific directional hypotheses instead of the general or omnibus null hypothesis and, whenever possible, specifying quantitatively the values to be nullified, instead of the "zero difference" null hypothesis), and worrying about the *generality*, the *interestingness*, and the *credibility* of research results.

As the reader was informed in the Preface and in the introductory paragraphs of this chapter, this is not a section on data analysis but rather a brief guide to the relevant connections between design and statistical issues in randomized experiments. The section begins with an overview of the probabilistic nature of random assignment mechanisms and ends with a synthesis of the trade-offs between local and statistical control in experimental and quasi-experimental research. In the two intermediate subsections, we give some guidelines for the analysis of intact and broken experiments.

4.2.1 Random Processes, Probabilities, and Assignment Mechanisms

At this point, we cannot resist quoting the best and shortest definition of randomization we have found: "Randomization is something that everybody says they do, but hardly anybody does properly" (Crawley, 2005, p. 10).

Perhaps because reference to randomization procedures in published research is often limited to a single sentence, such as "The participants have been randomly assigned to the experimental conditions," students and novice researchers tend to underestimate the true role of randomization in causal inference. We hope that the core contents of this monograph will help the reader to improve this state of affairs.

From a theoretical point of view, the true role of randomization or probabilistic assignment in experimental design can be best understood in the context of the missing data framework and the potential outcomes approach proposed by Rubin (1974, 2006, 2007; see also Little & Rubin, 2002). Suppose we want to compare the effect of a new experimental treatment (say T1) with an alternative treatment (say T2), and 20 participants are available. As explained in the introductory chapter, it is impossible to obtain counterfactual evidence at an "individual level": We are not able to apply two different treatments to an experimental unit at the same time. So we are obliged to estimate the differential effect of the experimental conditions T1 and T2 at a "group level," and for that we randomly assign the 20 participants to both conditions (10 participants per condition) using Method 3—*Forced Equal Sizes* (see Subsection 2.2.1). The actual assignment shown in the three left columns of Table 4.1 is one of the 184,756 equiprobable assignments under the procedural constraints of Method 3. Suppose also that all participants have complied with the assigned treatment and that we have collected the outcome measures depicted in the fourth and fifth columns of Table 4.1. Using Rubin's potential outcomes notation, a rapid inspection of these columns shows that half of the data are missing: Participants exposed to T1 (Units 11, 15, . . ., 14) have no outcome measures under T2, and the same is true for participants exposed to T2 (Units 5, 6, . . ., 2) in relation to the outcome measures under T1. In formal terms, what Rubin says is that the underlying probabilistic assignment mechanism in itself makes the *missing observations in the unassigned experimental conditions* into *missing completely at random* data, which are therefore nonimputable to any intrinsic characteristic of the experimental units that have been randomized. Under these circumstances, the average effect size calculated on the basis of the observed outcomes is a nonbiased estimator of the true effect size that would be obtained if the counterfactual evidence could be assessed at an individual level. In this example of an intact or nonbroken experiment, the nonbiased sample estimator of the population average effect size is $g = 0.65$ (Hedges's correction to Cohen's $d = 0.68$; see Analysis 1 in Table 4.1).

The number of possible assignments (NPA) using Method 3 is given by the formula $NPA = N!/(n!^t)$, where N is the number of available experimental units, n is the number of units per experimental condition, and t is the number of experimental conditions. If we apply this formula to our example in

Table 4.1 Assignment Mechanisms, Outcomes Notation, and Statistical Analysis of Intact and Broken Experiments

Random Assignment Mechanism (Method 3)			Potential Outcomes Notation		Observed Outcomes Notation			
Unit ID	RN	Treatment Assigned T_1 or T_2	DV under T_1 Y(1)	DV under T_2 Y(2)	Intact Experiment Treatment Compliance	Y_{obs}	Broken Experiment Treatment Compliance	Y_{obs}
11	.012	1	7	■	1	7	1	7
15	.229	1	11	■	1	11	2	11
18	.243	1	9	■	1	9	1	—
9	.261	1	8	■	1	8	1	8
17	.332	1	12	■	1	12	?	—
16	.411	1	14	■	1	14	1	14
1	.412	1	13	■	1	13	2	13
13	.576	1	11	■	1	11	?	—
19	.597	1	6	■	1	6	1	6
14	.662	1	16	■	1	16	1	16
5	.705	2	■	13	2	13	2	13
6	.733	2	■	6	2	6	1	6
7	.754	2	■	6	2	6	2	—
3	.764	2	■	11	2	11	2	11
8	.789	2	■	9	2	9	?	9
20	.791	2	■	9	2	9	1	9
4	.865	2	■	12	2	12	2	12
12	.879	2	■	5	2	5	2	5
10	.933	2	■	5	2	5	2	—
2	.947	2	■	10	2	10	1	10

	Treatment Level T_1										Treatment Level T_2									
ID	11	15	18	9	17	16	1	13	19	14	5	6	7	3	8	20	4	12	10	2

Analysis 1: Intact Experiment (Standard Analysis = ITT Analysis)

Y_{obs}	7	11	9	8	12	14	13	11	6	16	13	6	6	11	9	9	12	5	5	10

$M_1 = 10.70$; $M_2 = 8.60$; $d = 0.68$; $g = 0.65$; $t\,(18) = 1.53$, $p = .144$; 95% CI [−0.79, 4.99]

Analysis 2: Broken Experiment (ITT Analysis)

Y_{obs}	7	11	—	8	—	14	13	—	6	16	13	6	—	11	9	9	12	5	—	10

$M_1 = 10.71$; $M_2 = 9.38$; $d = 0.41$; $g = 0.38$; $t\,(13) = 0.78$, $p = .447$; 95% CI [−2.35, 5.03]

Analysis 3: Broken Experiment (Naive Analysis)

	Treatment Level T_1										Treatment Level T_2									
ID	11	9	16	19	14	6	20	2	—	—	15	1	5	3	4	12	—	—	—	—
Y_{obs}	7	8	14	6	16	6	9	10	—	—	11	13	13	11	12	5	—	—	—	—

$M_1 = 9.50$; $M_2 = 10.83$; $d = −0.39$; $g = −0.36$; $t\,(12) = −0.72$, $p = .485$; 95% CI [−5.36, 2.70]

Notes. ITT = Intention to treat. Bold numbers represent the data for each analysis. Shaded cells in Analysis 3 correspond to participants who have complied with the nonassigned treatment level.

Table 2.2 (Design 1: *Completely Randomized Design*, with 4 treatment levels, 20 experimental units, and 5 experimental units per treatment level), we will find NPA = $20!/(5!^4)$ = 11,732,745,024 possible assignments under Method 3 (for calculation of factorials, see Appendix 2). This formula is a shortcut for the general formula applied to "forced-sizes" SRA methods: NPA = $N!/(n_1! \times n_2! \times \cdots \times n_t!)$, where $n_1, n_2, \ldots, n_t$ are the intended number of units for the different experimental conditions. Applying this formula to our illustration of Method 4 (Design 1: *Completely Randomized Design*, with 4 treatment levels, 20 experimental units, and 7, 3, 3, and 7 units for Treatment Levels T1, T2, T3, and T4, respectively) results in NPA = $20!/(7! \ 3! \ 3! \ 7!)$ = 2,660,486,400 possible assignments.

When dealing with "a priori probabilities" SRA methods (Methods 1 and 2), the number of possible assignments are given by the so-called *rule of product* or *fundamental principle of counting*: NPA = t^N, where t is the number of experimental conditions and N the number of available experimental units. In the same example (see Table 2.2), the number of possible assignments are NPA = 4^{20} = 1,099,511,627,776. Please note that some of these assignments may correspond to situations in which one or more experimental conditions are empty; that is, no experimental units have been assigned to these conditions. In Method 1, all assignments are equiprobable. In Method 2, depending on the prespecified probabilities, some assignments are more probable than others. In the companion website of this monograph, under the link "Probabilities and Random Assignment Mechanisms," the reader can access a fully worked example showing a physical random assignment mechanism and containing all the details for counting the number of possible assignments in Methods 1 to 4. To conclude our example, we should note that if the reader uses Method 1 instead of Method 3, the probability of getting a random assignment with equal sizes ($n = 5$) per treatment level is $p = 11732745024/1099511627776 = .0107$. By the same token, if the reader uses Method 1 instead of Method 4, the probability of getting a random assignment with treatment levels sizes $n_1 = 7$, $n_2 = 3$, $n_3 = 3$, and $n_4 = 7$ is $p = 2660486400/1099511627776 = .0024$.

4.2.2 Statistical Analysis of Intact Experiments

As the reader would have realized in the previous subsection, an "intact" experiment is a randomized experiment in which the conditions introduced by the initial randomization are kept unchanged from the beginning to the end; that is, all participants comply with the randomly assigned experimental condition, and the researcher is able to collect reliable outcome measures from all of them. In these conditions, often assembled in short-duration laboratory experiments but seldom met in long-duration field experiments, modeling data and estimating relevant parameters are relatively simple tasks, providing that the statistical model is correctly specified and the computational algorithms are sufficiently accurate.

All truthful and pedagogically oriented statistical textbooks begin with one or more chapters focused on the proper use of descriptive statistics and the associated graphical displays. In addition to the efforts involved in planning the study and collecting reliable data, the first task a researcher is supposed to carry out before plunging into inferential statistics is a careful inspection of his or her raw data. This preliminary work of scrutinizing data is at least as important as obtaining the final results to be published and routinely takes much more time than the few seconds required to run a complex analysis via any standard statistical software. So it is always a good idea to advise students and novice researchers to begin by mapping raw data into convenient tabular and graphical displays (e.g., box-and-whisker, stem-and-leaf, and influence plots; informative and "sober" bar and line charts), avoiding the beautiful but almost always deceptive features of colored 3-D plots (see Wilkinson, 2005, for an outstanding discussion of graphical displays).

As indicated in Figure 4.1, the ultimate statistical analysis must also be preceded by relevant ancillary analysis (e.g., an *internal analysis* based on manipulation check measures) and, when necessary, by (admissible) data transformations required for meeting the assumptions underlying the statistical model. In addition to carefully checking these assumptions, the reader is also advised against the practice of relying on the default statistical models available from the GUI (graphical user interface) menus of standard statistical packages. In Table 4.2, we summarize the structural features and the statistical models underlying the five most basic one-factor designs, whose randomization was explained in Chapters 2 (Designs 1, 2, 3, and 5A) and 3 (Design 6N). If, for example, the reader uses IBM SPSS default options to run the analysis of Designs 2 and 5A, he or she gets an "ANOVA Table" filled with blanks telling that some parameters in the model cannot be estimated. The reason for this is trivial: By default, the program assumes interactive terms for all the main factors included in the model, as is the case with Design 3, in which the interaction ($\alpha\pi$) between the true experimental factor (α) and the blocking variable (π) can be estimated. To properly analyze Design 2 (one true experimental factor and one blocking variable) and Design 5A (one true experimental factor and two blocking variables), the user must delete the interactive terms from the default statistical models (see Table 4.2). Obviously, this can easily be done within the IBM SPSS GUI, but note that we are talking about the most elementary statistical models. For running complex models that include simultaneously fixed and random factors and have different error terms for relevant contrasts, it is

Table 4.2 Comparison of Randomization Procedures, Structural Features, and Statistical Models of Between-Subjects and Within-Subjects Designs (Illustration With One Treatment With Three Levels and Six Observations per Treatment Level)

Design	Between-Subjects				Within-Subjects
	Completely Randomized (Design 1)	Randomized Block		Latin Square (Design 5A)	Repeated Measures (Cross-Over) (Design 6N)
		Complete (Design 2)	Generalized (Design 3)		
Randomization procedure	Nonrestricted	Restricted	Restricted	Restricted	Counterbalancing
Structural features					
Units per study	$N = 18$	$N = 18$	$N = 18$	$N = 18$	$N = 6$
Treatments (IVs)	*One*	*One*	*One*	*One*	*One*
Treatment levels	$t = 3$	$t = 3$	$t = 3$	$t = 3$	$t = 3$
Units per treatment level	$n = N/t = 6$	$n = N/t = 6$	$n = N/t = 6$	$n = N/t = 6$	$n = N = 6$
Blocking variables	*None*	*One*	*One*	*Two*	*One (Subjects)*
Blocks	$b = 1$	$b = N/t = 6$	$b = N/(kt) = 2$	$b = t^2 = 9$	$b = N = 6$
Units per block	$u = N = 18$	$u = t = 3$	$u = kt = 9$	$u = N/t^2 = 2$	$u = N/b = 1$
Outcome measures (DVs)	*One*	*One*	*One*	*One*	*One*
Observations per study	$O = N = 18$	$O = N = 18$	$O = N = 18$	$O = N = 18$	$O = Nt = 18$
Observations per treatment level	$o = N/t = 6$	$o = N/t = 6$	$o = N/t = 6$	$o = N/t = 6$	$o = N = 6$
Statistical model	$Y = \mu + \alpha + \varepsilon$	$Y = \mu + \alpha + \pi + \varepsilon$	$Y = \mu + \alpha + \pi + \alpha\pi + \varepsilon$	$Y = \mu + \alpha + \pi_r + \pi_c + \varepsilon$	$Y = \mu + \alpha + S + \varepsilon$

Notes. k = Number of units per treatment within each block (any integer ≥ 2; in the example, $k = 3$). IV = Independent variable. DV = Dependent variable.

always a significant advantage to master the programming features of the statistical package (e.g., SAS and IBM SPSS syntax code) or to rely on flexible "computing environments," such as the free R software. Even if the user completely ignores the statistical coding potentialities, there is no GUI that can substitute for having a proper knowledge of the statistical model underlying the experimental design. Please note that what we are saying about IBM SPSS applies to the GUI menus of similar statistical packages, and the main point is not whether the analysis is conducted via "point-and-click" actions or via previously written code but rather the specification and estimation of the correct statistical model.

To express it in general terms, we can adopt the formulation given by Hinkelmann and Kempthorne (2008, p. 35), in which the outcome responses (i.e., the data) are a function of *explanatory variables* plus *random error*: Response = f(Explanatory variables) + Error. The model for explanatory variables includes treatment effects (i.e., the effects of the factors incorporated in the treatment design) and blocking/stratifying effects (i.e., the effects of the variables used in the error control design). Depending on both the nature of the treatment design and the nature of the error control design, interactive terms between explanatory variables may be included in the statistical model. The error term corresponds to the random variance that can be imputed to the unreliability of measures or of treatment implementation as well as to unintended variations in settings, and obviously to the "uncontrolled variability" of experimental units. What randomization effectively does is to make the error terms uncorrelated (i.e., independent) with the terms standing for the explanatory variables.

As the reader has already been informed, this is not a section on data analysis. So the next paragraphs will be limited to some guidelines and bibliographic orientations for the proper analysis of randomized experiments. Inevitably, these bibliographic orientations reflect our own teaching and research practice, but we do not intend in any way to disqualify other excellent books on experimental design and data analysis.

4.2.2.1 Between-Subjects Designs

Before proceeding with these guidelines, it should be noted that t tests, such as those included in Table 4.1, and ANOVA/ANCOVA models are special cases of the *general linear model* (GLM), which also includes correlation/regression analysis, as well as some interdependence models such as principal components and factorial analysis. Note also that t tests themselves are special cases (one experimental factor only with two levels) of the so-called one-way ANOVA models. Running an ANOVA on the example analyzed in the previous subsection gives an observed $F(1, 18) = 2.33$, $p = .144$ (i.e., $t^2 = 1.526^2 = F = 2.33$).

For an integrated approach to ANOVA and least squares regression under the GLM, the reader is referred to Cohen, Cohen, West, and Aiken (2003), Fox (2008), and Kutner, Nachtsheim, Neter, and Li (2004). In particular, Fox's book also covers *generalized linear models* (an extension of the GLM), which can be used with remarkable advantages over the traditional nonparametric alternatives to ANOVA in situations where outcome measures are taken as unordered or ordered categorical variables. Furthermore, it should also be stated that when the experimental factors are truly continuous variables, the analysis can be done via regression, without losing information by their artificial reduction to the status of nominal independent variables. As a matter of fact, statistical software packages can handle all ANOVA models via the so-called regression approach, in which the nominal independent variables are previously recoded into dummy variables.

With intact experiments, provided that the statistical model is correctly specified and the error terms are appropriate for the intended specific contrasts, all the general-use statistical packages mentioned in the introductory paragraphs of this chapter can be used for doing a proper analysis of between-subjects randomized experiments. As the reader has already been advised, the "point-and-click" actions and the help menus included in the chosen software do not excuse one from having knowledge of the underlying statistical models, which can be obtained only from authoritative sources. In addition to Fisher's (1925/1970, 1935/1966) seminal books, there are three classic sources, published in the 1950s, that remain irreplaceable references in experimental design and data analysis: Cochran and Cox (1957), Federer (1955), and Kempthorne (1952). Written without the assistance of present-day computers and statistical software, these books include fully worked examples, formulas, and supplementary materials that continue to be invaluable tools for the statistically skilled researcher. Among the updated editions of more recent "classics," our choice goes to Hinkelmann and Kempthorne (2005, 2008), Keppel and Wickens (2007), Kirk (1995, 2013), Maxwell and Delaney (2004), and Winer et al. (1991). As the reader has certainly noticed, Kirk (1995) gave us the explicit "layout" for the presentation of randomization methods in Sections 2.2 and 2.3. We finish this overview by recalling the experimental design and ANOVA QASS monographs whose serial numbers are mentioned in the Preface (the titles are given in the list included in the first pages of this monograph) and the new edition of Judd, McClelland, and Ryan (2009), focused on statistical models comparison, as well as the book by Tabachnick and Fidell (2007), which makes a fair trade-off between "hand calculations" and statistical packages procedures (IBM SPSS, SAS, and SYSTAT).

With specific regard to the estimation of effect sizes and the proper calculation of their confidence intervals, the reader can choose among several excellent books (e.g., Cortina & Nouri, 2000; Grissom & Kim, 2005; Kline,

2004; Rosenthal, Rosnow, & Rubin, 2000) and/or seek advice from systematic reviews such as Borenstein (2009), Fleiss and Berlin (2009), Kirk (2003b), or Thompson (2006). Reichardt (2000) discusses effect sizes in the context of the Campbellian "threats approach" to the validity of causal inferences.

4.2.2.2 Within-Subjects (Cross-Over) Designs

The considerations and the guidelines given regarding the statistical analysis of intact between-subjects designs are also valid for the analysis of intact cross-over designs. However, we must add two complementary notes.

The first note concerns the preliminary check of the assumptions underlying the statistical model. In between-subjects designs, these assumptions are *independence of errors*, *normality of sampling distributions*, and *homogeneity of variance*. The reader must realize that the *independence* assumption introduced by random assignment in between-subjects designs cannot be taken for granted in cross-over designs given that some degree of correlation between the measures collected on the same units in successive periods is always expected. Standard statistical packages generally include one or more routines (e.g., Mauchly's Test of Sphericity) to test if the magnitude of these correlations can compromise further analysis. In formal terms, this additional assumption, which includes separated but related components (*additivity* and *homogeneity of covariance*), is know as the *sphericity assumption*.

The second note concerns the choice of the statistical model itself. Even if the sphericity assumption holds, the reader must be advised against statistical packages with default options for the analysis of cross-over or repeated measures designs. These options are usually appropriate for the analysis of designs generated on the basis of Random Counterbalancing (Method 14; Design 6N) and Positional Counterbalancing (Method 15; Design 6M) but not for modeling direct and carryover effects simultaneously, as is the case with designs built by sequential counterbalancing (Methods 16–18; see Table 3.3 for the designations of designs). So, in addition to the bibliographic orientations given for between-subjects designs, in which Designs 6M and 6N are generally covered, we refer the reader to the sources where models for direct and carryover effects are fully explained and illustrated (e.g., Cotton, 1998; Jones & Kenward, 2003; Senn, 2003). In consonance with the presentation of cross-over designs randomization methods in Chapter 3, our first choice is Jones and Kenward (2003; in the companion website of this book, the reader can access XOEFFICIENCY, a GenStat module to calculate the efficiencies of direct and carryover contrasts in cross-over designs).

4.2.3 Statistical Analysis of Broken Experiments

As the expression suggests, "broken experiments" are randomized experiments in which the ideal conditions introduced by random assignment or counterbalancing are more or less compromised by unexpected threats to internal validity (e.g., attrition) and/or the violation of SUTVA components (e.g., treatment noncompliance).

4.2.3.1 Between-Subjects Designs

In the last two columns of Table 4.1, we show a hypothetical example of a between-subjects broken experiment (to be more precise, the same completely randomized design whose standard analysis is illustrated in Subsection 4.2.1). As the reader can easily verify, attrition has resulted in the absence of outcome measures for Participants 18, 17, 13, 7, and 10, and Participants 15, 1, 6, 20, and 2 and have complied with the unassigned treatment. Moreover, the follow-up on treatment compliance is uninformative for Participants 17, 13, and 8. In this situation, the assessment of the causal effect must be reframed to obtain the "least biased" estimator. One common procedure is to ignore treatment compliance information and analyze all cases without missing values on the outcome measure as if they have complied with the randomly assigned treatment (see Analysis 2 in Table 4.1). This analysis is called *intention-to-treat* (ITT) analysis, and the obtained effect can be thought of as the best available estimator of the *average treatment effect* (ATE) that would be obtained in an intact experiment (see Analysis 1). ITT analysis is always preferable to the temptation to estimate the ATE on the basis of treatment compliance information, ignoring random assignment. This is what is illustrated in Analysis 3 (see Table 4.1), and the obtained effect is called *naive* ATE (for consistent alternatives, see Angrist, Imbens, & Rubin, 1996).

Broken experiments fall somewhere in a gray area between intact randomized experiments and nonrandomized experiments (quasi-experiments or observational studies), and their statistical analysis could be improved by the sophisticated techniques developed in the context of *propensity score analysis*. We refer the reader to several fundamental sources on propensity score analysis (Imbens & Rubin, in press; Rosenbaum, 2002, 2010; Rosenbaum & Rubin, 1983; Rubin, 2006) and also to the excellent book by Guo and Fraser (2010), in which Rubin's approach and related techniques are fully explained and illustrated. For well-articulated presentations of Rubin's causal model, causal inference, and experimental methodology in the social and political sciences, see Morgan and Winship (2007) and Morton and Williams (2010).

4.2.3.2 Within-Subjects (Cross-Over) Designs

Treatment noncompliance issues and their implications for the validity of causal inferences are essentially the same in cross-over and between-subjects designs. On the contrary, whereas attrition (especially differential attrition) is a serious threat to the internal validity of causal inferences in between-subjects designs, its negative impact on cross-over designs can be more easily overcome. As we have already stated, omitting data from one or more participants in a cross-over design results in breaking the intended degree of balance for the whole design. If this happens, data coming from intact subsets of sequences can also be analyzed with statistical models appropriate for the degree of balance achieved in these intact subsets (e.g., subsets of Designs 6K: *Locally Balanced Designs*; more generally, all multiple-bricks designs or designs having two or more replications of the standard cross-over design).

4.2.3.3 Trade-Offs Between Design and Analysis

The core contents of this monograph (Chapters 2 and 3) relate directly to design features (random assignment, local control, and counterbalancing schemes) intended to maximize the internal and the statistical conclusion validity of local causal inferences. In this chapter and in the introductory chapter, the complementarity between Campbell's "threats approach" to causal inference and Rubin's causal model was conveniently highlighted. While the first approach is more centered in design issues, the second one is more focused on the probabilistic nature of assignment mechanisms and the formal assumptions underlying the specification and estimation of statistical models; however, there is no remarkable divergence on the very nature of randomized experiments and their central role in causal inference. This can be noticed in a recently published special section of *Psychological Methods* (Vol. 15, No. 1), with the benefit of first-hand accounts (Cook & Steiner, 2010; Rubin, 2010; Shadish, 2010). As stated in the introduction to the special section (Maxwell, 2010) and documented in the main articles (see also Imbens, 2010; West & Thoemmes, 2010), the two approaches are more dissimilar, yet not irreconcilable, with respect to causal inference in nonrandomized experiments, but this is not the place to elaborate on quasi-experimentation (observational studies). To conclude this short note, we must restate the intrinsic relationship between the randomization method used in the error control design and the specification of statistical models and error terms in the data analysis stage.

4.2.4 Randomization and Statistical Control

When previously measured covariates are continuous variables, ANCOVA may be a consistent alternative to local control (blocking and stratifying) in randomized experiments. By definition, random assignment procedures ensure the statistical assumptions (e.g., noninteraction between the covariable and the experimental factor) underlying ANCOVA models. Please note that we are not talking about the use of ANCOVA to infer causality in nonexperimental designs or about the inclusion of single or multiple covariates in quasi-experimental designs (see, e.g., the contribution of Reichardt to Cook & Campbell, 1979), in which propensity score analysis and related techniques can do a better job. For the same reasons, we were reticent about minimization as an acceptable method of randomization (see Subsection 2.5.4), regardless of whether and how prognostic factors are used in the data analysis stage (for consistent alternatives, see Berger, 2005).

4.3 Reporting Randomized Experiments

Even though the modes of production and transmission of academic knowledge in contemporary societies could depart significantly from the idealized Merton's (1942/1973) scientific ethos—in which organized skepticism is tied with the normative values of universalism, communalism, and disinterestedness—and can probably be best described by the Campbellian tribal model of the scientific social system (Campbell 1979), transparent communication of research findings continues to be a highly prized standard, as it is documented in the activities of organizations such as *The Cochrane Collaboration* (www.cochrane.org/) in the area of health care or its counterpart *The Campbell Collaboration* (www.campbellcollaboration.org/) in the domains of education, crime and justice, and social welfare. Both organizations focus on producing and disseminating systematic reviews of scientific studies and therefore helping policymakers and people in general make well-informed decisions on the basis of the "best available research evidence." This is also the most important mission of the *American Evaluation Association* (www.eval.org/) in the areas of evaluation studies and social experimentation (for systematic reviews, see Cook & Shadish, 1994; Shadish & Cook, 2009).

In this context, randomized experiments play a central role, and the effort to promote clear and truthful communication of their methodological details and results gave rise to the publication of well-systematized reporting standards, such as the *CONSORT Statement* (*Consolidated Standards of Reporting Trials*; see Schulz, Altman, & Moher, 2010) in the health sciences, *The American Psychological Association Journal Article Reporting Standards* (*JARS*, 2008) in psychology, and the *Standards for Reporting on Empirical Social Science Research in AERA Publications* (American Educational

Research Association, 2006) in education. Boutron, John, and Torgerson (2010) have also extended these guidelines to the political and social sciences in a recently published article in the official journal of the *American Academy of Political and Social Science*. Of course, this is not entirely new, since more or less explicit guidelines for research reporting have always been present in institutional publications (e.g., Standard 13 of the *Code of Ethics and Policies and Procedures of the American Sociological Association*, 1999), editorial and substantive pieces in scientific journals (e.g., a seminal version of the *Publication Manual of the American Psychological Association* was published as an article inserted in the 1929 volume of the *Psychological Bulletin*), and reference books that gave substance to and organized the various disciplines.

With the exception of the diagram embedded in Figure 4.1 showing the flow of participants through the different stages of a randomized experiment, we are not reproducing here the extended tables and checklists inserted in the aforementioned reporting standards, but the reader is referred to the companion website of this monograph, where an organized list—with direct links to the primary documents—is available. Warning against the mechanical use of these tables, checklists, and flowcharts and the implicit reification of the methods behind them, we encourage researchers to carefully read the explanations and elaborations given by the original authors (e.g., Cooper, 2011; Moher et al., 2010). An interesting appraisal of the impact of the *Consort Statement*—whose initial version was published by Begg et al. (1996)—on the quality of reporting randomized experiments in the health sciences is given by Plint et al. (2006).

If we had to summarize the contents of the various "reporting standards" in a single paragraph, we would say that a scientific report (e.g., a journal article) of a randomized experiment must comply with three basic requirements: (1) to allow for an exact or a conceptual replication of the experiment; (2) to give the theoretical, the methodological, and the contextual information needed for a fair evaluation of the main results, claims, and practical implications of the study; and (3) to provide the summary statistics required for a reliable meta-analysis. Briefly stated, any competent researcher in the field should be able to replicate, evaluate, or include the experiment in a meta-analysis relying exclusively on the published contents (comprising precise bibliographic references for complementary technical details), without the need to contact the author(s) of the study. The conflict between comprehensiveness and availability of space in scientific journals (Cooper, 2011) could be easily reduced by the current practice of providing supplementary materials in the journals' websites.

To conclude, we should also say that the randomization and local control procedures described in this monograph, as well as the "standardized statistical procedures" applying to data analysis, are "instrumental" and not "terminal" values. They are just devices that "supply the machinery for unambiguous interpretation":

> A clear grasp of simple and standardised statistical procedures will, as the reader may satisfy himself, go far to elucidate the principles of experimentation; but these procedures are themselves only the means to a more important end. Their part is to satisfy the requirements of sound and intelligible experimental design, and to supply the *machinery for unambiguous interpretation* [italics added]. To attain a clear grasp of these requirements we need to study designs which have been widely successful in many fields, and to examine their structure in relation to the requirements of valid inference. (Fisher, 1935/1966, p. vii)

APPENDIX 1. RANDOM NUMBERS

Definition. In the strong sense, a random number is a number generated by a noncausal or stochastic mechanism. In the weak sense, a random number is a number whose generating mechanism is ignored and about which no reliable predictions can be made. Formally speaking, a random number is a number drawn at chance from a uniformly distributed population of numbers or, which is the same, a number from an interval where all possible numbers have the same probability of being drawn.

True and Pseudo-Random Numbers. *True random numbers* can be produced by any physical mechanism whose behavior is completely unpredictable, such as flipping a coin, rolling a die, drawing a card from a traditional playing deck, or drawing a numbered ball from a lottery machine. Providing that all possible events are independent events having the same probability of occurrence (i.e., the behavior of the physical mechanism can be fully described by a uniform probability distribution), there are hundreds of physical devices that could be used for generating true random numbers. In some scientific areas and technological contexts (e.g., cryptography), true random numbers can be generated on the basis of radioactive decay or atmospheric noise.

However, in most situations, true random numbers can be substituted for the so-called pseudo-random numbers without serious disadvantages. *Pseudo-random numbers* are generated by special computational algorithms (e.g., the linear congruent function) whose behavior is unpredictable within predefined *cycles* or *periods* (i.e., sequences without repetition of the same uniformly distributed random series). The more extensive these cycles are, the better the algorithm is. In addition, the *initial seed* or *starting point* can be randomly set on the basis of some physical mechanism, such as the computer internal clock (e.g., the program reads the current date and time from the system clock and expresses this value in seconds or even in milliseconds). One relatively recent and very efficient RNG is the Mersenne Twister algorithm (period $= 2^{19937} - 1$), devised by Matsumoto and Nishimura (1998) and incorporated in statistical software such as IBM SPSS, R, and SYSTAT (for a very brief and clear presentation of RNG, see Schrodt, 2004; for a comprehensive presentation, see Gentle, 2010; for an evaluation of RNG used in statistical software, see McCullough, 1998, 1999).

Tables of Random Numbers and Details of the Procedure Used Through the Monograph. A table of random numbers is an array of r rows and c columns containing $r \times c$ integers between 0 and 9. The probability of their occurrence in each of the rc cells is equal for all integers, which means that the "physical" mechanism used for the production of the table must obey the rules of a uniform probability distribution. As in Table A1.1, the rows and the columns are numbered only for users' convenience, and the spacing between sets of three columns is a simple matter of readability. In fact, Table A1.1 was obtained by requesting from RANDOM.ORG (www.random.org/integers/), a true random numbers provider, a series of 2,250 uniformly distributed random integers between 0 and 9. As RANDOM.ORG states, the randomness of these numbers comes from atmospheric noise. To fit the page dimensions, the obtained series was arranged in 50 rows and 45 columns.

For pedagogical reasons (see the Preface and the introductory paragraphs of Chapter 4), Table A1.1 has been used through this monograph as one of the basic randomization tools. To extract series of random numbers from Table A1.1, the following general rules have been adopted:

a. Read the table vertically (columns instead of rows or diagonals), from top to bottom and from left to right.

b. Select random numbers with three digits (digits occurring in the random selected column and in the two immediately adjacent columns; in case we arrive at the bottom of the table, the series continues in the next three columns at the top of the table; in case we come to the right side of the table, we must come back to the left one).

c. Divide these numbers by 1,000 to obtain random uniform series between .000 and .999.

d. Select randomly the starting point (digit in the rth row and cth column) by closing your eyes and picking a digit with the tip of a pencil.

In all the randomization examples, the series of random numbers (RN) extracted from Table A1.1 are conveniently identified. For instance, the reference "RN: Table A1.1 (Rows 27–46, Columns 13–15)" in Table 2.1 (Design 1: *Completely Randomized Design*) means that the randomly picked starting digit was number 6 in the intersection of Row 27 and Column 13. According to the adopted rules, the series, containing 20 random numbers, begins in .621 (Row 27, Columns 13–15) and ends in .143 (Row 46, Columns 13–15). This random series is used to obtain a randomly permuted

Table A1.1   Random Numbers

RC	1-3	4-6	7-9	10-12	13-15	16-18	19-21	22-24	25-27	28-30	31-33	34-36	37-39	40-42	43-45
1	450	587	446	424	639	335	518	736	573	283	979	053	034	876	961
2	980	644	218	034	981	288	307	822	754	736	105	783	149	894	013
3	414	101	674	186	494	244	078	005	485	326	666	529	668	207	364
4	744	951	067	393	254	288	538	781	187	594	565	155	509	960	069
5	730	336	204	281	982	758	607	183	076	395	027	582	569	065	138
6	666	486	328	408	974	560	760	929	396	976	075	877	470	361	227
7	853	816	678	133	715	316	288	721	369	081	052	846	510	201	094
8	355	072	133	307	153	723	149	234	514	939	240	073	039	585	628
9	296	381	210	857	149	563	762	474	056	175	261	774	559	822	341
10	668	447	484	697	274	517	520	258	116	203	742	545	878	632	150
11	622	788	820	399	351	505	959	223	284	420	119	153	930	408	682
12	688	796	739	353	239	388	097	099	545	518	615	398	561	540	718
13	782	893	207	590	670	662	534	522	097	471	827	034	323	260	739
14	643	885	000	514	737	467	951	353	247	232	178	336	174	655	872
15	361	178	396	326	188	378	929	387	358	726	568	408	262	277	926
16	755	153	278	171	220	686	587	102	880	566	773	999	374	570	337
17	888	159	762	552	881	900	592	013	986	325	797	520	320	971	148
18	463	982	732	802	129	226	953	125	000	596	180	315	372	732	393
19	406	517	671	031	937	700	929	381	655	509	507	586	303	343	318
20	580	934	770	541	518	343	839	667	723	257	042	625	376	721	069
21	058	120	455	806	484	419	256	130	312	123	544	944	566	334	928
22	776	494	666	715	032	844	506	867	528	365	668	834	144	831	105
23	214	522	425	700	517	629	884	900	182	811	282	944	502	361	378
24	150	245	532	814	879	693	856	749	639	567	130	336	325	455	466
25	860	280	912	507	102	199	565	878	609	011	729	732	948	379	244
26	479	072	311	457	197	800	628	602	502	372	166	658	040	422	655
27	309	766	042	499	621	195	538	271	485	758	448	761	163	551	502
28	860	014	490	659	388	298	783	002	239	314	075	033	411	946	850
29	582	221	520	822	546	390	578	385	789	174	212	563	884	719	755
30	546	877	963	857	205	146	798	545	305	618	906	481	251	414	814
31	975	773	401	840	641	971	111	500	049	256	483	091	911	923	633
32	014	243	679	319	616	194	421	550	704	273	932	555	455	664	424
33	115	801	761	627	721	718	590	389	958	087	374	567	960	352	681
34	466	710	233	463	048	613	256	972	638	383	704	852	398	894	300
35	794	059	269	499	973	910	666	802	552	502	483	472	707	042	861
36	556	062	467	156	833	476	296	144	487	731	385	806	497	273	786
37	936	067	019	132	469	796	445	428	360	748	689	224	096	084	307
38	825	361	837	131	334	410	591	435	372	677	010	787	266	543	210
39	440	857	063	893	245	320	432	824	814	804	158	028	373	733	084
40	068	011	968	583	852	758	033	523	738	406	433	106	605	197	901
41	294	282	248	778	494	239	196	099	939	177	942	111	336	274	497
42	023	792	160	391	764	866	521	146	324	901	251	290	077	001	458
43	996	411	136	421	199	974	788	846	036	322	690	327	013	796	108
44	082	470	462	937	037	864	142	024	252	747	628	069	908	829	572
45	580	859	676	066	911	795	036	980	852	388	696	702	669	403	329
46	089	837	888	515	143	478	122	064	439	879	405	193	500	201	962
47	309	356	890	939	282	389	129	994	320	439	268	472	121	661	916
48	444	059	922	061	147	162	979	651	436	186	816	124	609	240	347
49	231	613	553	361	720	901	764	736	166	233	614	280	207	495	134
50	336	182	014	458	882	897	321	720	514	691	472	208	614	146	217

list of the ID numbers of experimental units, which is associated, term by term, to the ordered list of treatment replications (see Table 2.2). When a random series includes two or more identical numbers and this has influence on the process of randomization (i.e., after sorting the series, the identical numbers correspond to different treatment replications), the ties can be undone by using the digits in the column(s) immediately on the right of the randomly selected columns.

For substantially large tables of random numbers, the reader can either download a table with a *million random digits* from RAND Corporation (www.rand.org/pubs/monograph_reports/MR1418.html) or access the online version (http://digital.library.adelaide.edu.au/dspace/bitstream/2440/10701/1/stat_tab.pdf) of the classic *Statistical Tables for Biological, Agricultural and Medical Research* (Fisher & Yates, 1963, pp. 134–139).

Alternative Procedures for Using Tables of Random Numbers. As long as the rules of utilization are unambiguous and specified in advance and the choice of the starting point is truly random, there are many alternative procedures for using tables of random numbers. One of these procedures, commonly adopted in research methods textbooks, consists in establishing a system of correspondence between random digits and experimental conditions that ensures equal probabilities of assignment. For instance, with two experimental conditions and using digits 0 through 9, experimental units are assigned to Condition 1 if 0, 1, 2, 3, or 4 occurs in the random series and to Condition 2 if the digit that occurs is 5, 6, 7, 8, or 9 (see Table A1.2 for this and other examples).

The procedure illustrated in Table A1.2 corresponds to our Method 1— *Simple Random Assignment With Equal Probabilities*. If the reader wants to have an equal number of subjects (n_s) per experimental condition (Method 3: *Simple Random Assignment With Forced Equal Sizes*), he or she can use the same series, discarding occurring digits when an experimental condition is filled up. Taking the same example with two experimental conditions and 24 experimental units, Condition 1 is completed with the assignment of Unit 18. Accordingly, the random digit 4 associated with Unit 19 is discarded, and Condition 2 is assigned to this unit, as well as to the remaining experimental units (see Table A1.2).

To carry out Method 2—*Simple Random Assignment With Unequal Probabilities*, the system of correspondence between random digits and experimental conditions must be consonant with differential probabilities. For example, if we want to accomplish with this procedure the randomization we have done in Table 2.2 (*Completely Randomized Design* with four treatment levels), the system of correspondence would be 0, 1, 2, or 3 → T1 ($p_1 = .40$); 4 or 5 → T2 ($p_2 = .20$); 6 or 7 → T3 ($p_3 = .20$); and 8 or 9 → T4 ($p_4 = .20$).

Table A1.2 Alternative Procedures for Using Tables of Random Numbers (RN): Method 1—Simple Random Assignment With Equal Probabilities

| | Number of Treatments | | | | | | | | |
	Two		Three		Four		Five		Six	
Correspondence between treatments and random digits	T1 = 0,1,2,3,4 T2 = 5,6,7,8,9		T1 = 1,2,3 T2 = 4,5,6 T3 = 7,8,9 θ		T1 = 1,2 T2 = 3,4 T3 = 5,6 T4 = 7,8 θ,9		T1 = 0,1 T2 = 2,3 T3 = 4,5 T4 = 6,7 T5 = 8,9		T1 = 1 T2 = 2 T3 = 3 T4 = 4 T5 = 5 T6 = 6 θ,7,8,9	

Random Series	ID	T	ID	T	ID	T	ID	T	ID	T
3	1	T1	1	T1	1	T2	1	T2	1	T3
0	2	T1	—	—	—	—	2	T1	—	—
4	3	T1	2	T2	2	T2	3	T3	2	T4
5	4	T2	3	T2	3	T3	4	T3	3	T5
9	5	T2	4	T3	—	—	5	T5	—	—
4	6	T1	5	T2	4	T2	6	T3	4	T4
6	7	T2	6	T2	5	T3	7	T4	5	T6
7	8	T2	7	T3	6	T4	8	T4	—	—
2	9	T1	8	T1	7	T1	9	T2	6	T2
2	10	T1	9	T1	8	T1	10	T2	7	T2
4	11	T1	10	T2	9	T2	11	T3	8	T4
0	12	T1	—	—	—	—	12	T1	—	—
8	13	T2	11	T3	10	T4	13	T5	—	—
0	14	T1	—	—	—	—	14	T1	—	—
9	15	T2	12	T3	—	—	15	T5	—	—
2	16	T1	13	T1	11	T1	16	T2	9	T2
1	17	T1	14	T1	12	T1	17	T1	10	T1
1	18	T1	15	T1	13	T1	18	T1	11	T1
4	19	T1	16	T2	14	T2	19	T3	12	T4
6	20	T2	17	T2	15	T3	20	T4	13	T6
8	21	T2	18	T3	16	T4	21	T5	—	—
8	22	T2	19	T3	17	T4	22	T5	—	—
9	23	T2	20	T3	—	—	23	T5	—	—
5	24	T2	21	T2	18	T3	24	T3	14	T5
[. . .]	[. . .]	[. . .]	[. . .]	[. . .]	[. . .]	[. . .]	[. . .]	[. . .]	[. . .]	[. . .]

RN: Table A1.1 (Rows 26–49; Column 7)

Finally, the implementation of Method 4—*Simple Random Assignment With Forced Unequal Sizes* is similar to the implementation of Method 3, with the understanding that the digits corresponding to the conditions are discarded when the prespecified different n_s are attained.

Another alternative procedure, commonly recommended in the health sciences literature (e.g., Fleiss, 1986; Pocock, 1983; Zelen, 1974), used for forced equal sizes sequential simple random assignment is the *random permuted "blocks"* strategy. In this procedure, random digits between 0 and 9 are used for assigning sequences of treatments to equal-size blocks (*randomization fractions*, in the terminology adopted in this monograph; see Subsection 2.5.1 for an alternative conceptualization of randomization fractions) of experimental units. For example, if we have two treatment levels (A and B) and blocks of two units, sequence AB is assigned to the units when the occurring random digit is 0, 1, 2, 3, or 4 and sequence BA is assigned when the digit is 5, 6, 7, 8, or 9 (see Table A1.3 for this and other examples).

With more than three treatments or with blocks of larger size, the random permuted blocks strategy illustrated in Table A1.3 is time-consuming and not very practical. In these situations, the adopted solution is to generate a random permutation of the first *n* integers (see Appendix 2) and to establish a system of correspondence between the randomly permuted integers and treatments. Suppose we have four treatment levels (A, B, C, and D) and blocks of 20 units. Adopting the system of correspondence 1–5 → A, 6–10 → B, 11–15 → C, and 16–20 → D and having drawn the random permutation of the first row, the random assignment for the first block of 20 units is shown in the second row:

18	17	4	15	9	8	19	2	20	5	10	6	3	16	14	7	12	13	1	11
D	D	A	C	B	B	D	A	D	A	B	B	A	D	C	B	C	C	A	C

Random permuted blocks strategy is also applied in sequential stratified random assignment to ensure an equal number of treatment replications within each stratum. The procedure is similar to our Method 12—*Sequential Stratified Random Assignment With Time Blocking* (see Subsection 2.5.3).

Table A1.3 Alternative Procedures for Using Tables of Random Numbers (RN): Random Permuted "Blocks" (analogous to Method 5—Sequential Simple Random Assignment With Forced Equal Sizes)

	Treatments		
	Two		**Three**
	Units per *block* = 2	Units per *block* = 4	Units per *block* = 3
Correspondence between sequence of treatments and random digits	0, 1, 2, 3, 4 → AB 5, 6, 7, 8, 9 → BA	1 → AABB 2 → ABAB 3 → ABBA 4 → BBAA 5 → BABA 6 → BAAB 0̶, 7̶, 8̶, 9̶	1 → ABC 2 → ACB 3 → BAC 4 → BCA 5 → CAB 6 → CBA 0̶, 7̶, 8̶, 9̶

Random Permuted Blocks

RN	Block	ID	T	RN	Block	ID	T	RN	Block	ID	T
5	1	1	B	5	1	1	B		1	1	C
	1	2	A		1	2	A	6	1	2	B
0	2	1	A		1	3	B		1	3	A
	2	2	B		1	4	A	9	—	—	—
2	3	1	A	3	2	1	A		2	1	B
	3	2	B		2	2	B	4	2	2	C
3	4	1	A		2	3	B		2	3	A
	4	2	B		2	4	A	7	—	—	—
8	5	1	B	9	—	—	—		3	1	B
	5	2	A	4	3	1	B	4	3	2	C
9	6	1	B		3	2	B		3	3	A
	6	2	A		3	3	A		4	1	B
0	7	1	A		3	4	A	3	4	2	A
	7	2	B	1	4	1	A		4	3	C
6	8	1	B		4	2	A	7	—	—	—
	8	2	A		4	3	B		5	1	A
7	9	1	B		4	4	B	2	5	2	C
	9	2	A	9	—	—	—		5	3	B
	[. . .]				[. . .]				[. . .]		

RN (Two Treatments / Two Units per Block): Table A1.1 (Rows 12–20; Column 25)

RN (Two Treatments / Four Units per Block): Table A1.1 (Rows 7–12; Column 15)

RN (Three Treatments / Three Units per Block): Table A1.1 (Rows 34–41; Column 16)

APPENDIX 2. PERMUTATIONS, ARRANGEMENTS, AND COMBINATIONS

Permutations. A *permutation* of *n* distinct elements is an ordered arrangement of these elements. For example, the permutation {2, 3, 1} of the first *three* integers is different from the permutation {1, 3, 2}. The number of different permutations of *n* elements is given by the following formula:

$$P_n = n! = n(n-1)(n-2)(n-3)(\cdots)1,$$

where *n* is any integer equal to or greater than 1; by convention, 0! = 1.

For instance, with the first *three* integers, we have six different permutations:

$$[P_3 = 3! = (3)(2)(1) = 6]: \{1, 2, 3\}, \{1, 3, 2\}, \{2, 1, 3\}, \{2, 3, 1\},$$
$$\{3, 1, 2\}, \text{ and } \{3, 2, 1\}$$

In Table A2.1, all the permutations of two, three, four, and five elements (e.g., experimental conditions) are listed. These permutations are used for *nonrestricted sequential counterbalancing* (Method 16, Design 6E; see Tables 3.3 and 3.4) in within-subjects designs randomization (see Subsection 3.5.1).

A *random permutation* of *n* elements is a random selected arrangement of these elements from the population of all possible arrangements. One can easily select a random permutation by using tables of random numbers. If we want a random permutation of the first *six* integers, we pick a starting point randomly in Table A1.1 and read the table in accordance with the previous specified rules (see Appendix 1). For example, if we pick at random number 7 in the intersection of Row 2 and Column 25 of Table A1.1, we get the random series 7, 4, 1, 0, 3, 3, 5, 0, 1, 2, 5, 0, 2, 3, 8, 9, 0, and 6 (Rows 2–19; Column 25). Omitting zeros and integers greater than 6 and ignoring all repetitions, the intended random permutation is {4, 1, 3, 5, 2, 6}. This procedure is used through the monograph to obtain random permutations of rows, columns, and symbols of Latin squares (see Subsection 2.3.4 and Sections 3.3 and 3.4) or to obtain random permutations for the *last replication correction* in

Table A2.1 Permutations of Two, Three, Four, and Five Treatments (A, B, C, D, and E)

Two	Three	Four			
[1] AB	[1] ABC	[1] ABCD	[7] BACD	[13] CABD	[19] DABC
[2] BA	[2] ACB	[2] ABDC	[8] BADC	[14] CADB	[20] DACB
	[3] BAC	[3] ACBD	[9] BCAD	[15] CBAD	[21] DBAC
	[4] BCA	[4] ACDB	[10] BCDA	[16] CBDA	[22] DBCA
	[5] CAB	[5] ADBC	[11] BDAC	[17] CDAB	[23] DCAB
	[6] CBA	[6] ADCB	[12] BDCA	[18] CDBA	[24] DCBA

Five

[1] ABCDE	[21] AECBD	[41] BDEAC	[61] CDABE	[81] DBCAE	[101] EADBC
[2] ABCED	[22] AECDB	[42] BDECA	[62] CDAEB	[82] DBCEA	[102] EADCB
[3] ABDCE	[23] AEDBC	[43] BEACD	[63] CDBAE	[83] DBEAC	[103] EBACD
[4] ABDEC	[24] AEDCB	[44] BEADC	[64] CDBEA	[84] DBECA	[104] EBADC
[5] ABECD	[25] BACDE	[45] BECAD	[65] CDEAB	[85] DCABE	[105] EBCAD
[6] ABEDC	[26] BACED	[46] BECDA	[66] CDEBA	[86] DCAEB	[106] EBCDA
[7] ACBDE	[27] BADCE	[47] BEDAC	[67] CEABD	[87] DCBAE	[107] EBDAC
[8] ACBED	[28] BADEC	[48] BEDCA	[68] CEADB	[88] DCBEA	[108] EBDCA
[9] ACDBE	[29] BAECD	[49] CABDE	[69] CEBAD	[89] DCEAB	[109] ECABD
[10] ACDEB	[30] BAEDC	[50] CABED	[70] CEBDA	[90] DCEBA	[110] ECADB
[11] ACEBD	[31] BCADE	[51] CADBE	[71] CEDAB	[91] DEABC	[111] ECBAD
[12] ACEDB	[32] BCAED	[52] CADEB	[72] CEDBA	[92] DEACB	[112] ECBDA
[13] ADBCE	[33] BCDAE	[53] CAEBD	[73] DABCE	[93] DEBAC	[113] ECDAB
[14] ADBEC	[34] BCDEA	[54] CAEDB	[74] DABEC	[94] DEBCA	[114] ECDBA
[15] ADCBE	[35] BCEAD	[55] CBADE	[75] DACBE	[95] DECAB	[115] EDABC
[16] ADCEB	[36] BCEDA	[56] CBAED	[76] DACEB	[96] DECBA	[116] EDACB
[17] ADEBC	[37] BDACE	[57] CBDAE	[77] DAEBC	[97] EABCD	[117] EDBAC
[18] ADECB	[38] BDAEC	[58] CBDEA	[78] DAECB	[98] EABDC	[118] EDBCA
[19] AEBCD	[39] BDCAE	[59] CBEAD	[79] DBACE	[99] EACBD	[119] EDCAB
[20] AEBDC	[40] BDCEA	[60] CBEDA	[80] DBAEC	[100] EACDB	[120] EDCBA

nonsequential simple and stratified random assignment (see Subsection 2.2.1 and Section 2.4).

If we want a random permutation of 12 integers, we use two columns instead of one column and ignore zeros and all integers between 13 and 99. This is a tedious, error-prone task. A wiser procedure consists in listing sequentially the first 12 integers, selecting a random series of three-digit numbers between .000 and .999, and using this series to randomly sort the ordered list of integers. In practice, this is the procedure we have used throughout this book to randomly permute the ID numbers, in nonsequential assignment, or the sequence of treatment replications, in sequential assignment.

Arrangements and Combinations. An *arrangement* of n elements, k by k, is a special case of permutations where the k elements are a subset of the entire set. For example, $\{1, 3\}$, $\{3, 1\}$, $\{3, 2\}$, and $\{2, 3\}$ are different arrangements of first *three* integers. *Combinations* of n elements, k by k, are unordered arrangements of k elements, that is, arrangements where the order of the elements is negligible: $\{1, 3\}$ is not distinct from $\{3, 1\}$.

With arrangements and combinations, it is possible to have repeated elements. For instance, $\{1, 1\}$, $\{4, 1\}$, $\{1, 4\}$, and $\{2, 2\}$ are four possible *two-by-two* arrangements with repetition of the first *four* integers. In the same way, $\{1, 1\}$, $\{1, 4\}$, and $\{2, 2\}$ are three possible combinations with repetition. Arrangements and combinations with repetitions are named *complete arrangements* and *complete combinations* and are contrasted with *simple arrangements* and *simple combinations*, respectively. In Table A2.2, we give the formulas and an example of simple and complete arrangements and combinations of *four* elements, *two-by-two*.

Simple combinations are useful in incomplete block designs to determine the pattern of treatment combinations in each block (see Subsection 2.3.3). In the special case of $k = 2$ (see footnotes in Table A2.2), the formulas for combinations allow us to rapidly determine the number of *informative entries* in correlation and variance–covariance matrixes. For example, the correlation matrix of 10 variables has 45 off-diagonal correlations: $[(10)(9)]/2 = 45$ (simple combinations); the variance–covariance matrix of 10 variables has 45 off-diagonal covariances plus 10 variances in the diagonal: $[(10)(9)]/2 + 10 = 45 + 10 = 55$ (complete combinations).

The formula for complete arrangements is used when one attempts to determine the number of different samples of size n one can draw (with reposition) from a population of size N. On the other hand, the formula for simple arrangements gives this number for sampling without repositioning.

The relationship between permutations, simple arrangements, and simple combinations is given by the following formula:

$$C_k^n = \frac{A_k^n}{P_k}$$

$$C_2^4 = \frac{A_2^4}{P_2} = \frac{12}{2} = 6.$$

Table A2.2 Arrangements and Combinations

Ordered		Nonordered	
Without Repetition	With Repetition	Without Repetition	With Repetition
Simple Arrangements	*Complete Arrangements*	*Simple Combinations*[a]	*Complete Combinations*[b]
$A_k^n = \dfrac{n!}{(n-k)!}$	$A\,'^n_k = n^k$	$C_k^n = \dfrac{n!}{k!(n-k)!}$	$C\,'^n_k = \dfrac{(n+k-1)!}{(n-1)!k!}$
$A_2^4 = \dfrac{4!}{(4-2)!} = 12$	$A\,'^4_2 = 4^2 = 16$	$C_2^4 = \dfrac{4!}{2!(4-2)!} = 6$	$C\,'^4_2 = \dfrac{(4+2-1)!}{(4-1)!2!} = 10$
1, 2 3, 1	1, 1 3, 1	1, 2	1, 1 2, 3
1, 3 3, 2	1, 2 3, 2	1, 3	1, 2 2, 4
1, 4 3, 4	1, 3 3, 3	1, 4	1, 3 3, 3
2, 1 4, 1	1, 4 3, 4	2, 3	1, 4 3, 4
2, 3 4, 2	2, 1 4, 1	2, 4	2, 2 4, 4
2, 4 4, 3	2, 2 4, 2	3, 4	
	2, 3 4, 3		
	2, 4 4, 4		

[a] $C_k^n = C_{n-k}^n$. For instance, $C_2^5 = C_{5-2}^5 = C_3^5$. When $k = 2$, the formula simplifies to: $C_2^n = \dfrac{n(n-1)}{2}$. In the example, $C_2^4 = \dfrac{4(3)}{2} = 6$.

[b] When $k = 2$, the formula simplifies to $C_2^n = \dfrac{n(n-1)}{2} + n$. In the example, $C_2^4 = \dfrac{4(3)}{2} + 4 = 10$.

In the companion website of this monograph, under the link "Probabilities and Random Assignment Mechanisms" we use extensively the combinatorial formulas given above in the context of a fully worked example of probabilities of assignment and procedures for counting the number of possible assignments allowed by simple random assignment methods (Methods 1–4; see Subsection 2.2.1).

APPENDIX 3. LATIN SQUARES

A *Latin square* is an arrangement of n letters (A, B, C, . . .) in n rows and n columns so that each letter appears once in each row and once in each column. The designation comes from an ancient Roman puzzle whose aim was the determination of all possible arrangements of the first n letters in an $(n \times n)$-sided square. In addition to this recreational purpose, Latin squares have been used in many scientific and technological contexts, namely in cryptographic applications and experimental design.

A Latin square is said to be in its *standard form* (also called *reduced* or *normalized* form) when the letters in the first row and in the first column are alphabetically ordered. The number of different standard squares, $L(n, n)$, with *sides* (or *orders*) ranging from $n = 2$ to $n = 12$ are as follows:

n	$L(n, n)$
2	1
3	1
4	4
5	56
6	9408
7	16942080
8	535281401856
9	377597570964258816
10	7580721483160132811489280
11	5363937773277371298119673540771840
12	$\approx 1.62 \times 10^{44}$

Permuting the n columns and the last $n - 1$ rows of a standard Latin square gives rise to $n!(n - 1)!$ different Latin squares. So for a given order, the total number of Latin squares is obtained through the following formula: $N(n, n) = L(n, n)n!(n - 1)!$. For two-, three-, four-, five-, and six-sided Latin squares, $N(n, n)$ is 2, 12, 576, 161280, and 812851200, respectively (for the enumeration of Latin squares, see McKay & Rogoyski, 1995; McKay & Wanless, 2005).

Table A3.1 shows all standard Latin squares for orders 2 to 4 and one square from all possible standard Latin squares for orders 5 and higher. To randomly select a Latin square, the reader can adopt the common procedures recommended in the experimental design literature (e.g., Cochran & Cox, 1957, p. 121; Federer, 1955, pp. 140–142; Fisher & Yates, 1963, pp. 22–23, 86–88):

- *Order 2:* random permutation of the columns (or the rows) of the standard square
- *Order 3:* random permutation of the three columns and the last two rows of the standard square
- *Order 4:* random selection of one of the four standard squares and random permutation of the four columns and the last three rows of the selected square
- *Orders 5 and higher:* starting with the standard square given in Table A3.1 and randomly and independently permuting the order of the rows, the order of the columns, and the name of the letters (see illustration in Figure 2.2)

For orders 2 to 4, these procedures randomly select one square from all possible squares; for 5 and higher orders, one square is randomly selected from a sufficiently large subset of squares (if the reader uses SCRAED, he or she can also obtain one square from all possible squares of orders 5 and 6).

This appendix also includes tables of Graeco-Latin squares (Table A3.2), complete sets of mutually orthogonal Latin squares (Tables A3.3 and A3.4), and balanced Williams's squares (Table A3.5). The main properties of these squares and their use in experimental design are fully explained in Chapters 2 and 3. For complementary explanations and details, see the information under the link "Other Supplementary Materials/Latin Squares" in the companion website of this monograph.

Table A3.1   Selected Standard Latin Squares

2 × 2	3 × 3		4 × 4			
		1	**2**	**3**	**4**	
A B	A B C	A B C D	A B C D	A B C D	A B C D	
B A	B C A	B A D C	B C D A	B D A C	B A D C	
	C A B	C D B A	C D A B	C A D B	C D A B	
		D C A B	D A B C	D C B A	D C B A	

5 × 5	6 × 6	7 × 7	8 × 8
A B C D E	A B C D E F	A B C D E F G	A B C D E F G H
B A E C D	B F D C A E	B C D E F G A	B C D E F G H A
C D A E B	C D E F B A	C D E F G A B	C D E F G H A B
D E B A C	D A F E C B	D E F G A B C	D E F G H A B C
E C D B A	E C A B F D	E F G A B C D	E F G H A B C D
	F E B A D C	F G A B C D E	F G H A B C D E
		G A B C D E F	G H A B C D E F
			H A B C D E F G

9 × 9	10 × 10
A B C D E F G H I	A B C D E F G H I J
B C D E F G H I A	B C D E F G H I J A
C D E F G H I A B	C D E F G H I J A B
D E F G H I A B C	D E F G H I J A B C
E F G H I A B C D	E F G H I J A B C D
F G H I A B C D E	F G H I J A B C D E
G H I A B C D E F	G H I J A B C D E F
H I A B C D E F G	H I J A B C D E F G
I A B C D E F G H	I J A B C D E F G H
	J A B C D E F G H I

11 × 11	12 × 12
A B C D E F G H I J K	A B C D E F G H I J K L
B C D E F G H I J K A	B C D E F G H I J K L A
C D E F G H I J K A B	C D E F G H I J K L A B
D E F G H I J K A B C	D E F G H I J K L A B C
E F G H I J K A B C D	E F G H I J K L A B C D
F G H I J K A B C D E	F G H I J K L A B C D E
G H I J K A B C D E F	G H I J K L A B C D E F
H I J K A B C D E F G	H I J K L A B C D E F G
I J K A B C D E F G H	I J K L A B C D E F G H
J K A B C D E F G H I	J K L A B C D E F G H I
K A B C D E F G H I J	K L A B C D E F G H I J
	L A B C D E F G H I J K

Source. Cochran & Cox, 1957, pp. 145–146.

154

Table A3.2 Graeco-Latin Squares

3 × 3

A_1 B_3 C_2
B_2 C_1 A_3
C_3 A_2 B_1

4 × 4

A_1 B_3 C_4 D_2
B_2 A_4 D_3 C_1
C_3 D_1 A_2 B_4
D_4 C_2 B_1 A_3

5 × 5

A_1 B_3 C_5 D_2 E_4
B_2 C_4 D_1 E_3 A_5
C_3 D_5 E_2 A_4 B_1
D_4 E_1 A_3 B_5 C_2
E_5 A_2 B_4 C_1 D_3

7 × 7

A_1 B_5 C_2 D_6 E_3 F_7 G_4
B_2 C_6 D_3 E_7 F_4 G_1 A_5
C_3 D_7 E_4 F_1 G_5 A_2 B_6
D_4 E_1 F_5 G_2 A_6 B_3 C_7
E_5 F_2 G_6 A_3 B_7 C_4 D_1
F_6 G_3 A_7 B_4 C_1 D_5 E_2
G_7 A_4 B_1 C_5 D_2 E_6 F_3

8 × 8

A_1 B_5 C_2 D_3 E_7 F_4 G_8 H_6
B_2 A_8 G_1 F_7 H_3 D_6 C_5 E_4
C_3 G_4 A_7 E_1 D_2 H_5 B_6 F_8
D_4 F_3 E_6 A_5 C_8 B_1 H_7 G_2
E_5 H_1 D_8 C_4 A_6 G_3 F_2 B_7
F_6 D_7 H_4 B_8 G_5 A_2 E_3 C_1
G_7 C_6 B_3 H_2 F_1 E_8 A_4 D_5
H_8 E_2 F_5 G_6 B_4 C_7 D_1 A_3

9 × 9

A_1 B_3 C_2 D_7 E_9 F_8 G_4 H_6 I_5
B_2 C_1 A_3 E_8 F_7 D_9 H_5 I_4 G_6
C_3 A_2 B_1 F_9 D_8 E_7 I_6 G_5 H_4
D_4 E_6 F_5 G_1 H_3 I_2 A_7 B_9 C_8
E_5 F_4 D_6 H_2 I_1 G_3 B_8 C_7 A_9
F_6 D_5 E_4 I_3 G_2 H_1 C_9 A_8 B_7
G_7 H_9 I_8 A_4 B_6 C_5 D_1 E_3 F_2
H_8 I_7 G_9 B_5 C_4 A_6 E_2 F_1 D_3
I_9 G_8 H_7 C_6 A_5 B_4 F_3 D_2 E_1

11 × 11

A_1 B_7 C_2 D_8 E_3 F_9 G_4 H_{10} I_5 J_{11} K_6
B_2 C_8 D_3 E_9 F_4 G_{10} H_5 I_{11} J_6 K_1 A_7
C_3 D_9 E_4 F_{10} G_5 H_{11} I_6 J_1 K_7 A_2 B_8
D_4 E_{10} F_5 G_{11} H_6 I_1 J_7 K_2 A_8 B_3 C_9
E_5 F_{11} G_6 H_1 I_7 J_2 K_8 A_3 B_9 C_4 D_{10}
F_6 G_1 H_7 I_2 J_8 K_3 A_9 B_4 C_{10} D_5 E_{11}
G_7 H_2 I_8 J_3 K_9 A_4 B_{10} C_5 D_{11} E_6 F_1
H_8 I_3 J_9 K_4 A_{10} B_5 C_{11} D_6 E_1 F_7 G_2
I_9 J_4 K_{10} A_5 B_{11} C_6 D_1 E_7 F_2 G_8 H_3
J_{10} K_5 A_{11} B_6 C_1 D_7 E_2 F_8 G_3 H_9 I_4
K_{11} A_6 B_1 C_7 D_2 E_8 F_3 G_9 H_4 I_{10} J_5

12 × 12

A_1 B_{12} C_6 D_7 I_5 J_4 K_{10} L_{11} E_9 F_8 G_2 H_3
B_2 A_{11} D_5 C_8 J_6 I_3 L_9 K_{12} F_{10} E_7 H_1 G_4
C_3 D_{10} A_8 B_5 K_7 L_2 I_{12} J_9 G_{11} H_6 E_4 F_1
D_4 C_9 B_7 A_6 L_8 K_1 J_{11} I_{10} H_{12} G_5 F_3 E_2
E_5 F_4 G_{10} H_{11} A_9 B_8 C_2 D_3 I_1 J_{12} K_6 L_7
F_6 E_3 H_9 G_{12} B_{10} A_7 D_1 C_4 J_2 I_{11} L_5 K_8
G_7 H_2 E_{12} F_9 C_{11} D_6 A_4 B_1 K_3 L_{10} I_8 J_5
H_8 G_1 F_{11} E_{10} D_{12} C_5 B_3 A_2 L_4 K_9 J_7 I_6
I_9 J_8 K_2 L_3 E_1 F_{12} G_6 H_7 A_5 B_4 C_{10} D_{11}
J_{10} I_7 L_1 K_4 F_2 E_{11} H_5 G_8 B_6 A_3 D_9 C_{12}
K_{11} L_6 I_4 J_1 G_3 H_{10} E_8 F_5 C_7 D_2 A_{12} B_9
L_{12} K_5 J_3 I_2 H_4 G_9 F_7 E_6 D_8 C_1 B_{11} A_{10}

10 × 10

A_1 B_7 C_5 D_8 E_2 F_4 G_6 H_9 I_{10} J_3
B_2 J_9 F_3 A_4 H_{10} C_6 I_5 D_1 E_7 G_8
C_3 E_4 J_6 F_9 A_7 G_5 D_{10} I_8 H_2 B_1
D_4 F_5 I_7 G_2 J_8 H_1 E_9 A_6 B_3 C_{10}
E_5 G_1 A_8 H_3 I_6 B_{10} F_2 J_7 C_4 D_9
F_6 C_8 B_9 E_{10} D_5 I_3 H_7 G_4 J_1 A_2
G_7 D_3 H_4 I_1 C_9 J_2 B_8 F_{10} A_5 E_6
H_8 I_2 G_{10} J_5 B_4 A_9 C_1 E_3 D_6 F_7
I_9 A_{10} E_1 B_6 G_3 D_7 J_4 C_2 F_8 H_5
J_{10} H_6 D_2 C_7 F_1 E_8 A_3 B_5 G_9 I_4

Note. With the exception of the 10×10 Graeco-Latin square, all the squares were taken from Cochran & Cox (1957, pp. 146–147). There are no 2×2 and 6×6 Graeco-Latin squares.

Table A3.3   Sets of Mutually Orthogonal Latin Squares (MOLS): Standard Forms of Three-, Four-, Five-, and Eight-Sided Squares

3 × 3		4 × 4			5 × 5			
[1]	[2]	[1]	[2]	[3]	[1]	[2]	[3]	[4]
ABC	ACB	ABCD	ACDB	ADBC	ABCDE	ACEBD	ADBEC	AEDCB
BCA	BAC	BADC	BDCA	BCAD	BCDEA	BDACE	BECAD	BAEDC
CAB	CBA	CDAB	CABD	CBDA	CDEAB	CEBDA	CADBE	CBAED
		DCBA	DBAC	DACB	DEABC	DACEB	DBECA	DCBAE
					EABCD	EBDAC	ECADB	EDCBA

7 × 7					
[1]	[2]	[3]	[4]	[5]	[6]
ABCDEFG	ACEGBDF	ADGCFBE	AEBFCGD	AFDBGEC	AGFEDCB
BCDEFGA	BDFACEG	BEADGCF	BFCGDAE	BGECAFD	BAGFEDC
CDEFGAB	CEGBDFA	CFBEADG	CGDAEBF	CAFDBGE	CBAGFED
DEFGABC	DFACEGB	DGCFBEA	DAEBFCG	DBGECAF	DCBAGFE
EFGABCD	EGBDFAC	EADGCFB	EBFCGDA	ECAFDBG	EDCBAGF
FGABCDE	FACEGBD	FBEADGC	FCGDAEB	FDBGECA	FEDCBAG
GABCDEF	GBDFACE	GCFBEAD	GDAEBFC	GECAFDB	GFEDCBA

8 × 8						
[1]	[2]	[3]	[4]	[5]	[6]	[7]
ABCDEFGH	ACEGDBHF	ADGFHEBC	AEDHGCFB	AFBECHDG	AGHBFDCE	AHFCBGED
BADCFEHG	BDFHCAGE	BCHEGFAD	BFCGHDEA	BEAFDGCH	BHGAECDF	BGEDAHFC
CDABGHEF	CAGEBDFH	CBEHFGDA	CGBFEAHD	CHDGAFBE	CEFDHBAG	CFHADEGB
DCBAHGFE	DBHFACEG	DAFGEHCB	DHAEFBGC	DGCHBEAF	DFECGABH	DEGBCFHA
EFGHABCD	EGACHFDB	EHCBDAFG	EAHDCGBF	EBFAGDHC	ECDFBHGA	EDBGFCAH
FEHGBADC	FHBDGECA	FGDACBEH	FBGCDHAE	FAEBHCGD	FDCEAGHB	FCAHEDBG
GHEFCDAB	GECAFHBD	GFADBCHE	GCFBAEDH	GDHCEBFA	GABHDFEC	GBDEHACF
HGFEDCBA	HFDBEGAC	HEBCADGF	HDEABFCG	HCGDFAEB	HBAGCEFD	HACFGBDE

Table A3.4   Sets of Mutually Orthogonal Latin Squares (MOLS): Standard Forms of 9- and 11-Sided Squares

9 × 9			
[1]	[2]	[3]	[4]
ABCDEFGHI	ACBGIHDFE	ADGHBEFIC	AEIBFGCDH
BCAEFDHIG	BACHGIEDF	BEHICFDGA	BFGCDHAEI
CABFDEIGH	CBAIHGFED	CFIGADEHB	CDHAEIBFG
DEFGHIABC	DFEACBGIH	DGABEHICF	DHCEIAFGB
EFDHIGBCA	EDFBACHGI	EHBCFIGAD	EIAFGBDHC
FDEIGHCAB	FEDCBAIHG	FICADGHBE	FGBDHCEIA
GHIABCDEF	GIHDFEACB	GADEHBCFI	GBFHCDIAE
HIGBCAEFD	HGIEDFBAC	HBEFICADG	HCDIAEGBF
IGHCABFDE	IHGFEDCBA	ICFDGABEH	IAEGBFHCD

(Continued)

Table A3.4 (Continued)

[5]	[6]	[7]	[8]
AFHEGCIBD	AGDFCIHEB	AHFIDBECG	AIECHDBGF
BDIFHAGCE	BHEDAGIFC	BIDGECFAH	BGFAIECHD
CEGDIBHAF	CIFEBHGDA	CGEHFADBI	CHDBGFAIE
DIBHAFCEG	DAGIFCBHE	DBICGEHFA	DCHFBGEAI
EGCIBDAFH	EBHGDACIF	ECGAHFIDB	EAIDCHFBG
FHAGCEBDI	FCIHEBAGD	FAHBIDGEC	FBGEAIDCH
GCEBDIFHA	GDACIFEBH	GECFAHBID	GFBIEAHDC
HAFCEGDIB	HEBAGDFCI	HFADBICGE	HDCGFBIEA
IBDAFHEGC	IFCBHEDAG	IDBECGAHF	IEAHDCGFB

$$11 \times 11$$

[1]	[2]	[3]	[4]	[5]
ABCDEFGHIJK	ACEGIKBDFHJ	ADGJBEHKCFI	AEIBFJCGKDH	AFKEJDICHBG
BCDEFGHIJKA	BDFHJACEGIK	BEHKCFIADGJ	BFJCGKDHAEI	BGAFKEJDICH
CDEFGHIJKAB	CEGIKBDFHJA	CFIADGJBEHK	CGKDHAEIBFJ	CHBGAFKEJDI
DEFGHIJKABC	DFHJACEGIKB	DGJBEHKCFIA	DHAEIBFJCGK	DICHBGAFKEJ
EFGHIJKABCD	EGIKBDFHJAC	EHKCFIADGJB	EIBFJCGKDHA	EJDICHBGAFK
FGHIJKABCDE	FHJACEGIKBD	FIADGJBEHKC	FJCGKDHAEIB	FKEJDICHBGA
GHIJKABCDEF	GIKBDFHJACE	GJBEHKCFIAD	GKDHAEIBFJC	GAFKEJDICHB
HIJKABCDEFG	HJACEGIKBDF	HKCFIADGJBE	HAEIBFJCGKD	HBGAFKEJDIC
IJKABCDEFGH	IKBDFHJACEG	IADGJBEHKCF	IBFJCGKDHAE	ICHBGAFKEJD
JKABCDEFGHI	JACEGIKBDFH	JBEHKCFIADG	JCGKDHAEIBF	JDICHBGAFKE
KABCDEFGHIJ	KBDFHJACEGI	KCFIADGJBEH	KDHAEIBFJCG	KEJDICHBGAF

[6]	[7]	[8]	[9]	[10]
AGBHCIDJEKF	AHDKGCJFBIE	AIFCKHEBJGD	AJHFDBKIGEC	AKJIHGFEDCB
BHCIDJEKFAG	BIEAHDKGCJF	BJGDAIFCKHE	BKIGECAJHFD	BAKJIHGFEDC
CIDJEKFAGBH	CJFBIEAHDKG	CKHEBJGDAIF	CAJHFDBKIGE	CBAKJIHGFED
DJEKFAGBHCI	DKGCJFBIEAH	DAIFCKHEBJG	DBKIGECAJHF	DCBAKJIHGFE
EKFAGBHCIDJ	EAHDKGCJFBI	EBJGDAIFCKH	ECAJHFDBKIG	EDCBAKJIHGF
FAGBHCIDJEK	FBIEAHDKGCJ	FCKHEBJGDAI	FDBKIGECAJH	FEDCBAKJIHG
GBHCIDJEKFA	GCJFBIEAHDK	GDAIFCKHEBJ	GECAJHFDBKI	GFEDCBAKJIH
HCIDJEKFAGB	HDKGCJFBIEA	HEBJGDAIFCK	HFDBKIGECAJ	HGFEDCBAKJI
IDJEKFAGBHC	IEAHDKGCJFB	IFCKHEBJGDA	IGECAJHFDBK	IHGFEDCBAKJ
JEKFAGBHCID	JFBIEAHDKGC	JGDAIFCKHEB	JHFDBKIGECA	JIHGFEDCBAK
KFAGBHCIDJE	KGCJFBIEAHD	KHEBJGDAIFC	KIGECAJHFDB	KJIHGFEDCBA

Table A3.5 Williams's Designs: Standard Forms of Balanced Latin Squares (2 × 2 to 12 × 12) for the First-Order Carryover Effects in Cross-Over Designs

Even-sided squares Single carryover designs		Odd-sided squares Double carryover designs		
2 × 2	**10 × 10**	**3 × 3**	**5 × 5**	**11 × 11**
AB	ABCDEFGHIJ	ABC	ABCDE	ABCDEFGHIJK
BA	BDAFCHEJGI	BCA	BDAEC	BDAFCHEJGKI
4 × 4	CAEBGDIFJH	CAB	CAEBD	CAEBGDIFKHJ
ABCD	DFBHAJCIEG	ACB	DEBCA	DFBHAJCKEIG
BDAC	ECGAIBJDHF	BAC	ECDAB	ECGAIBKDJFH
CADB	FHDJBIAGCE	CBA	ACBED	FHDJBKAICGE
DCBA	GEICJAHBFD	**9 × 9**	BADCE	GEICKAJBHDF
6 × 6	HJFIDGBEAC	ABCDEFGHI	CEADB	HJFKDIBGAEC
ABCDEF	IGJEHCFADB	BDAFCHEIG	DBEAC	IGKEJCHAFBD
BDAFCE	JIHGFEDCBA	CAEBGDIFH	EDCBA	JKHIFGDEBCA
CAEBFD	**12 × 12**	DFBHAICGE	**7 × 7**	KIJGHEFCDAB
DFBEAC	ABCDEFGHIJKL	ECGAIBHDF	ABCDEFG	ACBEDGFIHKJ
ECFADB	BDAFCHEJGLIK	FHDIBGAEC	BDAFCGE	BADCFEHGJIK
FEDCBA	CAEBGDIFKHLJ	GEICHAFBD	CAEBGDF	CEAGBIDKFJH
8 × 8	DFBHAJCLEKGI	HIFGDEBCA	DFBGAEC	DBFAHCJEKGI
ABCDEFGH	ECGAIBKDLFJH	IGHEFCDAB	ECGAFBD	EGCIAKBJDHF
BDAFCHEG	FHDJBLAKCIEG	ACBEDGFIH	FGDEBCA	FDHBJAKCIEG
CAEBGDHF	GEICKALBJDHF	BADCFEHGI	GEFCDAB	GIEKCJAHBFD
DFBHAGCE	HJFLDKBIAGCE	CEAGBIDHF	ACBEDGF	HFJDKBIAGCE
ECGAHBFD	IGKELCJAHBFD	DBFAHCIEG	BADCFEG	IKGJEHCFADB
FHDGBEAC	JLHKFIDGBEAC	EGCIAHBFD	CEAGBFD	JHKFIDGBEAC
GEHCFADB	KILGJEHCFADB	FDHBIAGCE	DBFAGCE	KJIHGFEDCBA
HGFEDCBA	LKJIHGFEDCBA	GIEHCFADB	EGCFADB	
		HFIDGBEAC	FDGBEAC	
		IHGFEDCBA	GFEDCBA	

REFERENCES

Abelson, R. P. (1995). *Statistics as principled argument.* Hillsdale, NJ: Lawrence Erlbaum.

Abelson, R. P. (1997). A retrospective on the significance test ban of 1999 (if there were no significance tests, they would be invented). In L. L. Harlow, S. A. Mulaik, & J. H. Steiger (Eds.), *What if there were no significance tests?* (pp. 117–141). Mahwah, NJ: Lawrence Erlbaum.

Abelson, R. P., Frey, K. P., & Gregg, A. P. (2004). *Experiments with people: Revelations from social psychology.* Mahwah, NJ: Lawrence Erlbaum.

Alferes, V. R. (2012). A methodological classification of psychological studies: Implications for developing APA standards of research reporting and improving PsycINFO indexation. *Manuscript in preparation.*

American Educational Research Association. (2006). Standards for reporting on empirical social science research in AERA publications. *Educational Researcher, 35*(6), 33–40.

American Sociological Association. (1999). *Code of ethics and policies and procedures of the ASA Committee on Professional Ethics.* Retrieved from http://www2.asanet.org/members/coe.pdf

Anderson, I., & Preece, D. A. (2002). Locally balanced change-over designs. *Utilitas Mathematica, 62,* 33–59.

Anderson, N. H. (2001). *Empirical direction in design and analysis.* Mahwah, NJ: Lawrence Erlbaum.

Anderson, N. H. (2002). Methodology and statistics in single-subject experiments. In J. Wixted & H. Pashler (Eds.), *Stevens' handbook of experimental psychology: Vol. 4. Methodology in experimental psychology* (3rd ed., pp. 301–337). New York, NY: Wiley.

Angrist, J. D., Imbens, G. W., & Rubin, D. B. (1996). Identification of causal effects using instrumental variables (with discussion). *Journal of the American Statistical Association, 91,* 444–472.

APA Publications and Communications Board Working Group on Journal Article Reporting Standards. (2008). Reporting standards for research in psychology: Why do we need them? What might they be? *American Psychologist, 63,* 839–851.

Aronson, E., & Carlsmith, J. M. (1968). Experimentation in social psychology. In G. Lindzey & E. Aronson (Eds.), *The handbook of social psychology: Vol. 2. Research methods* (2nd ed., pp. 1–79). Reading, MA: Addison-Wesley.

Aronson, E., Ellsworth, P. C., Carlsmith, J. M., & Gonzales, M. H. (1990). *Methods of research in social psychology* (2nd ed.). New York, NY: McGraw-Hill.

Aronson, E., Wilson, T. D., & Brewer, M. B. (1998). Experimentation in social psychology. In D. T. Gilbert, S. T. Fiske, & G. Lindzey (Eds.), *The handbook of social* psychology (4th ed., Vol. 1, pp. 99–142). New York, NY: McGraw-Hill.

Barlow, D. H., & Hersen, M. (1984). *Single case experimental designs: Strategies for studying behavior change* (2nd ed.). New York, NY: Pergamon Press.

Bate, S. T., & Boxall, J. (2008). The construction of multi-factor crossover designs in animal husbandry studies. *Pharmaceutical Statistics, 7,* 179–194.

160

Bate, S. T., Godolphin, E. J., & Godolphin, J. D. (2008). Choosing cross-over designs when few subjects are available. *Computational Statistics & Data Analysis, 52,* 1572–1586.

Bate, S. T., & Jones, B. (2006). The construction of nearly balanced and nearly strongly balanced uniform cross-over designs. *Journal of Statistical Planning and Inference, 136,* 3248–3267.

Bate, S. T., & Jones, B. (2008). A review of uniform cross-over designs. *Journal of Statistical Planning and Inference, 138,* 336–351.

Begg, C., Cho, M., Eastwood, S., Horton, R., Moher, D., Olkin, I., . . . Stroup, D. F. (1996). Improving the quality of reporting of randomized controlled trials: The CONSORT statement. *Journal of the American Medical Association, 276,* 637–639.

Berger, V. W. (2005). *Selection bias and covariate imbalances in randomized clinical trials.* Chichester, England: Wiley.

Berger, V. W. (2010). Minimization, by its nature, precludes allocation concealment, and invites selection bias. *Contemporary Clinical Trials, 31,* 406.

Borenstein, M. (2009). Effect sizes for continuous data. In H. Cooper, L. V. Hedges, & J. C. Valentine (Eds.), *The handbook of research synthesis and meta-analysis* (2nd ed., pp. 221–235). New York, NY: Russell Sage Foundation.

Boring, E. G. (1954). The nature and history of experimental control. *American Journal of Psychology, 67,* 573–589.

Bose, M., & Dey, A. (2009). *Optimal crossover designs.* Hackensack, NJ: World Scientific.

Boutron, I., John, P., & Torgerson, D. J. (2010). Reporting methodological items in randomized experiments in political science. *Annals of the American Academy of Political and Social Science, 628,* 112–131.

Campbell, D. T. (1957). Factors relevant to the validity of experiments in social settings. *Psychological Bulletin, 54,* 297–312.

Campbell, D. T. (1963). Social attitudes and other acquired behavioral dispositions. In S. Koch (Ed.), *Psychology: A study of a science: Vol. 6. Investigations of man as socius: Their place in psychology and the social sciences* (pp. 94–172). New York, NY: McGraw-Hill.

Campbell, D. T. (1969). Reforms as experiments. *American Psychologist, 24,* 409–429.

Campbell, D. T. (1979). A tribal model of the social system vehicle carrying scientific knowledge. *Science Communication, 1,* 181–201.

Campbell, D. T. (1984). Foreword. In R. K. Yin, *Case study research: Design and methods* (pp. vii–ix). Beverly Hills, CA: Sage.

Campbell, D. T. (1986). Relabeling internal and external validity for applied social scientists. In W. M. K. Trochim (Ed.), *Advances in quasi-experimental design and analysis* (pp. 67–77). San Francisco, CA: Jossey-Bass.

Campbell, D. T., & Fiske, D. W. (1959). Convergent and discriminant validation by the multitrait-multimethod matrix. *Psychological Bulletin, 56,* 81–105.

Campbell, D. T., & Kenny, D. A. (1999). *A primer on regression artifacts.* New York, NY: Guilford Press.

Campbell, D. T., & Stanley, J. C. (1966). *Experimental and quasi-experimental designs for research.* Chicago, IL: Rand McNally.

Cochran, W. G. (1965). The planning of observational studies in human populations (with discussion). *Journal of the Royal Statistical Society, Series A, 128,* 234–265.

Cochran, W. G. (1977). *Sampling techniques* (3rd ed.). New York, NY: Wiley.

Cochran, W. G. (1983). *Planning and analysis of observational studies.* New York, NY: Wiley.

Cochran, W. G., & Cox, G. M. (1957). *Experimental designs* (2nd ed.). New York, NY: Wiley.

Cochran, W. G., & Rubin, D. B. (1973). Controlling bias in observational studies: A review. *Sankhyā: The Indian Journal of Statistics, Series A, 35,* 417–446.

161

Cohen, J. (1988). *Statistical power analysis for the behavioral sciences* (2nd ed.). Hillsdale, NJ: Lawrence Erlbaum.

Cohen, J., Cohen, P., West, S. G., & Aiken, L. S. (2003). *Applied multiple regression/correlation analysis for the behavioral sciences* (3rd ed.). Mahwah, NJ: Lawrence Erlbaum.

Cook, T. D. (1985). Post-positivist critical multiplism. In R. L. Shotland & M. M. Mark (Eds.), *Social science and social policy* (pp. 21–62). Beverly Hills, CA: Sage.

Cook, T. D. (1993). A quasi-sampling theory of the generalization of causal relationships. In L. B. Sechrest & A. G. Scott (Eds.), *Understanding causes and generalizing about them* (pp. 39–82). San Francisco, CA: Jossey-Bass.

Cook, T. D. (2000). Toward a practical theory of external validity. In L. Bickman (Ed.), *Validity and social experimentation: Donald Campbell's legacy* (Vol. 1, pp. 3–43). Thousand Oaks, CA: Sage.

Cook, T. D., & Campbell, D. T. (1979). *Quasi-experimentation: Design and analysis issues for field settings.* Boston, MA: Houghton Mifflin.

Cook, T. D., & Payne, M. R. (2002). Objecting to the objections to using random assignment in educational research. In F. Mosteller & R. Boruch (Eds.), *Evidence matters: Randomized trials in education research* (pp. 150–178). Washington, DC: Brookings Institution Press.

Cook, T. D., & Shadish, W. R. (1994). Social experiments: Some developments over the past fifteen years. *Annual Review of Psychology, 45,* 545–580.

Cook, T. D., & Steiner, P. M. (2010). Case matching and the reduction of selection bias in quasi-experiments: The relative importance of pretest measures of outcome, of unreliable measurement, and of mode of data analysis. *Psychological Methods, 15,* 56–68.

Cooper, H. (2011). *Reporting research in psychology: How to meet journal article reporting standards.* Washington, DC: American Psychological Association.

Cortina, J. M., & Nouri, H. (2000). *Effect size for ANOVA designs.* Thousand Oaks, CA: Sage.

Cotton, J. W. (1998). *Analyzing within-subjects experiments.* Mahwah, NJ: Lawrence Erlbaum.

Crawley, M. J. (2005). *Statistics: An introduction using R.* Chichester, England: Wiley.

Cronbach, L. J. (1982). *Designing evaluations of educational and social programs.* San Francisco, CA: Jossey-Bass.

Dattalo, P. (2010). *Strategies to approximate random sampling and assignment.* Oxford, MA: Oxford University Press.

Davis, A. W., & Hall, W. B. (1969). Cyclic change-over designs. *Biometrika, 56,* 283–293.

Efron, B. (1971). Forcing a sequential experiment to be balanced. *Biometrika, 58,* 403–417.

Faul, F., Erdfelder, E., Lang, A.-G., & Buchner, A. (2007). G*Power 3: A flexible statistical power analysis program for the social, behavioral, and biomedical sciences. *Behavior Research Methods, 39,* 175–191.

Federer, W. T. (1955). *Experimental design: Theory and application.* New York, NY: Macmillan.

Federer, W. T., & Balaam, L. N. (1973). *Bibliography on experiment and treatment design pre-1968.* New York, NY: Hafner.

Festinger, L. (1953). Laboratory experiments. In L. Festinger & D. Katz (Eds.), *Research methods in the behavioral sciences* (pp. 136–172). New York, NY: Holt, Rinehart, & Winston.

Festinger, L. (1980). Looking backward. In L. Festinger (Ed.), *Retrospections on social psychology* (pp. 236–254). New York, NY: Oxford University Press.

Festinger, L., & Katz, D. (Eds.). (1953). *Research methods in the behavioral sciences.* New York, NY: Holt, Rinehart, & Winston.

Fidler, F. (2011). Ethics and statistical reform: Lessons from medicine. In A. T. Panter & S. K. Sterba (Eds.), *Handbook of ethics in quantitative methodology* (pp. 445–462). New York, NY: Routledge.

Fisher, R. A. (1966). *The design of experiments* (8th ed.). New York, NY: Hafner. (Original work published 1935.) (Reprinted in *Statistical methods, experimental design, and scientific inference*, by J. H. Bennett, Ed., 1990, Oxford, England: Oxford University Press, 1990)

Fisher, R. A. (1970). *Statistical methods for research workers* (14th ed.). New York, NY: Hafner. (Original work published 1925.) (Reprinted in *Statistical methods, experimental design, and scientific inference*, by J. H. Bennett, Ed., 1990, Oxford, England: Oxford University Press)

Fisher, R. A., & Yates, F. (1963). *Statistical tables for biological, agricultural and medical research* (6th ed.). Edinburgh, Scotland: Oliver & Boyd. Retrieved from http://digital .library.adelaide.edu.au/dspace/bitstream/2440/10701/1/stat_tab.pdf

Fleiss, J. L. (1986). *The design and analysis of clinical experiments.* New York, NY: Wiley.

Fleiss, J. L., & Berlin, J. A. (2009). Effect sizes for dichotomous data. In H. Cooper, L. V. Hedges, & J. C. Valentine (Eds.), *The handbook of research synthesis and meta-analysis* (2nd ed., pp. 237–253). New York, NY: Russell Sage Foundation.

Fletcher, D. J. (1987). A new class of change-over designs for factorial experiments. *Biometrika, 74,* 649–654.

Fletcher, D. J., & John, J. A. (1985). Changeover designs and factorial structure. *Journal of the Royal Statistical Society, Series B, 47,* 117–124.

Fox, J. (2008). *Applied regression analysis and generalized linear models* (2nd ed.). Thousand Oaks, CA: Sage.

Fox, J. (2009). *A mathematical primer for social statistics.* Thousand Oaks, CA: Sage.

French, J. R. P. (1953). Experiments in field settings. In L. Festinger & D. Katz (Eds.), *Research methods in the behavioral sciences* (pp. 98–135). New York, NY: Holt, Rinehart, & Winston.

Gentle, J. E. (2010). *Random number generation and Monte Carlo methods* (2nd ed.). New York, NY: Springer.

Greenwald, A. G. (1976). Within-subjects designs: To use or not to use? *Psychological Bulletin, 83,* 314–320.

Grissom, R. J., & Kim, J. J. (2005). *Effect sizes for research: A broad practical approach.* New York, NY: Lawrence Erlbaum.

Groves, R. M. (1989). *Survey errors and survey costs.* New York, NY: Wiley.

Groves, R. M., Fowler, F. J., Couper, M. P., Lepkowski, J. M., Singer, E., & Tourangeau, R. (2004). *Survey methodology.* Hoboken, NJ: Wiley.

Guo, S., & Fraser, M. W. (2010). *Propensity score analysis: Statistical methods and applications.* Thousand Oaks, CA: Sage.

Harlow, H. F. (1958). The nature of love. *American Psychologist, 13,* 673–685.

Harlow, L. L., Mulaik, S. A., & Steiger, J. H. (Eds.). (1997). *What if there were no significance tests?* Mahwah, NJ: Lawrence Erlbaum.

Hedayat, A., & Afsarinejad, K. (1975). Repeated measurements designs, I. In J. N. Srivastava (Ed.), *A survey of statistical design and linear models* (pp. 229–242). Amsterdam, Netherlands: North-Holland.

Hedayat, A., & Afsarinejad, K. (1978). Repeated measurements designs, II. *Annals of Statistics, 6,* 619–628.

Hinkelmann, K., & Kempthorne, O. (2005). *Design and analysis of experiments: Vol. 2. Advanced experimental design.* Hoboken, NJ: Wiley.

Hinkelmann, K., & Kempthorne, O. (2008). *Design and analysis of experiments: Vol. 1. Introduction to experimental design* (2nd ed.). Hoboken, NJ: Wiley.

Holland, P. W. (1986). Statistics and causal inference (with discussion). *Journal of the American Statistical Association, 81,* 945–970.

Imbens, G. W. (2010). An economist's perspective on Shadish (2010) and West and Thoemmes (2010). *Psychological Methods, 15,* 47–55.

Imbens, G. W., & Rubin, D. B. (in press). *Causal inference in statistics, and in the social and biomedical sciences.* New York, NY: Cambridge University Press.

Iqbal, I., & Jones, B. (1994). Efficient repeated measurements designs with equal and unequal period sizes. *Journal of Statistical Planning and Inference, 42,* 79–88.

John, J. A. (1973). Generalized cyclic designs in factorial experiments. *Biometrika, 60,* 55–63.

Jones, B., & Kenward, M. G. (2003). *Design and analysis of cross-over trials* (2nd ed.). London, England: Chapman & Hall/CRC Press.

Jones, L. V., & Tukey, J. W. (2000). A sensible formulation of the significance test. *Psychological Methods, 5,* 411–414.

Judd, C. M., McClelland, G. H., & Ryan, C. S. (2009). *Data analysis: A model comparison approach* (2nd ed.). New York, NY: Routledge.

Kalton, G. (1983). *Introduction to survey sampling.* Beverly Hills, CA: Sage.

Kelley, K., & Rausch, J. R. (2006). Sample size planning for the standardized mean difference: Accuracy in parameter estimation via narrow confidence intervals. *Psychological Methods, 11,* 363–385.

Kempthorne, O. (1952). *The design and analysis of experiments.* New York, NY: Wiley.

Kenny, D. A. (2008). Reflections on mediation. *Organizational Research Methods, 11,* 353–358.

Keppel, G. (1991). *Design and analysis: A researcher's handbook* (3rd ed.). Upper Saddle River, NJ: Prentice Hall.

Keppel, G., & Wickens, T. (2007). *Design and analysis: A researcher's handbook* (5th ed.). Englewood Cliffs, NJ: Prentice Hall.

Kiess, H. O., & Bloomquist, D. W. (1985). *Psychological research methods: A conceptual approach.* Boston, MA: Allyn & Bacon.

Kirk, R. E. (1995). *Experimental design: Procedures for the behavioral sciences* (3rd ed.). Pacific Grove, CA: Brooks/Cole.

Kirk, R. E. (2003a). Experimental design. In J. A. Schinka & W. F. Velicer (Eds.), *Handbook of psychology: Vol. 2. Research methods in psychology* (pp. 3–32). Hoboken, NJ: Wiley.

Kirk, R. E. (2003b). The importance of effect magnitude. In S. F. Davis (Ed.), *Handbook of research methods in experimental psychology* (pp. 83–105). Malden, MA: Blackwell.

Kirk, R. E. (2013). *Experimental design: Procedures for the behavioral sciences* (4th ed.). Thousand Oaks, CA: Sage.

Kish, L. (1965). *Survey sampling.* New York, NY: Wiley.

Kline, R. B. (2004). *Beyond significance testing: Reforming data analysis methods in behavioral research.* Washington, DC: American Psychological Association.

Korn, J. H. (1997). *Illusions of reality: A history of deception in social psychology.* Albany: State University of New York Press.

Kutner, M. H., Nachtsheim, C. J., Neter, J., & Li, W. (2004). *Applied linear statistical models* (5th ed.). New York, NY: McGraw-Hill.

Lazarsfeld, P. F. (1959). Reflections on business. *American Journal of Sociology, 65,* 1–31.

Lenth, R. V. (2001). Some practical guidelines for effective sample size determination. *The American Statistician, 55,* 187–193.

Lenth, R. V. (2006–2009). Java applets for power and sample size [Computer software]. Retrieved from http://www.stat.uiowa.edu/~rlenth/Power

Lewin, K. (1997). Behavior and development as a function of the total situation. In *Resolving social conflicts & Field theory in social science* (pp. 337–381). Washington, DC: American Psychological Association. (Original work published 1946)

Lewis-Beck, M. S. (2008). Forty years of publishing in quantitative methodology. In J. M. Box-Steffensmeier, H. E. Brady, & D. Collier (Eds.), *The Oxford handbook of political methodology* (pp. 814–827). New York, NY: Oxford University Press.

164

Lindquist, E. F. (1953). *Design and analysis of experiments in psychology and education.* Boston, MA: Houghton Mifflin.

Little, R. J. A., & Rubin, D. B. (2002). *Statistical analysis with missing data* (2nd ed.). Hoboken, NJ: Wiley.

Lohr, S. L. (2010). *Sampling: Design and analysis* (2nd ed.). Boston, MA: Brooks/Cole.

Mark, M. M., & Lenz-Watson, A. L. (2011). Ethics and the conduct of randomized experiments and quasi-experiments in field settings. In A. T. Panter & S. K. Sterba (Eds.), *Handbook of ethics in quantitative methodology* (pp. 185–209). New York, NY: Routledge.

Matsumoto, M., & Nishimura, T. (1998). Mersenne Twister: A 623-dimensionally equidistributed uniform pseudo-random number generator. *ACM Transactions on Modeling and Computer Simulation, 8,* 3–30.

Maxwell, S. E. (2010). Introduction to the special section on Campbell's and Rubin's conceptualizations of causality. *Psychological Methods, 15,* 1–2.

Maxwell, S. E., & Delaney, H. D. (2004). *Designing experiments and analyzing data: A model comparison perspective* (2nd ed.). Mahwah, NJ: Lawrence Erlbaum.

Maxwell, S. E., & Kelley, K. (2011). Ethics and sample size planning. In A. T. Panter & S. K. Sterba (Eds.), *Handbook of ethics in quantitative methodology* (pp. 159–184). New York, NY: Routledge.

McCrae, R. R., & Costa, P. T. (1999). A five-factor theory of personality. In L. A. Pervin & O. P. John (Eds.), *Handbook of personality: Theory and research* (2nd ed., pp. 139–153). New York, NY: Guilford Press.

McCullough, B. D. (1998). Assessing the reliability of statistical software: Part I. *The American Statistician, 52,* 358–366.

McCullough, B. D. (1999). Assessing the reliability of statistical software: Part II. *The American Statistician, 53,* 149–159.

McGuire, W. J. (2004a). Appendix: Perspectivist worksheets for generating a program of research. In J. T. Jost, M. R. Banaji, & D. A. Prentice (Eds.), *Perspectivism in social psychology: The yin and yang of scientific progress* (pp. 319–332). Washington, DC: American Psychological Association.

McGuire, W. J. (2004b). A perspectivist approach to theory construction. *Personality and Social Psychology Review, 8,* 173–182.

McKay, B. D., & Rogoyski, E. (1995). Latin squares of order 10. *Electronic Journal of Combinatorics, 2*(#N3), 1–4. Retrieved from http://www.combinatorics.org/ojs/index.php/eljc/article/view/v2i1n3/pdf

McKay, B. D., & Wanless, I. M. (2005). On the number of Latin squares. *Annals of Combinatorics, 9,* 335–344.

Meehl, P. E. (1990). Appraising and amending theories: The strategy of Lakatosian defense and two principles that warrant it. *Psychological Inquiry, 1,* 108–141.

Merton, R. K. (1973). The normative structure of science. In N. W. Storer (Ed.), *The sociology of science: Theoretical and empirical investigations* (pp. 267–278). Chicago, IL: University of Chicago Press. (Original work published 1942)

Miller, A. G. (Ed.). (1972). *The social psychology of psychological research.* New York, NY: Free Press.

Moher, D., Hopewell, S., Schulz, K. F., Montori, V., Gøtzsche, P. C., Devereaux, P. J., . . . Altman, D. G. (2010). CONSORT 2010 explanation and elaboration: Updated guidelines for reporting parallel group randomised trials. *Journal of Clinical Epidemiology, 63,* e1–e37.

Mook, D. G. (1983). In defense of external invalidity. *American Psychologist, 38,* 379–387.

Morgan, S. L., & Winship, C. (2007). *Counterfactuals and causal inference: Methods and principles for social research.* New York, NY: Cambridge University Press.

Morton, R. B., & Williams, K. C. (2010). *Experimental political science and the study of causality: From nature to the lab.* New York, NY: Cambridge University Press.

Murphy, K. (2002). Using power analysis to evaluate and improve research. In S. G. Rogelberg (Ed.), *Handbook of research methods in industrial and organizational psychology* (pp. 119–137). Malden, MA: Blackwell.

Namboodiri, N. K. (1972). Experimental designs in which each subject is used repeatedly. *Psychological Bulletin, 77,* 54–64.

Newcombe, R. G. (1996). Sequentially balanced three-squares cross-over designs. *Statistics in Medicine, 15,* 2143–2147.

Neyman, J. S. (1990). On the application of probability theory to agricultural experiments: Essay on principles, Section 9. *Statistical Science, 5,* 465–480. (Original work published 1923)

Nickerson, R. S. (2000). Null hypothesis significance testing: A review of an old and continuing controversy. *Psychological Methods, 5,* 241–301.

Panter, A. T., & Sterba, S. K. (Eds.). (2011). *Handbook of ethics in quantitative methodology.* New York, NY: Routledge.

Patterson, H. D., & Lucas, H. L. (1962). *Change-over designs* (Technical Bulletin No. 147). Raleigh: North Carolina Agricultural Experiment Station.

Pearl, J. (2009). *Causality: Models, reasoning, and inference* (2nd ed.). New York, NY: Cambridge University Press.

Plint, A. C., Moher, D., Morrison, A., Schulz, K., Altman, D. G., Hill, C., & Gaboury, I. (2006). Does the CONSORT checklist improve the quality of reports of randomised controlled trials? A systematic review. *Medical Journal of Australia, 185,* 263–267.

Pocock, S. J. (1983). *Clinical trials: A practical approach.* New York, NY: Wiley.

Pocock, S. J., & Simon, R. (1975). Sequential treatment assignment with balancing for prognostic factors in the controlled clinical trial. *Biometrics, 31,* 103–115. (Correction: *Biometrics, 1976, 32,* 954–955)

Reese, H. W. (1997). Counterbalancing and other uses of repeated-measures Latin-square designs: Analyses and interpretations. *Journal of Experimental Child Psychology, 64,* 137–158.

Reichardt, C. S. (1979). The statistical analysis of data from nonequivalent group designs. In T. D. Cook & D. T. Campbell, *Quasi-experimentation: Design and analysis issues for field settings* (pp. 147–205). Boston, MA: Houghton Mifflin.

Reichardt, C. S. (2000). A typology of strategies for ruling out threats to validity. In L. Bickman (Ed.), *Research design: Donald Campbell's legacy* (Vol. 2, pp. 89–115). Thousand Oaks, CA: Sage.

Rosenbaum, P. R. (2002). *Observational studies* (2nd ed.). New York, NY: Springer.

Rosenbaum, P. R. (2010). *Design of observational studies.* New York, NY: Springer.

Rosenbaum, P. R., & Rubin, D. B. (1983). The central role of the propensity score in observational studies for causal effects. *Biometrika, 70,* 41–55.

Rosenberg, M. (1979). Disposition concepts in behavioral science. In R. K. Merton, J. S. Coleman, & P. H. Rossi (Eds.), *Qualitative and quantitative social research: Papers in honor of Paul F. Lazarsfeld* (pp. 245–260). New York, NY: Free Press.

Rosenthal, R. (1976). *Experimenter effects in behavioral research* (Enlarged ed.). New York, NY: Irvington.

Rosenthal, R., & Rosnow, R. L. (Eds.). (1969). *Artifact in behavioral research.* New York, NY: Academic Press.

Rosenthal, R., Rosnow, R. L., & Rubin, D. B. (2000). *Contrasts and effect sizes in behavioral research: A correlational approach.* Cambridge, England: Cambridge University Press.

Rosnow, R. L., & Rosenthal, R. (1997). *People studying people: Artifacts and ethics in behavioral research.* New York, NY: Freeman.

Rosnow, R. L., & Rosenthal, R. (2011). Ethical principles in data analysis: An overview. In A. T. Panter & S. K. Sterba (Eds.), *Handbook of ethics in quantitative methodology* (pp. 37–58). New York, NY: Routledge.

Rubin, D. B. (1973). Matching to remove bias in observational studies. *Biometrics, 29,* 159–183.

Rubin, D. B. (1974). Estimating causal effects of treatments in randomized and nonrandomized studies. *Journal of Educational Psychology, 66,* 688–701.

Rubin, D. B. (2004). Teaching statistical inference for causal effects in experiments and observational studies. *Journal of Educational and Behavioral Statistics, 29,* 343–367.

Rubin, D. B. (2006). *Matched sampling for causal effects.* New York, NY: Cambridge University Press.

Rubin, D. B. (2007). Statistical inference for causal effects, with emphasis on applications in psychometrics and education. In C. R. Rao & S. Sinharay (Eds.), *Handbook of statistics: Vol. 26. Psychometrics* (pp. 769–800). Amsterdam, Netherlands: Elsevier.

Rubin, D. B. (2010). Reflections stimulated by the comments of Shadish (2010) and West and Thoemmes (2010). *Psychological Methods, 15,* 38–46.

Russell, K. G. (1991). The construction of good change-over designs when there are fewer units than treatments. *Biometrika, 78,* 305–313.

Schrodt, P. A. (2004). Random number generator. In M. S. Lewis-Beck, A. Bryman, & T. F. Liao (Eds.), *The Sage encyclopedia of social science research methods* (Vol. 3, pp. 910–911). Thousand Oaks, CA: Sage.

Schulz, K. F., Altman, D. G., & Moher, D. (2010). CONSORT 2010 statement: Updated guidelines for reporting parallel group randomized trials. *Annals of Internal Medicine, 152,* 726–732.

Scott, N. W., McPherson, G. C., Ramsay, C. R., & Campbell, M. K. (2002). The method of minimization for allocation to clinical trials: A review. *Controlled Clinical Trials, 23,* 662–674.

Senn, S. (2003). *Cross-over trials in clinical research* (2nd ed.). Chichester, England: Wiley.

Shadish, W. R. (2010). Campbell and Rubin: A primer and comparison of their approaches to causal inference in field settings. *Psychological Methods, 15,* 3–17.

Shadish, W. R., & Cook, T. D. (2009). The renaissance of field experimentation in evaluating interventions. *Annual Review of Psychology, 60,* 607–629.

Shadish, W. R., Cook, T. D., & Campbell, D. T. (2002). *Experimental and quasi-experimental designs for generalized causal inference.* Boston, MA: Houghton Mifflin.

Sheehe, P. R., & Bross, D. J. (1961). Latin squares to balance immediate residual, and other order, effects. *Biometrics, 17,* 405–414.

Tabachnick, B. G., & Fidell, L. S. (2007). *Experimental designs using ANOVA.* Belmont, CA: Duxbury.

Taves, D. R. (1974). Minimization: A new method of assigning patients to treatment and control groups. *Clinical Pharmacology and Therapeutics, 15,* 443–453.

Thompson, B. (2006). Research synthesis: Effect sizes. In J. L. Green, G. Camilli, & P. B. Elmore (Eds.), *Handbook of complementary methods in education research* (pp. 583–603). Mahwah, NJ: Lawrence Erlbaum.

Thompson, S. K. (2002). *Sampling* (2nd ed.). New York, NY: Wiley.

Tukey, J. W. (1977). *Exploratory data analysis.* Reading, MA: Addison-Wesley.

Underwood, B. J. (1966). *Experimental psychology* (2nd ed.). New York, NY: Appleton-Century-Crofts.

Webb, E. J., Campbell, D. T., Schwartz, R. D., Sechrest, L., & Grove, J. B. (1981). *Nonreactive measures in the social sciences* (2nd ed.). Boston, MA: Houghton Mifflin.

Weiss, D. J. (2006). *Analysis of variance and functional measurement: A practical guide.* New York, NY: Oxford University Press.

West, S. G., & Thoemmes, F. (2010). Campbell's and Rubin's perspectives on causal inference. *Psychological Methods, 15,* 18–37.

Wilkinson, L. (2005). *The grammar of graphics* (2nd ed.). New York, NY: Springer.

Wilkinson, L., & Task Force on Statistical Inference. (1999). Statistical methods in psychology journals: Guidelines and explanations. *American Psychologist, 54,* 594–604.

Williams, E. J. (1949). Experimental designs balanced for the estimation of residual effects of treatments. *Australian Journal of Scientific Research, Series A, 2,* 149–168.

Williams, E. J. (1950). Experimental designs balanced for pairs of residual effects. *Australian Journal of Scientific Research, Series A, 3,* 351–363.

Wilson, T. D., Aronson, E., & Carlsmith, K. (2010). The art of laboratory experimentation. In S. T. Fiske, D. T. Gilbert, & G. Lindzey (Eds.), *Handbook of social psychology* (5th ed., Vol. 1, pp. 51–81). Hoboken, NJ: Wiley.

Winer, B. J., Brown, D. R., & Michels, K. M. (1991). *Statistical principles in experimental design* (3rd ed.). New York, NY: McGraw-Hill.

Woodworth, R. S. (1938). *Experimental psychology.* New York, NY: Henry Holt.

Yin, R. K. (1984). *Case study research: Design and methods.* Beverly Hills, CA: Sage.

Zelen, M. (1974). The randomization and stratification of patients to clinical trials. *Journal of Chronic Diseases, 27,* 365–375.

INDEX

Page references followed by (table) indicate a table; followed by (figure) indicate an illustrated figure.

174

175

176

178

180

ⓈSAGE research**methods**

The essential online tool for researchers from the world's leading methods publisher

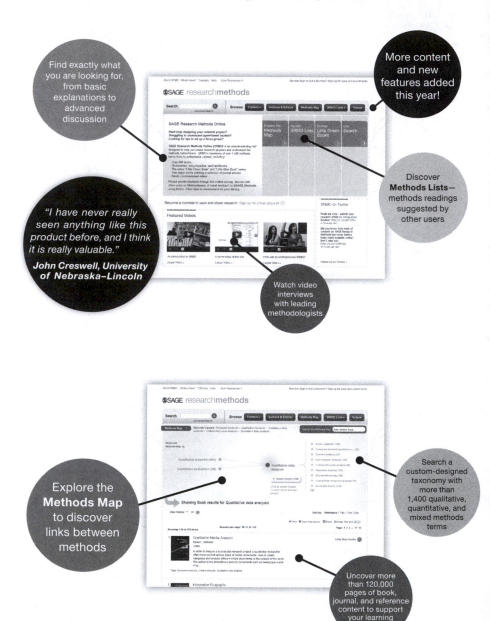

Find exactly what you are looking for, from basic explanations to advanced discussion

More content and new features added this year!

"I have never really seen anything like this product before, and I think it is really valuable."
John Creswell, University of Nebraska–Lincoln

Discover **Methods Lists**— methods readings suggested by other users

Watch video interviews with leading methodologists

Explore the **Methods Map** to discover links between methods

Search a custom-designed taxonomy with more than 1,400 qualitative, quantitative, and mixed methods terms

Uncover more than 120,000 pages of book, journal, and reference content to support your learning

Find out more at
www.sageresearchmethods.com